DEDICATION

To my wife Dawn; my severest critic, greatest admirer and best friend.

CONTENTS

Contents Continued:

READER'S NOTES:

Biblical quotations are taken from the Authorized King James' Version and are in *italics.*

Other passages in *italics* are extracts from contemporary documents.

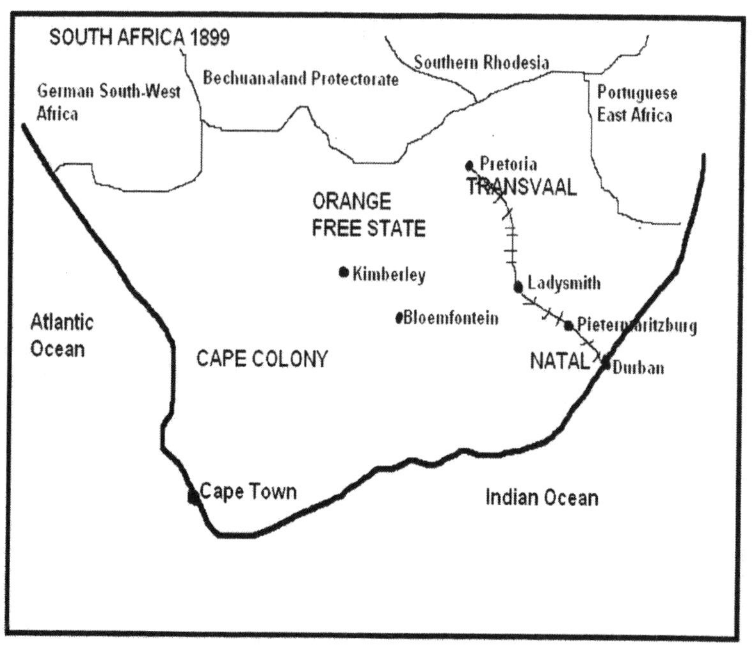
SOUTH AFRICA 1899
German South-West Africa
Bechuanaland Protectorate
Southern Rhodesia
Portuguese East Africa
Pretoria
TRANSVAAL
ORANGE FREE STATE
Kimberley
Ladysmith
Bloemfontein
Pietermaritzburg
Atlantic Ocean
CAPE COLONY
NATAL
Durban
Cape Town
Indian Ocean

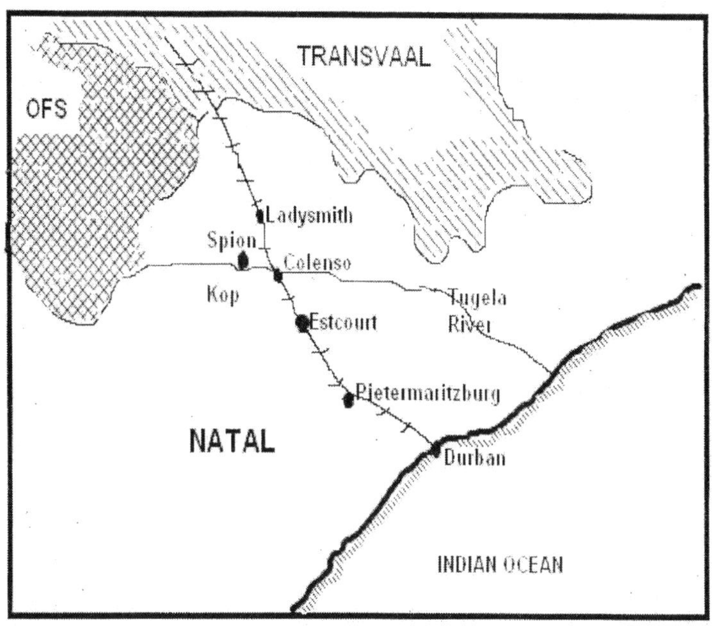
TRANSVAAL
OFS
Ladysmith
Spion
Kop
Colenso
Tugela
River
Estcourt
Pietermaritzburg
NATAL
Durban
INDIAN OCEAN

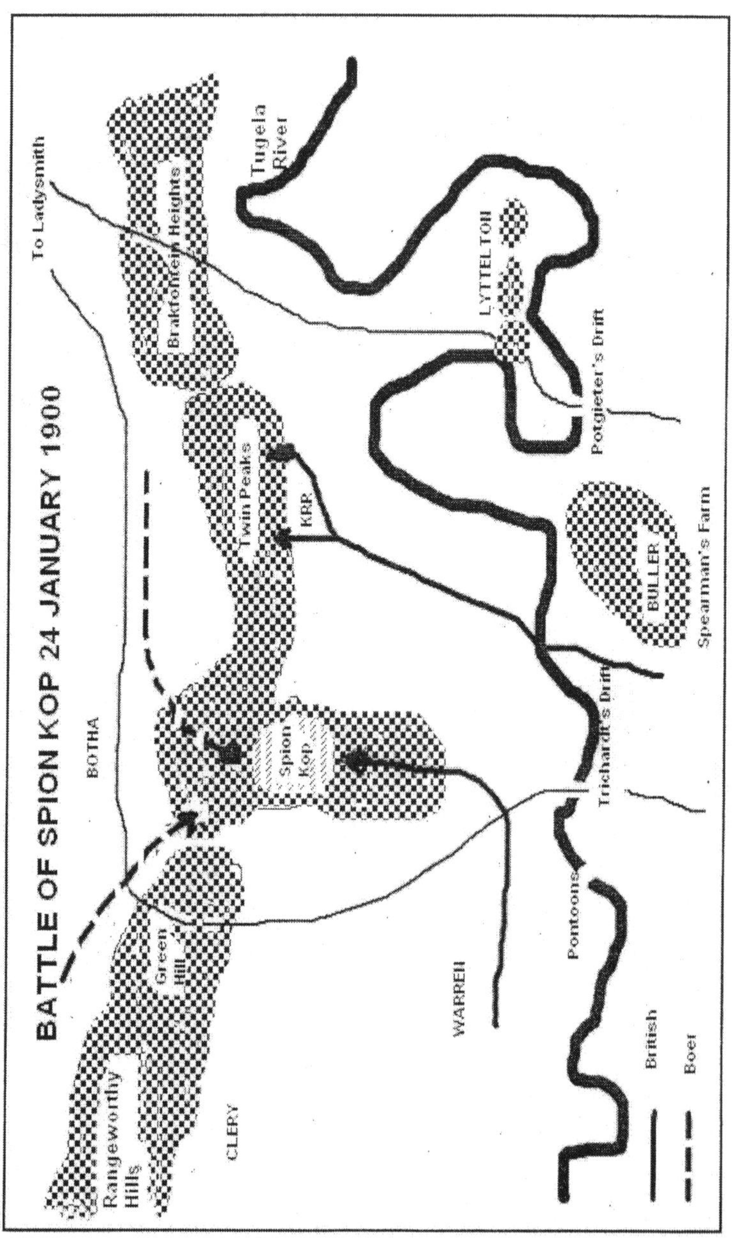
BATTLE OF SPION KOP 24 JANUARY 1900
To Ladysmith
Brakfontein Heights
Tugela River
LYTTELTON
Potgieter's Drift
Twin Peaks
KRR
BULLER
Spearman's Farm
BOTHA
Spion Kop
Trichardt's Drift
Green Hill
Pontoons
WARREN
Rangeworthy Hills
CLERY
British
Boer

PREFACE

Liverpool football fans are known as "kopites". In Liverpool, Blackpool, Preston, Sheffield and a dozen other stadia around the Country, fans sit, where they once stood, on steep terraces called "kops". The relevance of this Dutch word may be lost to the present generation, but at the birth of the twentieth century it was a word on the lips of every citizen of the Kingdom. It epitomised the inverted pride and poignancy, perhaps peculiarly British, which celebrates a glorious defeat; such as subsequent generations have come to venerate "the Miracle of Dunkirk".

The "Kops" are called after Spion Kop; the highest hill in a range of hills to be found in what is now Kwazulu Natal, South Africa. On the crest of that hill Dutch farmers – Boers – and British troops fought the bloodiest battle of the Boer War on 24 January 1900.

I first learnt of this hill and its battle when, at the age of fifteen, I joined the Rochdale Detachment of the Army Cadet Force which was affiliated to the local infantry Regiment, the Lancashire Fusiliers (LFs) – Twentieth of Foot. This Regiment took a leading part in the battle and suffered the most casualties. Forty-five years were to pass before I stood on the crest of that hill. There I looked along a four hundred metre line of piled rocks painted white, which originally had been a shallow trench, but now serves as a mass grave for approximately three hundred soldiers; many from Lancashire, some from Rochdale. I pondered; I left home on leaving school and, contrary to my parents wishes, joined the LFs. I fled the confines of a drab cotton town in a youthful quest for adventure. I was sent to fight my own small war, but three generations earlier I would, most probably, have been despatched with the Regiment to ultimately fight on this hill; as for so many it could have been my final resting place.

Spion Kop means Spy or Lookout Hill. From its prominence I could see to the north, about twenty miles away, the town of Ladysmith shimmering in the heat. To the south, at its foot, lay the meandering River Tugela, and beyond were the gentle pastoral hills of Natal. For several months a British Army - more than twice the size of that available to Wellington at Waterloo - battered itself against these hills trying to reach the town. They were held at bay by an unruly army of farmer-warriors. As I stood surveying an area no larger than Trafalgar square where once four thousand British soldiers struggled to survive a hellish onslaught, I felt a compelling conviction to tell the story. This was to be not only from the Generals' viewpoints, but also from the grass root perspective and experience – ex cotton workers and young Dutch farmers. As I researched I found that this was a battle which excited a furious debate in Parliament, and which precipitated the ultimate demise of the senior British generals involved.

This is an historical novel which relates true events told through the experiences of fictitious soldiers and real generals.

THE ABSENT-MINDED BEGGAR (1900)

When you've shouted "Rule Britannia," when you've sung
"God save the Queen,"
When you've finished killing Kruger with your mouth,
Will you kindly drop a shilling in my little tambourine
For a gentleman in *khaki* ordered South?
He's an absent-minded beggar, and his weaknesses are great-
But we and Paul must take him as we find him-
He is out on active service, wiping something off a slate
And he's left a lot of little things behind him!
Duke's son-cook's son-son of a hundred kings
(Fifty thousand horse and foot going to Table Bay!)
Each of 'em doing his country's work
(and who's to look after their things)
Pass the hat for your credit's sake,
and pay-pay-pay!

RUDYARD KIPLING

PROLOGUE

"(The Boers) ...have all the cunning and cruelty of the Kaffir without his courage or honesty ...they could not stand up against our troops for an hour."

General Sir Garnet Wolseley – October 1879

Majuba Hill - Northern Natal

27 February 1881

Boaz van den Berg paused to draw breath; he wiped his sweaty brow with his dirty sleeve. He had been climbing the hill for almost three hours, stomach pressed to the tussocks of grass and loose rocks, trying to be invisible. He looked about. The hillside was swarming with whiskered old men and young boys clambering up the steep slope, dressed in bark-tanned, leather breeches, open-necked, coloured, flannel shirts and loose-fitting, many-pocketed jackets. He was flanked by his two sons, Jacobus and Hendrick. They were just behind him, drawing level. He tightly grasped his single-shot, breech-loader and momentarily reflected upon the defiant words of the Commandant as he strode out ahead of them, goading the hesitant farmers into action: "Those who are not cowards must follow me."

The steepest part of the climb was immediately ahead, and the enemy were at the top. Shouting could be heard from the summit; the words unintelligible, but the taunting inflexion of the voices unmistakable. A volley of shots plunged downwards, but they were protected by the concave of the slope. He grinned alternatively at his sons in encouragement – at this point words were superfluous. He nodded, and together they renewed the ascent. As planned, others began to engage the enemy to keep their heads down and prevent them from returning fire. He was now just below the lip of the summit. He peered around a rock and saw that the basin-like plateau was teeming with redcoats, but they were in confusion. The Commandant stood up and waved his floppy, wide-brimmed hat to rally his men: "Come quickly, the English are flying!"

The shaggy horde surged over the rim stopping only to snap-shoot and reload. For a few minutes the redcoats held a line of rocks, but then they broke. Officers screamed: "Come back! Come back!" But the soldiers, consumed with fear, were not for staying. Boaz fired into their backs bringing them down abruptly. White, spiked pith-helmets rolled in the dust; kilts rode up on corpses to expose pale skin not yet reddened by the sun. One redcoat alone stepped forward to defy the rush; the gold braid and haughty bearing marked him as a senior officer. With pistol drawn he advanced firing repeatedly at the engulfing Boers until the inevitable "click" indicated that all chambers were empty. He stood, composed and resigned, awaiting his fate. Boaz aimed and squeezed the trigger. Major General Sir George Colley jerked backwards as the bullet hit his forehead.

"Boaz! Boaz!" He turned. It was his young friend and neighbour, Gerrit Pretorius, waving him back. He was crouched over a body. A sudden foreboding seized him; his stomach clenched; it was his son, Jacobus.

PART I

CHAPTER 1

On Commando

(Witberg, Transvaal - October 1899)

Gerrit Pretorius was dust covered and weary having been in the saddle since the first light of day. He coaxed his hardy Basuto pony down the steep bank of one of the many rain-gouged water-courses which furrowed the countryside, now in spate after the recent thunderstorm. The brown, gurgling water washed the belly of his short mount; he savoured the refreshing sensation as his hot feet, dangling in their loose stirrups, became submerged in the cooling torrent. He allowed his pony to pause mid-stream and drink while he sat patiently, slackly holding the reins. Suddenly his senses were quickened by an almost imperceptible movement on the far bank, a little down stream. At first it wasn't clear, but soon his experienced eye penetrated the mucky undergrowth to detect a python, its brown skin blotched with olive and tan markings acting as excellent camouflage. It was in the act of gorging a hapless, young warthog; only the victim's head had yet to be swallowed; its expression was mournful; its blank eyes bulged ready to burst from their sockets. The predator rested; it stared at Pretorius; he returned its hard look. It's the natural order of things, he mused, that the strong shall consume the weak. He knew pythons to be bad tempered and ready to bite if harassed. With a kick of his heels he urged his pony through the water and up the far bank.

The blood-red sun was sinking fast beneath the far horizon, casting long shadows over the Transvaal grasslands. The brief African dusk was giving way to the encroaching night. Pretorius was relieved to see the flickering lights beckoning to him. Ahead lay the farmhouse of the van den Berg family and rest, hospitality and friendship. He had known the family since before the War of Independence. Indeed, it was he who had carried the wounded Jacobus over his shoulder down Majuba Hill to the waiting ambulance. Jacobus had married his nurse, an attractive woman of French Huguenot stock, Anna, who had borne him four children; it was his joy to be an honorary uncle to them all. Now Pretorius was anxious to be with them and spurred his horse from a trot to a canter.

The farmhouse sat in a slight depression seeking protection from the winds which swept the vast, sprawling plains of the high veld. The mud walls were plastered and painted white, and the roof covered with corrugated, iron-zinc sheets. Mature fruit trees clustered in a nearby orchard, evidence that this was the homestead of one of the original pioneering families. A small wall protected the vegetable plot with its hedges of quince, peach and pomegranate. There was a clump of bamboo cultivated for whip-stocks. To one side, in a shallow fold, lay a dam of puddled clay which trapped the rain water. Close by and prominent towered a hillock of dry dung - the only available fuel in this virtually treeless landscape.

It was dark as Pretorius dismounted. A black face lit with bright eyes and gleaming white teeth appeared from the gloom. Instinctively, he handed the reins to the servant, "Wipe him down good and give him plenty of water."

"Yes, Bwana."

Pretorius mounted the semi-circular steps to the veranda and front door. He was about to knock and enter, but hesitated; inside the dim interior he could hear voices singing: male and female, some strident others gentle and melodic. Then he recognized Boaz's voice; he was reading a portion of scripture. Pretorius removed his hat and stood with bowed head straining to catch a word or phrase. He identified Psalm number 121: "*I will lift up mine eyes unto the hills, from whence cometh my help....*"

Involuntarily, Pretorius began to mouth the words in unison: "*My help cometh from the Lord, which made heaven and earth....*" He had been raised on the Bible, in fact even now, it was the only book in his house, and like many Afrikaners he saw no need for others. Repeated reading had implanted the words of Scripture on his heart: "*The Lord shall preserve thy going out and thy coming in from this time forth, and even for evermore...*"

When he judged the evening devotions to be finished, he knocked and entered the candle-lit voorhuis. Heads turned.

"Uncle Gerrit! Uncle Gerrit!"

The two youngest children, Adrian who was ten and Hannie eight, surged forward excitedly. He crouched to their level and swept them up in his strong arms, "Now how are my two favourite little people?"

"I have a new pony!" exclaimed Adrian.

"I have a new best dress!" competed Hannie.

"My, you're both blessed! Now let me greet your family." He released the clinging children and entered the broad room with its stinkwood furniture, ancestral paintings and haze of tobacco. Vigorously he embraced Boaz and Jacobus before warmly shaking the hand of the latter's eldest son, Jan. He then turned to the women, Anna, and the eldest daughter, Ruth; he kissed them fondly on their cheeks.

"Take off your cloak and come and sit by the fire, the nights still bring a chill," urged Boaz. "You look exhausted. What you need is a drink to put new life into you." He turned to his daughter-in-law, "Anna, let's have a sup of the peach-brandy." She quickly brought an earthenware jug and cups from the kitchen and poured the home-made brew for the men."

"Can I have some, father?" enquired Jan hopefully.

Boaz sensed the purpose of Pretorius' visit, "Anna, I think it's time for Jan to join the men."

Pretorius drew up to the glowing embers oblivious to the pungent smell of burning manure, and threw back the drink in one; he sucked his teeth noisily as the fiery liquid burnt his throat and stomach. "That was good!" Instinctively, Anna refilled his cup. Once he had farmed nearby, but when cholera had carried off his wife and three children he had plunged into a pit of despair, losing heart and purpose, and had sold off his land. Boaz had adopted him into his family where he had been loved and supported during that turbulent time of emotional and spiritual torment. Gradually he had recovered, and with Boaz's encouragement put himself forward as a candidate for the post of Magistrate or Field-Cornet. With Boaz's strong endorsement he was inevitably swept into office with a massive lead over his opponents. Now it was his responsibility to maintain the register of the fit fighting men within the Ward, and to ensure that each burgher was capable of mustering with the Commando complete with rifle, ammunition, pony and supplies. He had last visited his friends about two months ago. On that occasion he had come to enrol Jan and his two cousins, Pieter and Hans - twins. He had personally presented them with their own new Mauser rifle and bandolier of ammunition. It had been a simple ceremony, but an important rite of passage, for now the three youths were considered ready to defend the Republic in times of danger.

"So what's the news out of Pretoria?" enquired Boaz. "We heard that the commandos there had mobilised."

Pretorius looked across the hearth at the elderly and recently widowed patriarch whom he not only respected but loved. He was a large man and tall, perhaps six foot six inches, though now he drooped with the burden of age and the legacy of hard work. Beneath a long, straggling, white beard his face was leathery and sun-scorched. He had a rugged exterior, but Pretorius knew through his own life experience that this belied a practical kindliness, courage and simplicity. Boaz was a child of the Great Trek - that iconic event so pivotal in the moulding of the Afrikaner character.

"Let's eat while you talk," interrupted Anna, "the meal's ready." Boaz took his cue and led his guest and family to the large wooden table at the other side of the room; the children sat at the far end. For a moment conversation ceased as everyone sat quietly, heads bowed expectantly. Boaz thanked God for Pretorius' safe arrival before giving thanks for the food and placing the conversation into God's care. The ritual concluded Anna, assisted by Ruth, ladled out bowls of ragged-mouton stew and vegetables swimming in sheep's-tail fat.

Pretorius took a mouthful of stew, the gravy dribbling into his beard. He began, "The English are still intent on tearing up the Conventions of Pretoria and London which secured our independence after Majuba. The British High Commissioner in South Africa, Sir Alfred Milner, is being egged on by Cecil Rhodes to champion the cause of the uitlanders – the foreigners."

"You'd have thought that Rhodes had had enough after the farce of the Jameson raid and his failure to incite a revolt in the goldfields," interjected Jacobus.

"Not so; that rampant imperialist and his cronies want to roll up the Republics just like they have Mashonaland." Pretorius paused to chew and swallow a troublesome piece of gristly meat before continuing, "and he has the audacity and arrogance to call the territory after himself; Rhodesia – bah!" He made no attempt to conceal his contempt for the English. "They will not stop until we are compliant vassals in a South African Federation – they would swallow us. Since the discovery of gold at Witwatersrand and the influx of all these fortune hunters, we Boers have become a minority in our own land. The English insistence on equal political representation would surely mean that we lose control of our own country."

"How would that be?" enquired Jan.

Boaz looked across to his grandson and sought patiently to explain, "We are about thirty thousand enfranchised burghers. The newcomers number between sixty and seventy thousand. If we give them the franchise tomorrow, then we might as well give them the Republic."

Jacobus added with undisguised emotion looking firmly at Jan, "We fought for our freedom and believed we had won, but what the English couldn't take by force they're now trying to take by subterfuge."

"What does President Kruger say to all this?" asked Ruth.

Pretorius paused to take another mouthful of food before answering, "President Kruger has offered concessions, but always the English want more. However, at the last meeting in Bloemfontein, the President was adamant saying that he's not ready to hand over his Country to strangers." He hesitated before adding in softer tones, almost conspiratorially, "It's reported that Kruger shed tears as he left the negotiations."

Jan scrutinised the bulky figure seated down the table with his wide face, brown eyes and bulbous nose. He hung on every word spoken, sensing that this was the beginning of a momentous time. His older sister, Ruth, also listened intently, while the two youngsters ate eagerly, oblivious to the import of the conversation.

Pretorius continued, "The British Government is now insisting upon a joint enquiry to investigate the alleged grievances of the uitlanders, while simultaneously reinforcing its garrisons in Natal and the Cape. Troops are arriving from the colonies and Britain as we speak. They're playing for time."

"What became of the Government's appeal to Queen Victoria and the President of the United States?" asked Anna who had been straining to follow the conversation whilst carrying out her domestic duties. .

"The old lady didn't even have the courtesy to reply," responded Pretorius in disgust. "As for the President, McKinley is engrossed in his own imperialistic adventure in the Philippines for which he desperately wants British support – he won't intervene to help us." In frustrated anger he added, "It seems as if the Colonial Secretary, Joseph Chamberlain, and Milner are acting without restraints and are growing increasingly intransigent."

"So it's war," stated Boaz resignedly.

"As before," sighed Pretorius. "To survive the Republics must strike before the English grow too strong. It's been prudent to await the spring grass on the veld in order to sustain the horses and ponies of the commandos, but now the rains are here the moment has come. All day I've been visiting the steads, and tomorrow I'll alert the remainder. We muster in two days time and then move south to the border with Natal."

There was a silence as the severity of the news struck home. The older family members knew the cruelty of war and were saddened. Jan felt an almost uncontainable excitement.

"Then let it be Majuba again!" cried Jacobus emphatically, shattering the quiet. "The only difference is that this time Tommy is wearing khaki and not red." He grinned, "It makes him slightly more difficult to shoot."

....

Jan was not thick-set and muscular like the typical Afrikaner; instead he had inherited the influence of his mother's more delicate features. He was tall, but clean-limbed, of florid complexion with dark hair, blue eyes and just the beginnings of facial hair. However, despite his lighter build he was physically tough and resilient - characteristics born of his time on the veld. While growing up he and his cousins had roamed the game-covered plains on tough, surefooted ponies, hunting, fishing and sleeping under the moody skies. They had learned to shoot and ride almost as quickly as they had learned to walk and read. Such skills were second nature. The emptiness of the veld with its searching heat and its unpredictable, vicious storms, held no fears for them. Even as they grew older and assumed greater responsibilities on the farms, their expeditions had never ceased completely; they remained close friends bound by kinship and affection.

As he attempted to bridle his Basuto pony, he found that his hands shook involuntarily; he was excited by the looming adventure, if not a little fearful. He might not fully understand the intricacies of the politics, just that as a Boer he had to fight for his Country. From the earliest age he had been inculcated with a strong sense of identity, a love of God-given freedom, and the knowledge of inescapable duty; and now the time for action had arrived. He tried to hide his nervousness by exuding an air of calm and resolve, while struggling with the leatherwork – why were the buckles so unusually tricky? Soon they would be joined by his uncle Hendrick and his two cousins. His cousins were slightly older by a few months making them eighteen. He reflected on their recent enrolment into the Witberg Commando; now they were considered to be men, and every able-bodied male, man and youth from sixteen to sixty, was required to defend the homeland. He knew that the life which he had known and enjoyed was about to be interrupted; would it ever be the same again?

The familiar, acrid smell of smouldering dung wafted from nearby cattle kraals. Jan adjusted the bit in his pony's mouth; she jerked back awkwardly, fearfully; he held her tightly. He caught sight of a puff-adder leisurely slithering away into the lengthening grass after a night's hunting of the many rats which haunted the kraals - no doubt returning to cool shelter before the sun reached its zenith. He had been taught to be wary of the venomous snakes and now understood his pony's unusual skittishness. "Steady girl, steady," he gently reassured her. Ruth came from the stable carrying her tack and leading her mount; she tethered him to a fence nearby and threw on the saddle. She stooped to fasten the leather straps, self-consciously and deliberately avoiding his glance. They didn't speak. The previous evening she had confided in him, and now he felt an instinctive tenseness as he anticipated the inevitability of the approaching clash.

Jacobus came around the corner having watered his horse. "What're you doing?" he asked brusquely of his daughter, knowing the answer full well. He was conscious that just below the surface of this dutiful daughter lurked the Latin passion of her mother. Ruth could be feisty and strong-willed, and possessed a dormant volatility which occasionally erupted in a manner so alien to the Dutch character.

"I'm going on commando," Ruth replied bluntly, busying herself with the harness, not looking up.

"Women don't go on commando, and certainly not my daughter."

Ruth felt the heat of frustration and anger welling up inside her. She knew that she was as capable as the men, but it had always been the same; Jan and her cousins could roam the veld rounding up cattle and sheep and hunting white-bellied impala, while she was restricted to domestic chores about the house and gardens. They could fight the Khakis, but as a woman she was to be confined to the farm. It seemed that the boys had preordained freedoms denied to her. "Grandfather is too old to go on commando; he'll be here to organise the Kaffirs. Whereas I can ride and shoot as good as Jan and Pieter and Hans."

Jacobus was well aware of her prowess. Frequently, when she was younger, he had overruled Anna's concerns and disquiet to permit Ruth to join the boys on their forays across the veld. Begrudgingly, the boys had come to acknowledge that she could ride and shoot with the best of them.

"And who is to care for your Uncle's farm?" His voice rose sternly. "You know there are two farms to run. Do you expect your grandfather to do everything? We'll be away for a few months and you're to help him and your mother."

"As you say, it's only for a short time … they don't need me."

Jacobus released his horse and strode over to his daughter. He took her by the arm and firmly, not aggressively, pulled her around to face him. "I'm your father," he spoke slowly and resolutely trying to control a surging anger. "You're not going on commando. You stay here and run the farms …that's your duty so that we are released to fight the enemy. There can be no further discussion." Stubbornness had collided with iron will.

She flushed with fury and resentment, but experience had taught her that when her father was in this mood nothing would budge him. She breathed out heavily and audibly, deflating as if releasing her very spirit. "Then can I come with you to the muster point?"

"Yes; all the family must come. Tell the servants to get the cart ready."

Jan pulled the strap tight on the pony's bridle; he was ready. Perfect timing he thought as he looked up to see riders approaching in the distance. His uncle Hendrick and cousins would soon be with them.

Hendrick, like Jacobus and their father, was powerfully built; his full unkempt beard and unruly side whiskers hid a face scored by premature ageing. A clear, deep gouge ran from his left ear across his cheek to his nose - a memento following a struggle with a crazed buffalo. He was proud to have his sons by his side. He was only too aware that in the past his attitude to Pieter and Hans had been ambivalent. In their early years he had regarded them as poor compensation for the loss of his young wife whom he had loved so dearly during their short time together, and who had died at their birth. He had given over his sons to the care of his black, female servants. Yes, he had provided for them physically, they never wanted for food, clothes or shelter. He had even enlisted the help of their cousin, Ruth, to teach them to read and write in the absence of their mother. But affection? He had only recently reconciled the contradictory emotions of love and resentment which had tormented him and caused an inner turmoil. But now, at the moment of their Country's need, they were men together

The family united amid much back-slapping, kissing and bravado. It was a time of heightened emotion as the love of kinship and the fear of the unknown merged. "We'll soon eat fish in Durban!" declared Jacobus; the others roared with approval. But beneath this swashbuckling was the knowledge, born of bitter experience, that even victories can exact a high price.

Anna hovered with a jug of peach-brandy refilling mugs as the genial reunion grew ever more vocal and boisterous, until finally Boaz declared that it was the time to depart for the muster point. The men trotted ahead riding with an easy familiarity, while Ruth followed driving the light Cape cart with her mother and two younger siblings on board.

....

The predikant stood on the back of the ox wagon in the dusty market square and surveyed his congregation of warrior farmers and beardless boys; some accompanied by their women folk who had come to see them off to war. He wore the customary frock-coat of black broadcloth buttoned tightly to the neck with trousers to match. His felt hat of wide brim and low crown was pulled down firmly on his head, seemingly held in place by protruding ears. He sprouted a white beard and whiskers which contrasted with the darkness of his lined face. His sunken, brown eyes accentuated his stern countenance - in appearance he was the archetypical Calvinist minister. Like his flock, he had been bred in a creed that had more of the Old Testament in it than the New; a harsh, uncompromising faith in which the events of everyday life were interpreted in terms of Scripture.

He held up his Bible and entreated those carrying theirs, mainly the older men, to turn to the First Book of Samuel from where he read the story of David and Goliath:

> *"This day will the Lord deliver thee into mine hand; and I will smite thee, and take thine head from thee, and I will give the carcasses of the host of Philistines this day unto the fowls of the air, and to the wild beasts of the earth; that all the earth may know that there is a God in Israel……………"*

He spoke loudly with irrepressible zeal, convinced of the solid certainties of the ancient texts. He gesticulated freely to reinforce his belief that the English were the modern Philistines, and that the Boer Republics represented the new tribes of Israel. He had no doubt about the virtue of their cause and so he confidently anticipated God's support. Once again David would defeat Goliath, and the harbingers of God's wrath were arrayed before him. Had not God smitten the English in the War of Independence? Would He not do it again? Would He not use His God-fearing servants as the instruments of His justice and righteousness?

The exhortation became a noisy back-drop in which the individual words merged as Jan's concentration wandered. He cast his eyes over the people gathered in the market place: family, friends, neighbours; people who normally led isolated, self-sufficient lives, and yet people bound by a common language, religious beliefs, occupation, heritage, and a fervent and unquenchable yearning for freedom. Then he noticed, standing just a little apart from the crowd, a young man so obviously a stranger, awkward among the farming community. He was older than himself, perhaps late twenties. His face was ruddy from the wind and sun, but the skin was not yet weathered. He sported a scruffy moustache and an embryonic beard, immature and ungroomed. His clothes, though of the Boer style, looked new, hardly soiled by the veld dust or stained from the labours of the farm. His facial features were not those of the Afrikaner; they were gentler, moulded not hewn. He carried a rifle and slung ammunition belt as did the majority of the men present. Jan assumed him to be a city-dweller and a volunteer, but how did he get to Witberg? Momentarily their eyes met; both nodded acknowledgement and then self-consciously they looked away.

Henry Barnham felt rather conspicuous as he hovered on the edge of the Commando muster listening to the rousing sermon. He might not understand the strident, guttural words, but the sentiments needed no translation. As the attention of the crowd was held by the animated preacher, he furtively scrutinized the farmers in their wide-brimmed, felt hats, tweed jackets and corduroy trousers; some he noticed were even in suits and neckties as if dressed for office or church. A few older men wore high-crowned hats and frock-coats with claw-hammer tails; people seemingly of authority. For most, their clothes had that lifeless, misshapen appearance suggesting that they had been slept in, as well as frequently soaked through and dried on the body. In contrast his clothes were relatively new and clean. These were big men, rough, half-savage, with tanned faces and blue eyes. Many had unkempt beards or untidy facial hair; only the young boys still had uncluttered faces.

He found it difficult to believe that barely six weeks ago he had been cosseted in the comforts of middle-class Boston, New England. It was literally a world away. He reflected momentarily: he had not joined his father in his printing business with all its commercial uncertainties and worries, but instead had chosen the less stressful and more lucrative legal profession. He had been taken on as a junior partner in his uncle's chambers, but had soon realised that his heart was not in it. The work had proven to be mundane, tedious and without challenge. He had soon become bored of pampering to the petulant, vindictive and selfish demands of shallow, elderly clients. For distraction and excitement he had turned to gambling, drinking and the favours of lesser-principled young ladies. He had known that he was drifting aimless through life. His gambling debts were mounting; demands from creditors were becoming increasingly uncompromising, and he was staggering from one inconsequential relationship to another.

"Soon decent families will have nothing to do with you," warned his distraught mother. "How are you ever to get a good wife … to raise a family?"

Each morning en route to his office he would buy a copy of the *Boston Times* from the newspaper-boy on the corner. He would drink his first coffee of the day and read the paper putting off the unavoidable return to the mind-numbing minutiae of work. For months the paper had been reporting the tensions between the Boers and the British in South Africa; with the breakdown of the talks in Bloemfontein between Milner and Kruger, war was looking inevitable. He could still remember the moment of realisation as if being struck by an imperceptible flash of understanding and certainty. The hairs had stood up on his back; excitement and fear dovetailed; he had felt physical palpitations.

There had been an inexplicable stirring of emotion; a sense of impending injustice and a desire to help the fledgling Republics. The imminent fight between unequals had served to accentuated the frivolous nature of his existence; his life suddenly seemed trivial and irrelevant. He would travel to South Africa and join the Boer forces in their struggle against imperialistic Britain. He would break out of the constricting straight-jacket which was his life in Boston, and embrace something worthy. He would fight for the freedom of an oppressed people – and escape hassling creditors and broody women.

In those days he didn't often dine with his parents, preferring to visit a club or a restaurant with friends of either gender. But that evening he had an announcement to make, "I'm off to South Africa to join the Boers."

There was a moment of silent disbelief. His father spoke, "Why would you want to do that? If it's excitement you must have, then the West needs all the good young men it can get to settle it and bring stability and enterprise – but South Africa!"

"And the British!" exclaimed his mother. "There'll be fighting there!"

"Precisely, that's why I must go. We once fought for our independence, now I must help the Dutch farmers do the same."

His parents had not understood. Disapproval and bewilderment radiated from them as they stood on the quayside and forlornly waved farewell. He took the steamer for London and so to Cape Town. From there he travelled by train to Pretoria.

He remembered his eagerness to stretch his legs, and the joy of escaping the claustrophobic railway carriage after five monotonous days of crossing seemingly endless veld. As he descended he was confronted by platforms crowded with turbulent and noisy refugees - mostly British it seemed. They were burdened with suitcases and bundles of all shapes and sizes, anxiously jostling to escape the coming war. Clearly the rolling stock was unequal to the demands being made upon it. Many wretched uitlanders scrambled into open cattle trucks or coal-dust layered tubs amid pushing and shoving, resigned to travel in discomfort south to Cape Town, or east to Portuguese Delagoa Bay. The Dutch ignored the pitiful aliens as they hurriedly loaded artillery onto flat trucks and horses into boxes.

He carefully picked his way through the flotsam of war and emerged onto the adjacent street. He wandered into the town and found himself in Church Square by the Volksraad – Parliament buildings. Across the open space rode commandos from the countryside on their way to the Natal border. Impromptu crowds cheered and the riders saluted by waving their hats or rifles. It was chaotically carnival-like. It was apparent that with most shops boarded up normal commercial activity had ceased; only the official business of preparing for war seemingly ground on relentlessly.

Tentatively, he entered unchallenged into a government building, which after the commotion of the frenzied streets was an oasis of calm. He lingered in a corridor unsure of his next move, when a slight-built man burdened with files addressed him as he attempted to squeeze by. Having failed to communicate in Afrikaans he broke into perfect English, "Can I be of help?" Henry hurriedly explained that he had come to join the Boers in their struggle against the British. To his surprise, he was ushered without ceremony into the office of no less a person than the State Secretary himself, Mr Francis William Reitz; an unpretentious man, and one ready to welcome freedom-loving volunteers from overseas. His reception was warm and relaxed, lacking any formality, "Pity, you've just missed the Irish Brigade commanded by Colonel Blake - an American of Irish descent. He trained at West Point and served in the cavalry; fought against the Apaches in Arizona. Do you know him?"

Henry wondered how he was meant to know this one man from a vast country of millions. "I'm afraid not, sir. It's never been my pleasure."

"Well, he set off for the Natal border two days ago. It's mostly Irish in the Brigade, but there are a sprinkling of your countrymen and about ten Frenchmen; you'd probably feel at home there. The local Pretoria Commando mobilised last week and will already have reached the assembly point." He thought for a few moments. "We have a messenger leaving shortly with important instructions for the Field-Cornet in charge of the Commando at Witberg. In the circumstances I think it best if you ride with him. The journey will get you accustomed to the veld and your new mount, and there you can join the local Commando. I'll give you a letter of introduction, also a letter to present at the armoury here where you will be issued with a Mauser rifle and a bandoleer of ammunition. You will leave in the morning; you can buy a pony from the kraal behind the station."

He had bought an Arab bay in preference to the diminutive ponies so loved by the Boers, and had spent the remainder of the day frenetically procuring stores and equipment. He considered himself to be a competent horseman - many holidays had been spent on an uncle's ranch. However, he had never before ridden continuously for two days over a distance of about one hundred and twenty miles. His companion – a simple rustic - seemed to have no need for food or rest. He spoke little English which had made their relationship rather awkward; they communicated by hand gestures and grinned a lot. He had filled his two panniers with all possible items trying to anticipate every contingency, but he soon felt embarrassed by his apparent extravagance. His escort was content to carry a blanket and rifle on the saddle-bow, and strips of dried buck meat – biltong - tied to his harness. As dusk descended they had halted for the night. His companion quickly and expertly prepared coffee; it was thick and black, and he gave Henry a crystal of sugar-candy to suck as he sipped it. Henry sat quietly to one side while his friend read eagerly from the Scriptures. On completion, Henry offered to share his bread, beans, tinned meat and fruit, but his companion was content to chew the biltong. With the chill of night they wrapped themselves in their blankets and lay with their saddles behind their shoulders. He arrived in Witberg aching and sore, and there was introduced to Gerrit Pretorius, whom he soon learned was the Field-Cornet for the local Commando. He was greeted with a strong handshake, but the body language was distinctly cold.

"Mr Barnham, I have read the letter from Pretoria. We are humbled to think that you've come half way across the world to join us in our fight for freedom." Pretorius scrutinised the American. Why would he be willing to die for a cause which was not his own? Would he stay when the going got tough? He had little time for foreign adventurers. He went on, "Thank you for coming." The cynicism hit Henry like a bolt. "But please don't imagine that we have need of you. The Transvaal wants no foreign help, but if you wish to fight for us, so be it." He paused deliberately, the momentary silence giving weight to his words. "What a pity some of your countrymen see fit to join the English irregulars, motivated no doubt by promises of future riches from our gold mines, rather than by worthy principles and a sense of justice. I hope when it comes to the fight you can see them as your enemy." He starred at Henry unflinchingly.

Henry was unsettled and struggled vainly to compose a suitable response; he failed.

Pretorius disregarded his visitor's visible discomfort and continued tersely, "The message which you've helped to deliver from the Capital calls us to war. I and my assistants will be away for the next couple of days as we alert the burghers. We muster at the end of the week. I suggest you find a room in the town and recover from your ride until we assemble." With that he concluded the meeting.

Henry remembered mumbling something about it being his privilege to help fight tyranny, but in the circumstances it had seemed trite and inadequate.

Now, as he studied the crowd, his eyes met those of a young man; they exchanged a hesitant nod of introduction before diverting their glances with slight embarrassment. He paused, and then looked back surreptitiously trying not to be obvious. Standing amid a family group, which included the young man, was an attractive young woman. She was dressed in a sweeping, ankle-length skirt and a white high-necked blouse, both joining at a broad belt around a trim waist. Her hair was pulled back tightly revealing an elegant face of smooth, olive complexion. On her head was a straw boater. She held the hand of a girl, perhaps eight or nine years old, who was becoming restless at the proceedings. She bent down to the child and passed an unheard comment; they both giggled as if party to some shared secret. At that moment a previous tenseness dissipated and her face beamed bright and full and compassionate.

Heads bowed in solemn prayer, and with a resounding "Amen" the service concluded.

Jan sought out the newcomer, "Hello, I'm Jan", he said speaking instinctively in English and holding out his hand. "You're not one of us?"

Henry shook the proffered hand, "I hope to be; I'm an American come to join you in your fight against the British," he replied smiling. He went on to briefly explain how he came to be in Witberg.

"Have you been allocated to a corporalship?" asked Jan.

"A corporalship?"

"Yes," explained Jan, "a commando is made up of several field cornetcies, which in turn are split into a number of corporalships, normally between twenty and twenty five men. We then elect our own leader. Our corporal is my uncle Hendrick. He fought in the last war against the English and is very brave; sometimes he can be moody, but he's a good leader - just and reliable. Would you like to join us?"

"Very much," responded Henry. He was eager to be included and accepted.

Hendrick's warm greeting was sealed by a crushing handshake, and Jan's insistence that he should join his uncle's group was agreed with a condescending smile of encouragement. Jan was excited by his coup; here was a real American to ride and shoot with them. He eagerly introduced him to the family. Henry was pleased to be so readily received, and somewhat relieved to find that everyone spoke a degree of English - in some cases heavily accented, but understandable. His introductions also brought him into brief contact with the attractive young woman. They shook hands and smiled politely; their eyes searching each other intensely.

"So you've come to show us how it's done," she said with a mischievous glint in her eye."

"How what's done?" countered Henry, faking a lack of understanding.

"Why of course, how to defeat the English and ensure our independence."

"Naturally," he parried. "Family tradition and folklore place my great uncle at the celebrated and infamous Tea Party."

"So you know all about taxation without representation – the uitlanders grievance of course."

And the rallying cry which had mobilised the American colonists against the English, Henry mused. She was teasing him.

There followed a period of general milling as farewells were said: clinging, hugging, embarrassed kisses, shouts of encouragement, defiant protestations. Then from the chaos emerged order as Gerrit Pretorius, Hendrick and the other corporals, shouted brusque commands and the Boers responding, mounted their stocky, shaggy ponies. They set off, complete with preacher, at a rocking-chair canter, erect, proud, confident. Boaz, now too frail to fight, stood with his daughter-in-law and grandchildren and watched in the sudden, foreboding silence until the two hundred men or so were lost in the billowing dust; and when it settled there was a solemn emptiness. No one spoke.

Ruth, fired by her patriotism and intrigued by the handsome American, vowed inwardly that she would follow.

After three days of hard, monotonous riding, Jan was glad to reach Sandspruit, a small railway station about ten miles from the Natal border. It was here that the commandos were massing. The surrounding veld was teeming with tents and wagon laagers of varying size, and he could hear the crack of rifle fire on the outskirts as men practiced their marksmanship. The Commando trotted through the encampment and was greeted with welcoming shouts and jovial comments; old acquaintances were renewed - some reaching back to the last conflict. Everywhere there seemed to be an air of expectancy and excitement. Prominent amidst this amorphous sprawl was a large white marquee where flew the "vier kleur" flag of the Transvaal with its three horizontal stripes of red, white and blue, with a vertical green stripe at the hoist. This, he learnt, marked the headquarters of the ageing Commandant-General, Piet Joubert, and his wife, for she habitually accompanied him in the field.

The dusty horsemen halted short of the marquee. Pretorius dismounted, entered and enquired of their allocated space. They then moved off to a vacant plot close to the spruit. Until their laager wagons arrived they had no tents and only limited equipment. Some prepared a rudimentary meal and coffee, whilst others took the ponies for watering. Afterwards most threw their water-proof capes onto the tall grass and slept, but Jan was restless, consumed by a feeling of nervous energy; sleep was impossible. He decided to explore the encampment. It was crowded and busy; he had never seen such intense activity and commotion. Perhaps as many as fifteen thousand burghers had already assembled. He noticed a train standing at the crude platform heralding the arrival of further commandos. Horses and ponies were disembarking; boxes and sacks of supplies were being unloaded by sweating black Africans and stacked by the track. Close by was a group of guns belonging to the Transvaal Staats Artillery which, on enquiry, Jan found to be Krupps from Germany and Creusots from France. In attendance were the grey-uniformed gunners, the only regular soldiers of the Republic's forces. On the periphery of this great assembly were large herds of long-horned cattle; these he knew to be slaughter animals which would follow the commandos and provide fresh meat. As he wandered about he was fascinated and absorbed by the self-assured, confident, unruly farmers and their incessant activity as they prepared for war.

It was early the following day when the news circulated that an ultimatum had been passed to the English giving them forty-eight hours to withdraw their forces from the borders of the Republics. That same evening Hendrick summoned his corporalship, "We muster in twenty minutes over by the hill. The deadline has passed and the Commandant-General will speak with us."

Jan kept close to his father as they jostled amid the largest body of mounted men ever seen in Southern Africa. A path was cleared for Piet Joubert as he rode to a vantage point accompanied by his staff. "Make way for the Royal Family!" joked his father disapprovingly, for Joubert's staff was mostly relatives. Jan knew from his father that Piet Joubert was, like his mother, a descendent of French Huguenots. He had long been active in politics, but always overshadowed by Kruger. He had been Commandant-General during the War of Independence, and crucially at Majuba Hill. But many wanted a younger, more resolute commander; they thought it insufficient for him to be an honourable, old gentleman. Now the stocky, bushy-bearded, square-faced Commandant sat on his horse beneath an embroidered banner and addressed the resolute mass.

Jan strained to hear. Joubert reminded them of the long history of English treachery: of the continuous bullying of the Republics; of the earlier annexation of Natalia; of the seizing of the Kimberly diamond fields; of the unreasonable demands regarding the enfranchisement of the uitlanders; of the unacceptable meddling in the affairs of the Boer sovereign states:

"Even now," he proclaimed, "English troops are menacing our borders and thousands more are arriving from across the seas. It's necessary to move pre-emptively before the English become too strong. As in the War of Independence, we will move quickly and defeat the English in Natal. Then following our victory we will negotiate peace from a position of strength. Ours is a just cause! God is with the righteous!"

Joubert's words roused the Boers to visible elation. After the waiting and tensions of the previous months, everyone was spoiling for a fight. With the others, Jan stood in his stirrups, waved his hat and shouted until he was hoarse. Some fired a ragged *feu de joie*. Encouraged by Joubert, they sang the *Volkslied.* The noise of thousands of stentorian, male voices reverberated around the hills. Together they cheered as the Commandant-General and his staff shoved through the crowd cutting a path back to his marquee. Quickly orders cascaded down the chain of command. Eight days' rations were to be collected from the supply dumps by the railway track. Bandoliers were to be fully replenished. Wagons were to assemble in a central laager. All commandos were to be ready to ride at dawn.

It was 12 October 1899. It was raining heavily and too wet to make a fire, so Jan, with everyone else, forfeited his customary black coffee. He sat on his pony lingering in the freezing dawn, chewing the ubiquitous biltong. He pulled his cape tightly around his shoulders, but still the drumming rain penetrated; soon he was soaked. The signal was given and with friends and family he took his place in the marching column. Through the misty greyness of the emerging day he looked with awe at the slowly advancing mass which spread over several miles: thousands of mounted fighters, guns drawn by oxen, great herds of slaughter cattle resignedly bringing up the rear. The Natal border was barely two hours ride away. Soon they would pass over Laings Nek with Majuba Hill on their right, and drop down from the high veld into the rolling hills below. Khakis were known to be in the town of Aberdeen, about fifty miles distant.

CHAPTER 2

The Call of Empire

(Southampton - 2 December 1899)

The third-class, wooden railway carriage was full of men in khaki. The atmosphere was thick with smoke from woodbines and smouldering clay pipes; a condition exacerbated by the pungent smells of sweat and acrid body-odours which exuded in the stuffy heat. The nervous laughter, shouting and ribaldry faded away as the occupants settled down in their cramped compartment - ten soldiers elbowing for space where eight civilians might have travelled. Equipment was stored on luggage racks, harnesses eased, rifles pushed under seats, legs stretched and carefully dovetailed between those of friends sitting opposite – muddy boots ignored. Gradually, in the maturing silence, men became introspective and pensive as they thought of loved ones left behind, and quietly contemplated their uncertain future.

Jack Clegg sat by the window. He was tired after the intensive preparations of the past weeks, and the 3 a.m. start that morning. With his sleeve he wiped clear the condensation on the glass and peered at the rain splashing onto the pane. As if hypnotized, he watched with weary fascination as most drops bounced off the window, swept away by the forceful slip-stream. A few hopelessly congregated to form rivulets which trickled downwards before they too were abruptly scattered. In the sedative quiet he became aware of the rhythmic clatter of the iron wheels on the track: "clackety-clack, clackety-clack, you're-going-to-war, clackety-clack". He looked out at the grey, wintry landscape which was barely visible through the murky weather and the gusting smoke which poured from the labouring engine. It was an unfamiliar landscape with rolling hills, clustered villages and rustic cottages; so very different from home.

....

There was a persistent tapping on the window: "tap-tap, tap-tap". "Cum on lads, keep us right, I've got others to see to'.

Again the knocker-up banged on Jack's window with the umbrella wires tied on the end of his long pole. Wearily Jack rolled over on his straw mattress, unwillingly slid out of bed, raised the window and shouted down, "'Ave 'eard yer!" With this acknowledgement the knocker-up moved on to his neighbours, the Naylors. The "tap-tap, tap-tap" disturbed the quiet of the morning; the sound gradually receding down the courtyard as the community stirred. Jack noticed that it was raining. He closed the window, gave his younger brother, Fred, a rough shake before opening the bedroom door and taking the two steps across the tiny landing. He banged on the door of the other upstairs room and received a reluctant response: "Alright … comin'!"

The house grudgingly came to life. His mother went down stairs first and lit the single gas-mantle above the fire-place; it cast an eerie and barely adequate light across the room which served as living space and kitchen - the focus of all family activity. She drew hot water from the kettle hanging from a top-bar by the black fire-range and brewed a pot of tea. During the cold months the fire was banked up and kept alight throughout the night in an attempt to keep the damp at bay. She riddled the embers and shovelled on the remaining coal from the scuttle sitting in the hearth. Oats were mixed with water and seasoned with salt. This porridge would tide over the family workers before the short, mid-morning halt for breakfast in the mill. For this meal she now cut chunks of bread and covered them with beef dripping. In the good times she would include cold fish: haddock or kipper. There were six children in all, four boys and two girls. The boys shared one bedroom; two single, metal beds crunched together with barely room to manoeuvre around the edges; two to a bed. In similar fashion the grown-ups occupied the second bedroom together with their two daughters. Jack and Fred were old enough to work as was Sally, the eldest girl. Together, with their father, they were employed at the Albert Street Mill just around the corner. The Mill towered like a giant, dwarfing the courtyard in which they lived: dirty, red-bricked, grim and menacing.

Jack dressed quickly and headed for the outdoor privvy in the small cobbled yard. The ashen pit was in a small brick building roofed with heavy, stone flags. He didn't linger; it was too cold. Besides, it was too dark to read from the pieces of newspaper which were pierced by a nail and swung on a length of string from the ceiling. The cold-water tap was also in the yard; he washed perfunctorily oblivious to the sweet, oily smell of cotton which permeated his clothes, hair and skin pores.

On returning to the kitchen he found his dad, Fred and Sally already eating their porridge and drinking the hot tea.

"'Urry up lad, we're off in a few minutes," urged his dad.

Jack gobbled down his food. "Any fish this mornin' mam?" he

enquired hopefully. "You'll see lad wen yer open's yer

'aversack."

"Cum on ...time to go." And with that Jack's father rose from the scrubbed, wooden table, threw on his jacket, pressed on his oil encrusted cap, slung his haversack over his shoulder and led the scurrying procession through the door. They burst into the dark, damp morning.

In the courtyard others were also on the move. The boys and men emerged wearing flat caps, with the collars of jackets turned up to keep necks dry and provide protection from the cold. Young women and girls too disgorged from the cottages, their long, colourless dresses sweeping the cobbles, while black shawls covered their heads and shoulders providing warmth. Few older women appeared. Once married with children their responsibilities were in the home. From the courtyard the workers turned left into Albert Street and joined the trickle of hunched humanity which quickly became a stream, became a river and washed through the mill gates. This flowing tide was accompanied by the clatter of clog-irons on the uneven cobbles. On entry Jack nodded casually to Sally; she veered off with the other girls to the carding room, whilst the men climbed the stairs to the spinning machines. The long, monotonous day had begun.

At 6:30 a.m. precisely, the enormous steam engine sprang into life; its powerful, shiny, oiled pistons moving to and fro driving a baffling array of shafts, cogs and drive-belts; all naked and unprotected. They in turn powered the spinning mules. The noise was deafening. On arrival the men stripped to collarless shirt tucked into trousers held up by string and broad braces. Mr Clegg began to "mee-maw" - passing instructions to his sons by over emphasising his lip movements. Jack and Fred expertly negotiated the carriages of the mules in order to join the broken yarn without interrupting the flow of the machinery as it moved backwards and forwards across the floor. They worked bare-footed to avoid slipping on the oil splashed from the spindles, and were adept at picking up the yarn ends between their toes; this greatly speeded up the repair. After all, it was piece-work, and wages depended upon output. Soon in the warm, moist room dusty sweat dripped off the end of Jack's nose, but he knew these conditions to be necessary if the fine cotton thread was not to snap. He looked up at the humidifiers spewing out steam. At least it wasn't summer when he and Fred would have to douse the floor with water from buckets to ensure sufficient humidity.

Everyone remarked that Jack was like his dad; he looked across at a small reserved man of slight build, but a hard worker and one who was proud of his skills. He had sharp facial features half hidden behind a trimmed moustache. He was a Lancashire spinner, and in a good week might earn a full pound. Jack and Fred worked for their dad as "piecers", and were dependent for their remuneration on his generosity. It had been that way since Jack was twelve and a part timer - school half a day and then in the mill for the remainder - but since the age of thirteen he had worked full time. In due course he too would become a spinner; his life was preordained.

Jack was aware that he belonged to the first generation of working-class children to receive free elementary education in one of the new board schools. His father had learnt to read at the Methodist Sunday School, but his mother remained illiterate. Jack had enjoyed his schooling. In his final years he had been enthralled and inspired by his teacher, Mr Brown, who was a champion of the Empire. Before being sucked into the burgeoning school system, he had previously been a soldier in the Twentieth of Foot, and had fought in the Crimean War at Balaclava and Inkerman. He would regularly re-enact his significant part in the battles to the delight of his young audience. With swelling chest he would recount the General's accolade when the Russians had been driven off at the point of the bayonet: "Nobly done, Twentieth!" From Russia to India, and as a sergeant he had been at the siege of Lucknow and in the thick of the fighting for the famous "engine house". It was there he was wounded with a musket ball to the thigh; thereafter he walked awkwardly, dragging his distorted leg. But he remained proud of his exploits and regaled his pupils with past glories. A large map of the world was displayed on the classroom wall with its ever expanding pink, reflecting the unstoppable increase in the spread of Queen Victoria's domains.

At 12:30 p.m. the steam engine rested; gradually the whirring wheels and slapping belts slowed to a stop, and the silence became almost palpable. This was the cue for his two younger brothers to appear carrying a hot-pot of potatoes, vegetables and herbs; sometimes even bits of meat. Jack took the food and sitting on the floor ate amid the machinery. If the weather permitted he might eat in the mill yard or more pleasantly on the banks of the mill lodge. In the winter, the lunch hour offered the only possible glimpse of daylight, for it would be dark as he trudged between mill and home.

That night the cigarette smoke was dense in the Spinners' Arms as Jack gathered with Fred and his neighbours, Bill and John Naylor. The four were life-long friends and almost inseparable. They were of a similar age, and had all grown up together in Joseph's Courtyard: scruffy, ragged, shoeless, unwashed urchins. They had progressed from hop-scotch and marbles to carving out the Empire in Africa and India with little more than crude, wooden swords, stick-muskets and a good dollop of courage. As they got older they had naturally cohered into the Joseph's Court gang; Jack's assertiveness made him the undisputed leader. Their sisters, Sally and Mary, being mere girls, had been admitted under sufferance. They had all attended the same school before being engulfed by the insatiable appetite of the mills. The lives of both families were inextricably interwoven in their tight community; they would even share digs in Blackpool during the wakes.

Jack elbowed a path through the noisy crowd while expertly balancing two jugs of Thwaite's Ale in each hand. He placed them roughly on the stained, wooden table without spilling the precious contents. Fred held up his beer and examined the brownish liquid; a self appointed connoisseur, "T'as a good 'ead on it," he announced, "An' it's clear. Aye, tha' does a grand pint 'ere." With the ritual inspection over, they each raised their jugs, "Yer good 'ealth."

"See there's some good turns on at Circus this week," Bill pointed to a poster hanging askew on the wall opposite him. The others turned to look. The Circus of Varieties was a place of entertainment for the workers close to the town centre on Newgate. It was in sharp contrast to the nearby competing Theatre Royal with its opulent décor and productions of opera and serious drama. The Circus provided proper entertainment.

"Lancashire Lads are on. There's a new young un called Charlie Chaplin; suppose to be best clog dancer about. An'," Bill held the floor, "the Chocolate Coloured Coone's back." The latter was a local Rochdale lad who was currently the top turn on the variety circuit. His family had taken him as a child to America in search of a better life, but he had returned to his roots and now, as a black-faced singer, he crooned the songs of the Deep South in a dramatic, bass voice. "Tomorrow is lasses night. We can take Sally and Mary for nowt; are we goin'?"

These days Jack found that one of the few places where he could find release from the daily drudgery was at the Circus; he would immerse himself in the songs, dancing, slap-stick and magic. Also it was an opportunity to be with Mary in a more intimate setting; they always sat together on these occasions. Like Sally, she was a carder at the Albert Street Mill. She shared the same pale, anaemic complexion which characterized most girls in the cotton mills who were deprived of sunlight. She was plagued by a persistent mill-cough, or perhaps it was a trace of consumption – a too common ailment of those living in the damp, jerry-built, back-to-back cottages. She was a trim, petite girl and rather plain, but her bubbly character and impetuous laugh attracted him. She could be stubborn and forthright in the Lancashire mould, but also warm and caring.

"Aye, let's go," asserted Jack, carrying the agreement of the others.

The Circus was a large, wooden building heated by two open, coke-burning stoves with tall, metal chimneys which protruded through the roof. It was shabby with peeling paint, but sympathetically in character with its surroundings and working-class clientele. The men paid their six pence and the party took their seats in the stalls. It was a full house, and soon the sour reek of warming bodies and smouldering coke produced a fetid stench which pervaded the whole atmosphere. But no-one seemed to notice. The erudite Master of Ceremonies, in his swirling tailed-coat, banged his gavel, called the audience to order, and in his pompous, flamboyant language announced the first turn; it was the comedian. He soon had them all laughing uninhibitedly with his audacious tongue twisters: "She sells sea shells on the sea shore …", and with his droll monologues: "It must have been the lobster, it couldn't have been the booze ..."

Jack was spell-bound by the male mentalist and his young beautiful assistant. She moved among the audience collecting objects which the blind-folded mentalist identified by apparently reading her mind. Everyone was mesmerized. Jack knew it was trickery, but he couldn't fathom how it was done.

The clog dancing was impressive. The Lancashire Lads cleverly mimicked the movements made by the cotton machinery. They carried sticks symbolic of the cotton bobbins which were colourfully decorated with ribbon strands. And the youngest, Charlie, gave a spectacular solo dance of exceptional speed and complexity.

As billed, the star turn was the Coloured Coone. He was dressed in immaculate frock-coat and top hat, and seduced his audience with his soulful rendition of the songs of the slaves: Old Folks at Home, Gospel Train, Swing Low sweet Chariot. He brought the night to a raucous conclusion as everyone was invited to join in singing, "Michael, Row the Boat Ashore". Thwaite's Ales had clearly moistened a few throats.

Jack was sorry to see his time of escapism drawing to a close. He awaited the drum-roll which ritually announced the national anthem and concluded the entertainment. The Master of Ceremonies once again banged his gavel; some people shuffled on the wooden benches glad to ease growing aches, and in anticipation of the invitation to stand, but instead he introduced an unscheduled turn.

"Ladies and Gentlemen," he began rapidly. "It is my unadulterated, unostentatious, unornamented, patriotic duty and irrepressible, indubitable pleasure to introduce to you one of the 'eroes of our glorious Empire; one of the Queen's envoys who 'as travelled the world to subdue the noble savage, and to establish our incomparable, unparalleled, unsurpassed civilization in the darkest reaches of the known world; a true bearer of the white-man's burden."

Jack tensed in surprise and with an unexpected anxiety, as if his hidden hopes were to be revealed.

"Tonight 'e's come from Bury to exhort and encourage the young men among us to consider a glorious and worthy career, to 'elp in the further inexorable, unstoppable, irrevocable expansion of Empire. Without further ado …" he banged his gavel with demonstrative force on his small table, his voice rising, "I present Sergeant Grindrod!"

On cue the seven-piece band struck up, "Soldiers of the Queen". The audience responded to the jingoistic prompting and burst into song. It was a heady performance of arrogant zeal. Amid this cacophony of sound, a stern figure marched onto the stage. With an exaggerated slide of the left foot and driving-in of the right he thundered to a halt. He swivelled, repeated the forceful drill movements and faced his audience. He was fairly short in the ilk of Lancashire men, but slim, fit and physically robust. He was dressed in a smart red tunic, blue trousers and a "fore and aft", which balanced precariously on his head. He stood still waiting for the band and singing to end, and when it did he commanded the silence. He moved his head slowly and deliberately from left to right, his eyes searching out the young men, his polished moustache quivering. People waited for him to break the spell. He owned the audience and held the tension like the professional actor he was; until he deemed it appropriate to speak.

"God 'as given to the British nation the solemn mission to go out to farthest corners of the world in order to spread civilization, Christianity, and commerce. Isn't this wat Livingstone told us. The Queen's Empire extends from India to Zanzibar, from Egypt to Jamaica." He paused, relishing his power, "Those natives wat don't know better and resisted these benefits, 'ave been shown the errors of their ways by the British Army, unbeatable and unbeaten. Why, only a few months ago the cowardly death of Gordon of Khartoum were amply avenged with destruction of the Mahdi's vast army at Omdurman by the great General Kitchener. It were a glorious victory shared by local Rochdale men servin' with Lancashire Fusiliers."

Mr Brown's proud boasts echoed in Jack's mind. As he listened to the immaculate sergeant and observed his every gesture, he felt that the piercing eyes were boring into him personally; it was to him that the sergeant was speaking.

"Now me lads, yer can be a part of this sturrin' adventure. Yer can soldier for Queen and Country and 'elp make 'istory just like yer mates. Down the road in Bury is the barracks of the Lancashire Fusiliers, the unequalled Twentieth of Foot, born of the Glorious Revolution of 1688. Cum and join us!" he urged. "Cum and take Queen's shillin'! I'll be in Mason's Arms after show, and will be for next three nights."

Again as rehearsed, the band picked up its cue, the drums rolled and it launched into the national anthem. "Gerr up!" urged Mary tugging at Jack's arm, "Are yer sleepin'?" In his thoughts Jack was marching through the mountains of the North-West Frontier, or struggling through the dripping jungles of Africa. Grasping reality he struggled to his feet and sang with gusto, "God save the Queen".

As they spilled out into the street, the cold night air hit them like a rushing wind; they pulled up collars or tightened shawls. "Let's call at chippy," prompted Bill.

"Four fish 'n chips … ta."

They sauntered through the streets eating from newspaper wrappings. They snatched with bare fingers at the hot chips and fleshy batter, their nostrils assaulted by the reek of the acid smell of vinegar on hot grease. The excited chatter was of the turns, each with their favourite: John the comedian, Bill the mentalist, Fred the clog dancers, the girls the Coloured Coone. Jack said little. The girls were sent home while the men headed for the Spinners' Arms. There they sat at a table in the smoking room, Thwaite's Ale to hand.

"Yer've been quiet since we left the Circus Jack. Is owt troublin' yer?" enquired Fred.

Jack didn't answer immediately; he was chewing over his thoughts. "There's more to life than these 'ere mills," he said reflectively. "Wouldn't it be grand to travel, to see world and new countries and people and things. 'Ere's just drab and borin'" He had aired his discontent to his friends before, but now he realised that his feelings were solidifying. He had become increasingly disillusioned with the dreariness and predictability of life, and with the stifling and suffocating environment of the cotton town.

"That's nowt new. Yer always goin' on about it," retorted John.

"Hi, but now there's a chance to do summat about it," replied Jack. "Tha could join the Army."

"Aye," added Fred eagerly, "We'd 'ave smart uniforms and th' opportunity to serve Queen and country – we'd be the envy of all wen us cum 'ome."

"Aye, and yer get yersel killed for nine pence a day – we'll all soon be spinners an' get twice that money," injected John.

"If we don't die of consumption or mill-cough first," countered Jack. "It's like livin' in a prison."

"D'yer think parents will agree?" Bill spoke for the first time; slowly as if seriously considering the proposition.

"Don't know. But I'll soon be twenty one, and then I can make up me own mind."

The discussion swirled around until closing time. Gradually a consensus emerged. It was decided to coordinate their actions; both sets of parents would be asked together after tomorrow's tea. Jack knew that he would break free from this oppressive existence with or without parental blessing.

"Join the army, yer must both be soft in the 'ead! Look at the Hargreaves lad on Nelson street. Where d' he go? Africa? Egypt? Sudan? Don't matter. Tha' point is, yon lad's cum 'ome an' he's as daft as a brush. The army gives 'im a pittance and expects 'is mum and dad to look after 'im for rest of 'is life. War 'appens when they're dead … loony-bin?" Jack's dad was angry. He banged his pipe on the table to empty the burnt residue and continued, "'Ave worked me backside off to bring yer up; for all of yer. Yer've been me piecers for seven years and more; we're a good team and pick up a good wage. War 'appens wen yer gone? 'Ow do I pay bills 'ere?"

"Yer can train other piecers," offered Jack

"Aye; and in meantime output drops and so does the pay packet."

"It won't be long afore Fred and me are spinners in our own right. You'll 'ave to train new piecers any road." Jack decided to be bold. "I don't wanna be a spinner for the rest of me life. I wanna go past Blackpool. I wanna see other countries; do things; soldier for Queen and Country."

"Ne'er mind Queen and Country, yer've got a family 'ere." His voice was rising.

"Always thought yer were proud of Queen and Country. Yer talks a lot about th'empire and 'ow we own much of the world, and teach heathens the right way to live. Yer always goin' on about the Jubilee celebrations, street parties and all. Is that beer talkin', or would yer be proud of a son who's 'elping to carve out the empire?" Jack had never spoken like this to his dad before.

Jack's dad was thrown by this unaccustomed assertiveness in his son. For a moment he was quiet. He pressed the fresh tobacco into his pipe. "And wat about yon lass? Do yer expect 'er to wait seven years for thee?"

"Which lass?" countered Jack defensively.

"Are yer blind as well as soft in the 'ead? Wen the lass from next door cums for a cup of sugar, she really cums to see thee."

Since making his decision to leave, Jack had been strangely concerned about Mary and her reaction. What's it matter? he had thought, there's nowt between us. And yet he was nagged by strange feelings stirring within as if exposing a self deception; but he was not to be deflected. "Am goin'dad."

"I son yer goin', I can see that. I can't stop thee, you'll soon be a man. But Fred stays; he's nor old enough."

Fred had been quite happy up to this point to leave the argument to Jack. Now he interjected, "Am eighteen, am old enough!"

Their dad was fuming, and struggling to control himself. He spoke deliberately, "I'll only lose one son and one piecer; that's wer it ends." He turned to face the fire with his back to the two brothers. The discussion was over.

Fred knew that it was pointless to protest, and sullenly resigned himself to staying, at least for now

Dad lit his pipe and puffed, the smoke swirled upwards in the hot current. He spoke into the fire and into the awkward silence which now filled the room. "And I 'opes yer cum back, and in one piece lad."

There had been a heated argument in the Naylor family too, but both John and Bill had had their way. Together the three of them went to the Mason's Arms and met Sergeant Grindrod. That Monday morning they nervously joined with eight others at the station, and travelled by train the seven miles to Bury. Grindrod was a happy man as he contemplated the bounty which was his due for each new recruit - not an inconsiderable sum; although he would have to share it with the accommodating Master of Ceremonies.

John Naylor almost failed the medical on account of his childhood rickets which had left him slightly bowed-legged. Jack's occasional rasping was tolerated as mere mill-workers' cough - fresh air and solid food was the Army's remedy. Bill's chest expansion, or lack of it, didn't impress the doctor, but the Army was eager for recruits and the marginal could be accepted. The three became Lancashire Fusiliers on the 21st February 1899.

....

"We're 'ere lads; get yer kit together!"

Still groggy from the clinging sleep and soporific atmosphere the soldiers stood up, stamped their feet to encourage blood circulation, and began to pull on their harnesses and haversacks. Rifles were retrieved from beneath the seats. Bodies jostled for space. Jack looked out of the window and saw vast, red-bricked warehouses and numerous heavily-laden, horse-drawn wagons running on metal tracks. There were crowds of excited people. The train slowed, groaning and screeching to a gradual halt. He saw the sign: *Southampton.*

CHAPTER 3

The Reunion

(Frere, Natal - 26 December 1899)

The Irish, single-malt whiskey was smooth and warming, not fiery as some could be, particularly the indiscriminate blends. His love of Irish whiskey was a consequence of his earlier service in Ireland where he had been sent to pursue the *Moonlighters* - ruthless, vicious gangs of disenchanted peasants. He reached for the nearby decanter and half-filled his tumbler. From a small jug he added a tear-drop of water - just sufficient to tease out the flavour. He sipped his drink and involuntarily winced at the sharp pain. His ribs still ached and the bruises were still raw from the shell fragment which had struck his side during the recent fighting at Colenso. He had been unable to shake of the despondency which weighed heavily following the disasters of the previous weeks - frequently the muscles in his forehead twitched uncontrollably. So far he had spent a miserable Christmas in his railway carriage, harassed by the heavy rain and burdened with his own gloom.

It was in these moments of loneliness that his thoughts drifted naturally towards his mother. Even now, so many years after her death, her memory induced a sense of warmth, comfort, security. She was the most gentle, affectionate, patient and amusing person that he had ever encountered. He remembered how she would teach him and his siblings nursery rhymes; she was exciting, full of lively expression as she brought characters alive. She would accompany them on the piano or read them Bible stories. Her brood were the focus of her life. She was often ill, but as a youth he had not appreciated the severity of her condition; not until that fateful day when he had gone to the railway station in Exeter to meet her as she returned from a shopping expedition. He was with her when she collapsed on the platform, struck down by a lung haemorrhage. He recalled his panic and fear. With others he helped to carry her into the waiting room. She was too ill to be taken home. A bed and linen were summoned and she lay barely conscious in the waiting room. During all that time he sat by her bed fanning her and wiping her brow. He left only to allow her privacy when the nurse attended to her more intimate needs. He slept fitfully in a chair in the corner of the room wanting to be close; fearful of losing her. He held her hand when after three days she sighed as her spirit finally abandoned her frail body. Redvers Henry Buller had been 16 years old.

He felt melancholic. He poured another drink.

His thoughts wandered to another lady, the Queen. He had once been her aide-de-camp and had enjoyed a frank but respectful relationship. It was scarcely two months ago when she had summoned him to Balmoral for a private audience - how quickly time had passed.

"General Buller, my dear friend, how pleased we are to see you again." She had welcomed him warmly. "Congratulations! We are heartened by your appointment as Commander-in-Chief, South Africa. I know that as the General Officer Commanding the Aldershot Garrison, you should expect the appointment, but I want you to know that you are also your Sovereign's choice. You are our most trusted General." She had been clear: "The eyes of the Empire are upon you. Our supremacy in Southern Africa is at stake. There can be no failure; we are certain that you will teach those troublesome Boers a lesson."

"For certain Mam, it will not be a long affair," he had reassured her. "There will not be much hard fighting."

But he was sixty years old and only too aware that he had become softened by a decade of sedentary appointments. Now, in the autumn of his military career when he was eagerly anticipating retirement to manage his extensive estates in Devon and Cornwall, he had unexpectedly been given his first independent field command. His innate honesty had come to the fore; hadn't he candidly admitted to the Secretary of State for War, Lord Lansdowne, that he was inexperienced in the command of large formations in the field, and that he was more comfortable as the number two? Hadn't he been unequivocal in saying that he was sick of Africa, and that if forced to go out he would come away as soon as he could? But he had failed to cut through their mutual loathing. His ally and mentor, Lord Wolseley, Commander–in-Chief of the Army, was sinking into senility and of no support. He had put on a brave public face, but he didn't want the job.

The streets of Southampton had been thronged with union-jack waving crowds; bands had played, people had sung jingoistically. The political and military hierarchies had come to bade him farewell. He was to command an Army twice the size of Wellington's at Waterloo - the largest British expeditionary force since the Crimea. He was to dictate history in Africa. What a privilege had been bestowed upon him by the mightiest nation in the world; what a responsibility!

How could he forget the chaotic situation that had greeted his arrival at Cape Town? The British High Commissioner, Sir Alfred Milner, was beside himself with fear. He predicted an imminent insurrection in Cape Colony by the majority Afrikaner population following the defeat of the British Army. The Boers had besieged and neutralized the in-country forces at Mafikeng, Kimberly and Ladysmith, and both Cape Colony and Natal were anticipating the Boer columns sweeping down across the wide undefended plains to the coastal towns. He had decided to stabilize the situation by splitting his reinforcing Corps; the main body to secure Cape Town and then strike northwards to relieve Kimberley, while he hurried to Natal with a Division to secure that Colony and break the siege of Ladysmith. But it had all gone wrong. His Generals, Gateacre and Lord Methuen, had been defeated in the Cape, while he had been checked on the march to Ladysmith at Colenso. He was still furious with General White for allowing himself to be cooped up with almost 14,000 men in a town of absolutely no strategic worth. Now the relief of the garrison had become a political imperative; the British public, whipped up by the press, was clamouring for the restoration of imperial pride. But the encircled garrison was an encumbrance which diverted him from other more pertinent lines of advance. He once more refilled his empty glass and turned the file on his desk to the telegram which he had sent prior to the battle at Colenso; he had clearly forewarned London of his misgivings:

> *It will be better to lose Ladysmith altogether than to throw open Natal to the enemy. The real fact is the enemy have the whip hand of us ever since the war*

began, and we have had to attack with inferior force their superior forces in selected positions. I certainly hoped to have found the relief both of Ladysmith and Kimberley less difficult than it has proved to be. I appear to have failed at Kimberley, and the undertaking in front of me is a very grave one.

In the fight that followed he been badly let down by his subordinates who had blatantly disregarded orders. That damned gunner, Colonel Long, had foolishly established his firing line well in front of the protecting infantry, and consequently lost ten of the guns to the Boer – an unpardonable disgrace. Hadn't he watched with misgivings as General Hart drilled his brigade as if on a parade ground before marching them off in close formation into a loop in the river Tugela? There they had been decimated by accurate Mauser rifle fire from three sides. He, Buller, had been left with no viable option other than withdrawal. He brooded; with that reverse what could he do? He had been convinced that the best plan was to let Ladysmith go and to take up a defensive position south of the river in order to contain the enemy and secure the Colony. He threw back the whiskey and recalled his fatigue, pain and raging temper at the time he had sent a signal to the beleaguered White in Ladysmith. He re-read it:

I tried Colenso yesterday but failed; the enemy is too strong for my force. Can you last long? If not, how many days can you give me in which to take up a defensive position? After which I suggest you firing away as much ammunition as you can and making the best terms you can.

He had conveyed his plan to London, but this had been decisively rejected:

The abandonment of White's force and its consequent surrender is regarded by the Government as a national disaster of the greatest magnitude. We would urge you to devise another attempt to carry out its relief.

Not only had he been rebuffed by London, but he had been humiliated. His political, military and Court enemies had conspired against him. He read on:

> *The prosecution of the campaign in Natal is being carried out under quite unexpected difficulties, and in the opinion of Her Majesty's Government it will require your presence and whole attention. It has been decided to appoint Field-Marshall Lord Roberts as Commanding-in-Chief South Africa.*

He replenished the empty whiskey tumbler and added water. He was being provoked into resignation. Lansdowne and Roberts were as thick as thieves and were scheming together with the king-in-waiting. He was only too aware of how peeved the Prince of Wales had been by his refusal to associate with the immoral Court following - "The Marlborough House Set". He recalled how, as Adjutant General, he had declined to facilitate favours for the Prince and so compromise his own integrity. Throwing Edward out of his office had irrevocably soured relationships; not the wisest of actions – even dangerous for his future career. But he was safe as long as the Queen lived. Yes, for one moment, at his time of ignominy, he had thought seriously about resignation; but how could he return to England so soon and as a failure? Was he forever to be known as the man defeated by the Boers at Colenso? How his enemies would gloat. The Queen's reaction to these setbacks had been surreptitiously relayed to him by a friend: "We are not interested in the possibilities of defeat; they do not exist." He must bide his time and await other opportunities. He had graciously replied to London:

> *I entirely agree with the reasons that guided the actions of Her Majesty's Government. I have for some time been convinced that it is impossible for one man to direct active military in two places distant 1,500 miles from each other.*

And so, after only three months he had been replaced as overall Commander-in-Chief South Africa, and his theatre of action limited to Natal.

Buller took out his pocket-watch and studied it. He was expecting a visit from Lieutenant-General Sir Charles Warren, the commander of the Fifth Division newly arriving in theatre from England. The Division was the War Office's response to his plea for reinforcements, and it was now concentrating at Estcourt, some nine miles down the railway track from his headquarters at Frere. He knew Warren well; he was stubborn and opinionated, hardly his choice. He had been resurrected from retirement to command - an engineer! He was famous for his excavations under Jerusalem and had been hailed as the first biblical archaeologist. He had also had a controversial period as Commissioner of the Metropolitan Police. He was a renowned surveyor having delineated territory around Bechuanaland and Griqualand West in the Northern Cape, but these were hardly the qualifications to command a fighting division. What he found particularly galling was that Warren had been given the Dormant Commission - should anything happen to him, Buller, be he a military or political casualty, then Warren would take command.

It was getting late.

....

More than a year had passed since Lieutenant-General Sir Charles Warren GCMG, KCB, FRS had relinquished command of the Thames Military District. He had bought a modest house in Ramsgate where he lived on half pay with his wife, Fanny, whilst awaiting the recall to duty. He was sixty years old, but remained fit and active; every morning he walked briskly for an hour either along the Esplanade to the harbour, or through the streets and around the common land adjacent to the boy's school on Chatham Street. He immersed himself in writing of his biblical excavations and African adventures, but remained restless to serve his Country again. He monitored with intense interest the deteriorating situation in South Africa; fighting was inevitable. Immediately following the Boer incursions into the

Cape and Natal, he wrote to the Commander-in-Chief, Lord Wolsey, reminding him of his availability. He was delighted and honoured to have been given command of the newly formed Fifth Division. After all, he was universally acknowledged as one of the principal authorities on South African military and administrative problems. No one could match his long record of distinguished service in that country; his wars against the natives and his familiarity with the Boers made him the natural choice.

As he disembarked from the ***SS Mohawk*** in Durban on Christmas Day, he was handed a note from the Governor of Natal, Sir Walter Hely-Hutchinson. He was requested to break his rail journey northwards at the Capital, Peitermaritzburg, and to dine with him at Government House. As the train zigzagged up and down the lush hills and contorted into curves that horrified Warren as an engineer, he wondered about the reason for the invitation; it was not as if they knew each other. If there are military concerns, shouldn't the Governor be speaking directly with Buller? After about four hours he reached the Capital and was met at the railway station by the Governor's Secretary; it was 7 p.m. As he climbed aboard the elegant, hand-crafted landau he could but admire the two magnificent, black Friesian stallions and the smart, black, red-liveried coachman. It was his first visit to Pietermaritzburg and he was suitably impressed with this thriving city of red-bricked buildings which nestled at the foot of a range of densely wooded hills. As they trotted on, his escort proudly pointed out the sights of this miniature metropolis: churches, hotels, banks, museum, library, the labyrinth of narrow streets which comprised the financial and legal district of the city. Most impressive was the newly completed City Hall with its imposing domes, stained windows and clock tower - reputedly the largest all-brick building in the southern hemisphere. In contrast, he was struck by the homely appearance of Government House. Far from being palatial, it resembled an English vicarage.

Warren was ushered into a reception room where the Governor, his wife and a select group of their friends were already present, aperitif in hand. The hum of conversation stopped as he entered; all eyes were upon him.

"So pleased that you could make it, General," Hely-Hutchinson stepped forward. "Let me introduce you to my wife and our guests." As the formalities unfolded, Warren began to feel decidedly underdressed in his khaki uniform - albeit smartly cut by his London tailor. The men wore formal evening dress with tailcoat and white, high-collared shirts. Warren's wife was adamant that the real influence in fashion was Princess Alexandra, the Prince of Wales' wife. Despite the remoteness of the Colony from London, it was clear that the ladies were mimicking the Court with the same popular, flowing dresses of sumptuous fabric and extravagant cut pulled in tightly at the waist by a narrow belt. Sleeves were puffed at the elbow where they met the obligatory long kid gloves. There was a profusion of colour: maroon, blue, green.

The preliminaries over, the Governor offered Warren a drink, "Gin and tonic?"

"A long one, thank you."

Light, inconsequential small-talk resumed until adjoining doors were opened by an Asian servant; the gesture indicating that the meal was ready. Each man linked arms with the lady designated to sit on his right, as per the seating plan, and escorted her into the dining room. The Governor led the way. His wife offered her arm to Warren which he accepted courteously. Her grip was soft; a little sensuous. He glanced surreptitiously at this attractive brunette – a good ten years younger than her husband. Her hair was gently waved and drawn back into a small, high chignon which exposed smooth, pale skin and bright, grey-blue eyes; she was warm and feminine. Together they brought up the rear. The dining room was of modest size, in fact he thought it somewhat cramped. The walls displayed water-colours of typical African landscape and local animals; at the far end French-windows were slightly ajar inviting the cooler air to intrude. The table was lavishly laid with Lincoln House, sterling-silver cutlery and Waterford crystal glassware. However, the food was uncomplicated; Warren thought it a simple menu with only six courses. The hors d'oeuvres of smoked eel presaged a thick soup followed by a local fish. The main course was a joint of bush-meat - impala he was informed - accompanied by a variety of fresh seasonal vegetables. Anchovy aigrettes heralded a final dish of fresh, dried and crystallised fruit with an array of sweets and biscuits. However, despite it being the festive season, the atmosphere around the table was strained and sombre.

Each course demanded a complimentary wine. "More red wine, sir?" The black, liveried footman hovered.

Warren covered the almost-empty glass with his hand, "I've had sufficient."

"You are not enamoured with our wines, Sir Charles?" It was his hostess.

"Not at all, I think this Constantia is excellent: full bodied with a fruity aroma. It reminds me of a fine Bordeaux. And how are the Cape winemakers recovering after the damaging phylloxera epidemic?"

"They have planted new disease free vines," interjected one of the male guests sitting opposite, Edward Grey was a developer with interests in expanding the docks and extending the infrastructure of the Colony; he was also known to dabble in vineyards. "That's the easy part. The wine industry is still struggling to find suitable markets after the imposition by the British Government of penal taxes in its favouring of the French producers."

Warren chose not to be drawn into a contentious discussion and simply sipped the remainder of his wine appreciatively. He summoned the attendant waiter, "A glass of water please." He looked across at a bemused Grey and explained, "While I was the Commissioner of the Metropolitan Police I saw much abuse of alcohol. I believe drunkenness to be a major cause of increasing poverty, unemployment and crime in our burgeoning cities and towns. So I drink in moderation and encourage others to do so."

"Didn't I hear that you were a supporter of the Temperance Movement? Doesn't it advocate total abstinence; or is that for others?" challenged Grey.

"That is the nonconformist position. I think we all agree that drunkenness is a disgusting personal habit and a social vice; it's a sin with eternal consequences. However, the Anglican Church's approach is that alcohol may be consumed wisely and in moderation."

"Were you not the Police Commissioner at the time of the infamous Whitechapel Murders?" asked the Governor, pointedly changing the subject.

"Just so."

"I understand that the murderer was never officially found … didn't you accuse one of the Queen's grandsons?"

Yes, reflected Warren to himself, and earned her bitter animosity. "The murderer was probably a young doctor known to be on the borderline of insanity. He disappeared for some days after the last murder and his body was later found in the Thames."

There was an uneasy silence.

"You have much experience of Africa?" asked another male guest.

"I commanded the Diamond Fields' Horse in the Transkei War against the Xhosa through seventy-seven and seventy-eight; that's until I was badly wounded. Subsequently, I frustrated the Boers as they attempted to encroach into Bechuanaland. I know certain parts of South Africa very well …. and I know the Boer."

"Then you will know that he wishes to place the whole of South Africa under his hegemony." The speaker was another entrepreneur, George Miller. He was an importer of all kinds of goods, of growing influence in the young colony, and alert to every business opportunity. "Until the discovery and exploitation of gold by Englishmen at Witwatersrand, those primitive Dutch farmers had nothing of any worth. In fact, you'll be aware that on several occasions they went cap-in-hand to the British Government begging for a hand out. Then they were poor. Now like leaches they suck the life-blood out of business men with debilitating taxes. Their government, once inefficient and incompetent, is additionally corrupt, oligarchic and arrogant." He was becoming heated. "What sticks in my gullet like a fish bone is the sale of monopolies to their cronies. Honest business men like me can't trade in dynamite, timber, iron and much else. Everything they practice runs contrary to the principles of free trade. Boer ministers flaunt their corruption and see this accumulation of personal wealth as their God-given dues. And while incomers provide the innovation, sweat and enterprise, they are allowed no say in the laws that govern them. You may be aware that in April of this year 21,000 uitlanders petitioned the Queen begging for the direct protection of the British Government."

No one was eating; everyone was listening earnestly as their grievances were enunciated.

Warren strove to reassure his fellow diners, "These complaints are well known to Her Majesty's Government. Isn't that why I'm here? Isn't that why our soldiers are dying …to bring the Boer to heel and to impose justice in government and trade?"

Miller was not appeased, "We have watched incredulously as again those bigoted Calvinists thrashed the British Army: Stormberg, Magersfontein, Colenso. We live in daily fear of an insurrection by the thousands of Boers living among us in Natal. Will they rise in support of their brothers to the north? Will they kill us in our beds? Will they oust the Government and take control of the Colony? Can we expect the Boers to come sweeping south into Peitermaritzburg and down to the port of Durban? If so, then the war is lost. After Majuba the British Government capitulated. What miserable concessions will it make this time at our expense?"

"It's interesting, don't you think General?" the calmer voice of the Governor's wife interrupted. "The previous policy of compromise after Majuba offered no chance of restoring Britain's power in South Africa. And the clumsy attempt to annex the Transvaal by Rhodes with the raid by his stooge, Jameson, was a fiasco. So now we have the situation where the Cape Colony is inhabited with a white majority of Afrikaners, but seemingly the Transvaal is inhabited by a white majority of British sucked in by the gold rush." She leant forward and held his eyes, "The Boers call the Transvaal "The South African Republic", and have taken to themselves a four-coloured flag as emblem of the future union of the Transvaal, Orange Free State, Cape Colony and Natal. The question being asked is: "Who is to have paramountcy in South Africa – Britain or the Boers?""

Warren responded firmly, casting around the table as he spoke, "Let me assure everyone, that the British Government will make no concessions to the Boer. It is totally unacceptable to have belligerent, uncooperative and unfriendly neighbours on the borders of our colonies. It has become an imperial imperative to establish a federation of homogeneous states in South Africa such as has occurred in Canada and is planned for Australia. Only then can British power be consolidated and the African Continent subdued. The Boers will be defeated; you have my assurance."

Grey returned to the discussion with an exaggerated politeness, almost mocking, "General, from the very beginning during long negotiations with the Boer, we warned that our territories would be invaded and that has happened. Our towns have been shelled or captured; thousands of head of cattle have been driven off; White is confined to Ladysmith; Buller is reeling; and the possibility of the whole Colony being overrun stares us in the face. We have intelligence that thousands of Natal Afrikaners have joined the Boer forces. But you should know that those loyal Englishmen from this Colony capable of bearing arms have responded. Irregular units have been raised such as the Imperial Light Horse, and Thorneycroft's Mounted Infantry. We will fight for our very existence even if Buller will not!"

The Governor sensed that his guests were becoming belligerent; he interjected, "This evening is for celebration not an occasion to harangue our guest. Let us enjoy ourselves, after all as the Scriptures say: "Tomorrow has enough worries of its own."" And so with cultivated tact the meal continued.

At a measured time following the dessert, the hostess rose and bowed slightly to the other ladies. Reacting to this cue, they demurely put on their gloves and withdrew to the drawing room to drink tea. The men stood for the departure of the ladies before relaxing back into their chairs to drink port, smoke cigars and talk leisurely. Eventually Hely-Hutchinson pushed back his chair and stood to indicate that it was time to join the ladies. He waved the others before him, but motioned discreetly yet firmly to Warren and led him onto the veranda.

The African night was in full chorus; the rhythmic, deep-throated belching of the bull frogs competed with the high-pitch scratching of thousands of crickets and other insects to fill the vacuum of awkward silence between the two men.

For a few moments the Governor stared into the blackness with his back to his guest. He turned, hesitated as if summoning confidence, then spoke deliberately and firmly; "I'm sorry that you were berated during dinner, but you needed to understand the depth of concern felt by the colonists." He paused before continuing: "As the Governor of this colony I am required to display steadfastness, hope, an unshakeable conviction in the coming victory, but my façade grows thin. When Buller passed through here he brought with him a spirit of depression, and now I am receiving alarming reports about the state of the Army. Officers, the wounded, war correspondents and the like are all passing through the Capital and bring discouraging news. Some say that Colenso was a shambles. That Buller became so engrossed with the attempts to recover the field guns that he lost sight of the overall battle. Apparently, the cavalry under Lord Dundonald had success in their grasp at Hlangwe, but Buller refused reinforcements. The infantry assault was conducted by Hart as if on parade at Aldershot; his men massacred in close formation - didn't we learn anything in our first war against the Boers?" His exasperation was too apparent.

"Often the truth is distorted and there are many facets of the battle which will not be known to us," offered Warren defensively, but he was unsure of his ground. He too had heard disgruntled murmurings.

The Governor continued in a severe, controlled tone, "Did you know that Buller invited General White to surrender his garrison together with its guns and supplies? I have it from one of his staff officers. Fortunately, White thought it a Boer ruse and refused to comply." An uncomfortable silence descended. Hely-Hutchinson eventually spoke, "The battle was ten days ago; what has Buller done since then? His army sits in Chieveley licking its wounds, whilst he hides in his railway carriage at Frere … doing what? In the meantime General White and his men in Ladysmith starve or die of disease. And the Boers? They strengthen their defences behind the river Tugela. Buller tells all that his infantry has poor morale; that they collapsed in the face of the enemy; whilst they in turn are hurt by his criticism and are restless for the opportunity to fight. We can't help worrying about what's going on. You heard Miller at the table; will the Army hold? Can we expect the Boer hordes to come galloping down the main street?" His body grew tense; the practiced outward calm of a diplomat displayed for his dinner guests was evaporating; he became agitated. He paused to offer Warren a cigar taken from a nearby box; the latter refused. The Governor flicked his ornate, silver lighter into life, lit his cigar, and slightly more composed by the soothing effect of the nicotine continued, "I hear that his men call him "Sir Reverse Buller" behind his back. You know the saying, "The higher the monkey climbs, the more he shows his arse." We are worried. I have informed London of my concerns. I invited you here tonight Sir Charles to impress upon you one thing; we are counting on you to restore leadership to our Army, to defeat the Boer, and to secure Natal."

....

"General Sir Charles Warren?" The affirming question did not invite an answer. "General Buller is waiting for you in his railway carriage, this way please, sir." The confident young staff officer strode out. It was a short distance to the carriage set apart in an adjacent siding. They mounted the steps. The young officer knocked on the door before opening it, "Sir Charles to see you, sir." He motioned for Warren to enter before withdrawing closing the door behind him.

Warren squinted briefly as he entered the brightly lit carriage; the abundant gas lights hissed contentedly. The Natal Railway Company had patriotically provided the Commander-in-Chief with a first-class carriage. The dining compartment had been stripped of its fixed tables and seats and replaced with a sturdy, oak writing table and green leather chairs. The original mahogany panelling and bold, shiny brass fittings gave an opulent but masculine appearance to the interior.

Buller looked at his watch with an expansive gesture reflecting his irritation; it was almost 10 p.m. "So pleased to see you Sir Charles after all this time." He indicated an arm-chair without offering his hand, "Remind me, when was it we last met?"

"Ninety-four I believe; on my return from commanding the garrison in Singapore. I visited you in the War Office to brief you on the situation there. You were still Adjutant General."

"Yes, of course. Would you like a drink? I'm enjoying a whiskey; or perhaps you prefer champagne?"

"A small whiskey, thank you." Warren sat down and looked across at Buller as he poured the drinks. When they had first met back in seventy-eight during the Transkei War, Buller was commanding an irregular unit like himself, the Frontier Light Horse. They had worked closely together, and at that time had become good friends; yes, on occasions they might differ greatly on the conduct of operations, but arguments and good natured chaff had never spoiled their relationship. Then Buller had been a handsome, lean, hyper-fit individual; much sought after by the young ladies. He had gone on to fight in the Zulu Wars and there won the Victoria Cross; his bravery was legendary and it was said that he earned the accolade twenty times over. He was known to be tough and brusque, but his soldiers had always loved him as an officer who shared their dangers and discomforts. But the man with the whiskey glass in his hand was bulky, heavy-jowled and thick necked; a stereotypical John Bull. His face was tired and strained. He had a lugubrious expression; his movements were weighted and deliberate.

"Water?" inquired Buller.

"No, neat thank you."

Buller sat facing his guest; he handed him a tumbler, "Your good health sir." They both drank.

"Cigar?" offered Buller, "or do you still prefer a pipe of Boer tobacco?"

Warren was surprised and impressed that Buller could recall his distant smoking habit. "I gave up that pleasure when I last left Africa. Perhaps I shall take it up again, but for the moment nothing, thank you."

"You had a good journey?" probed Buller. He had heard that Warren had stayed at Government House and was curious.

"Yes, everything went smooth enough. I spent last night with Hely-Hutchinson."

"The man's in a funk!" grunted Buller sharply. "Everywhere he sees the enemy: the local Boers are about to revolt; those facing us are about to sweep us into the sea; the Zulus are poised to take advantage of our defeat and ally themselves with the Dutch. Disaster is imminent!"

"There is an air of ...shall I say, concern, in the Capital," confirmed Warren. "Hely-Hutchinson remains unconvinced that we are able to drive the Boer out of Natal. I strove to be reassuring. However, I hear everywhere that the troops are dispirited. It would be good to have first hand authority for contradicting this .... my men are just coming up and would hear this gossip."

Their eyes met. "My troops are dispirited!" affirmed Buller forcefully. "Half of them are reluctant reservists called up a couple of months earlier. They are unfit, ill-fed, and have barely recovered from a long voyage packed into troopships. They were thrown into the scorching heat of an African summer, and have not yet had time to weld into units, never mind a field force – the largest expeditionary force sent overseas since the Crimea, and I was not even allowed to manoeuvre on Salisbury Plain for fear it would appear provocative. The damage caused by an unseen enemy has shattered morale. At Colenso, I and my staff had to drag them from their places of shelter and pull them back."

Warren listened alarmed. He offered advice, "After a defeat, troops can quickly get out of sorts if they have nothing to do. Have the men been practising skirmishing with the enemy? I recommend immediate exercising as a remedy."

"They have plenty of exercising in athletics and sports," retorted Buller.

"But what of practising contact with the Boer? Habit makes second nature," urged Warren.

"Another drink?" Buller moved to replenish his glass as if ignoring his visitor's suggestion.

"No thank you. I've had sufficient."

Warren sensed his advice was unwelcome and changed the subject, "I take it, Sir Redvers, that you have a plan of attack in which my Division will gladly play its part?"

Buller scrutinized the dapper General opposite him; the pretender to his throne. He had no plan. He addressed his visitor with an air of condescension, "Let me appraise you of the situation in which I find myself. The northern side of the Tugela River at nearly every point commands the southern bank. Ranges of high hills rise abruptly from the water forming a mighty rampart for the enemy. Before this the river, a broad torrent with a few narrow fords – drifts - flows rapidly; a great moat. Before the river, on our side, there stretches smooth, undulating, grassy country in full view from the hills making covert manoeuvre impossible." By now he was pacing the carriage. "My intelligence services estimate that there are between twelve and fifteen thousand Boers in those hills. That is twelve to fifteen thousand of the best riflemen in the world, armed with beautiful magazine rifles, an inexhaustible supply of ammunition, and fifteen to twenty excellent guns – Creusots and Krupps. All the drifts across which I must advance are surrounded with concealed trenches and rifle pits from which converging fire can be directed - this I learnt at Colenso." He collected a rudimentary map from his desk which had been hastily drawn by his engineers, and spread it on the table before them. "No doubt with your surveyor's eye you have studied the ground in detail. So tell me Sir Charles, where would you strike?"

Before leaving Cape Town, Warren had scoured the town for all available mapping of the area. During the four day sea journey to Durban, he had conducted war-games with his staff. They had studied every drift, every line of approach, all possible Boer defensive positions, and all reasonable locations for artillery. In his mind he was clear. "After due consideration I propose that we attack here," he pointed on the map to the hill at Hlangwe.

Buller exploded, "Hlangwe! What do you know about it?"

Warren was taken aback by this aggressive response, but was not to be intimidated, "General knowledge and war games. It's the extreme left of the Boer defence line. There the hill sits on the home bank of the Tugela unlike elsewhere; the defenders have the river behind them which is in spate and which hinders either their withdrawal or reinforcement. Once in our hands we can enfilade the whole Boer position with our artillery and pound them into retreat or surrender. Sir, I believe that Hlangwe is the key that will open the door to Ladysmith."

Hlangwe had been among the failed objectives of the Colenso battle. Buller felt his guts tighten; he was unnerved at the prospect of returning to the scene of his recent defeat.

"This is where we attack, sir!" indicated Buller brusquely, his finger on Potgieter's drift. This had been his first plan before he subsequently abandoned it for Colenso. Then he had hesitated to move away from the railway and his only line of supply and communication, but now he had little choice. "Here we will cross and fight our way through the hills to Ladysmith."

Warren was horrified. He knew this point well from his studies. Even if the crossing was successful, to exit would mean advancing surrounded by high ground on three sides held by Boer marksmen; they would be dominated like actors in an amphitheatre. "Sir Redvers," protested Warren, "with our marching columns and logistic tail we may cover ten miles in a day. The Boers on their ponies cover that distance in two hours. Wherever we assemble to attack, the Boers will concentrate to defend. We can never achieve surprise. These farmers are natural good shots reared on the veld and accustomed to the long ranges of the wide-open plains. Our men are trained to shoot over short distances and in volleys. We must, therefore, use our strengths to our advantage. Sir, we should pound the enemy with artillery until they are broken and demoralized, and then choose the best opportunity to close quickly and so deny them the advantage of range. Our best chance to achieve that is among the bush and scrub of Hlangwe."

Buller looked sternly at Warren. He was not going to be dictated to, "Whilst I thank you for your analysis Sir Charles, you are to understand that we will attack at Potgieter's. Your Division is to march forward from Estcourt to Frere and onwards to concentrate at Springfield. You should leave on the 6th January."

Warren became taut, "Sir Redvers, my infantry are concentrating as we speak, and my artillery is still moving up the track from Durban. I need more time. I would suggest 8th or 9th January."

Buller knew that he was not prepared to move without the Fifth Division complete. "The 9th and no later. I will issue your orders for the movement in due course." He emptied his glass and rose. "Now it's late and no doubt you'll need to rest after your long journey. We'll talk again."

Warren understood that he was dismissed. He drained his glass, stood up, nodded slightly, "Good night Sir Redvers. I thank you for your hospitality." Buller nodded tersely in acknowledgement.

It was raining. Warren descended from the carriage grasping the hand-rail to steady himself on the wet, slightly oily steps. At the bottom he paused momentarily to replace his helmet and fasten his Macintosh. The cool night air blew fresh in his face bringing a welcome relief from the smoke-stuffed, whisky-tainted interior. The young staff officer appeared out of the darkness, "Sir, can I escort you to your train?"

"My train?" Warren was thrown. "Have no arrangements been made for my overnight accommodation?"

The young officer stumbled over his reply, "I'm afraid General Buller gave no instruction on the matter."

Warren turned up his collar to deflect the drips now falling from his helmet and running down his neck. With a bad tempered shrug he abruptly launched into the darkness ignoring his would-be guide. His path was illuminated by the ambient light from scores of soldiers' flickering camp fires.

"Who does this dug-out ex-policeman think he is?" murmured the young officer to an unseen companion.

Back in his carriage Warren spread full length along the seat struggling to find warmth under a blanket. His great-coat acted as a pillow. He couldn't sleep. He was full of misgivings. The proposed plan was too hazardous; Buller nervous and irrational. He had seen men in that condition before. During the excavations under Jerusalem there had been several tunnel collapses and miners had been dragged to safety barely alive. They had subsequently manifested similar symptoms, and experience had shown him that the best cure was rest. Buller, he thought, needs a month's recuperation after the trauma of Colenso.

CHAPTER 4

Pastures New

(Estcourt in Natal & Rochdale in Lancashire - Christmas 1899)

Jack and friends quickly dumped their kit on their allocated bunks and pushed their way onto the deck of the Union Line Steamer, *SS Norman.* They jostled through the milling soldiery to gain a place by the rails. It was a damp, dull day, but the cold drizzle had not deterred the many well-wishers who packed the Southampton quayside to cheer them on their way. A band struck up and the crowd began to sing the familiar music-hall favourites of the day: “Dear Old England”, “Tommy Atkins” and “The Girl I Left Behind Me”. They sang until they were hoarse. Finally, the steamer slipped anchor and nudged away from the quay; the crowd gave a mighty cheer. Jack, Bill, Fred, everyone on board shouted back appreciatively until they could no longer be heard. The crowd became ghostly dots through the hazy rain. An odd silence descended on the ship as the finality of the situation dawned.

It was his first time on a boat – you couldn’t count the steamer on Hollingworth Lake. The first days were awful. The ship wallowed drunkenly across the Bay of Biscay where the heavy seas pounded the boat and the rain-filled winds lashed the decks. Jack, like most, felt wretched with sickness, and moaned and writhed in his bunk – death would have come as a welcome relief. But gradually his strength returned, his stomach stopped whirling around, the vice gripping his head released its hold; he began to feel human again.

By the time they docked in Las Palmos in the Grand Canary, everything changed. Grey, angry skies and cold, penetrating winds gave way to the warm, azure skies of the tropics. Jack and friends climbed on deck seeking the sunshine and fresh air, eager to escape the stale, befuddling atmosphere below. A matelot shouted through a loud-hailer that the ship would dock only for a few hours whilst the crew took on coal, soon evidenced by the swirling black dust that began to settle everywhere. Within minutes of arriving the ship was circled by bustling natives in a variety of seemingly flimsy craft selling fruit, cigars and cigarettes at ridiculously low prices.

Bill took out a penny and held it up high; with a shout he drew the attention of a couple of almost-naked, young boys before throwing the coin into the sea. Unhesitatingly, the boys dived into the water and disappeared below the surface; the water settled over them. At first the spectators jabbered excitedly, but soon the noise dissipated as now they anxiously searched the spot where the boys had submerged. "They must of drowned," uttered Bill guiltily, but then like corks bursting from a champagne bottle they erupted into the sun laughing, one of them holding up the penny triumphantly.

"Ere lad, catch this!" Now Fred threw a coin into the water. Again the boys dived only to emerge a few minutes later beaming with the coin held high. And so they dived again and again retrieving coins for the amusement of the soldiery. For Jack, that was one of the few highlights of a fairly miserable four week voyage.

As the ship steamed south, the sailors erected awnings as protection from the sun, and beneath these a regime of gymnastics and musketry practice was introduced – firing at cans and boxes thrown overboard and trailed by ropes behind the ship. But there was a lot of dead time; Jack read out-of-date magazines or played "house" or seven-card brag, anything to relieve the numbing boredom. Meal times offered no relief; breakfast alternated between black bread and hard biscuits with sugarless black tea. Dinner was bully beef with preserved potatoes or rice. Tea was as for breakfast.

It was a beautiful summer's day when the steamer carefully manoeuvred into Table Bay, Cape Town. Sweating black labourers heaved on chunky hawsers to pull the ship alongside the quay. With practised ease they wrapped the ropes around the sturdy capstans.

"Look! Look yonder!" Bill pointed animatedly at a prominent mountain knoll in the distance. It stood alone, majestic and proud, covered by an isolated, fluffy cloud which clung to its summit as if reluctant to reveal its nakedness. Everyone crowded on the decks hungry to experience the new sights, sounds and smells; their excited, incessant chatter was almost child-like.

Lively newspaper boys shouted loudly. At first the words were indistinguishable, but as Jack's ear began to cut through the unaccustomed dialect, he became alarmed at the emerging headlines: "Black week! Black week! Read all about it!" The boys held out open hands inviting payment. Jack tossed a two-penny piece which was expertly caught, and in return a rolled paper flew through the air. He grasped it and read eagerly.

"Wat's it say?" demanded Bill straining to catch a glimpse for himself.

Jack read aloud: "Black Week … A Big Battle … Gatacre's and Buller's reverses … Great fighting by the Boers … Heavy losses on the British side."

"Bugger me!" exclaimed John in despair, "looks like we've been beat everywer!"

"Good job I didn't bet on the war bein' over by Christmas," muttered Bill, conscious of the sweepstakes which were running on the concluding date of the conflict.

The mood changed. Their buoyant confidence was shattered. A palpable gloom descended with the realisation that there was to be no quick and easy victory over primitive farmers after all. Soon the order came to disembark. "We're off to see the sights of Cape Town," encouraged Bill as they clumped down the gangway and formed up on the quayside: "Right turn! …Quick march! …Halt! …Left turn! …Up the gangway!" And so into the bowels of the ***SS Roslin Castle*** which was moored barely five hundred yards further along the quay. "A bloody sharp trip that was," concluded Bill, voicing everyone's bitter disappointment. "We're up and down gang-planks like the Grand Old Duke of York."

In the failing light the ship steamed away for the port of Durban where they arrived four days later. They were ferried ashore in small, single-stacked lighters before being crammed into open, railway cargo-tubs. They sat on their packs waiting for the engine to lock-on and pull them into the hills.

"Look wat I've got!" Bill had slipped away unnoticed by the non-commissioned officers (NCOs), ostensibly to urinate, and was now scrambling back over the side of the truck. Jack pulled him in by his harness. A large object dropped to the floor with a squelching thud. Bill quickly gathered it up and drew his friends into a corner where they sat in a conspiratorial huddle. "Round the corner there's some posh women givin' out presents to "gallant soldiers"." He mimicked their refined accents. "That's us in it? So I gladly relieved 'em of a pineapple – any 'ow, that's wat they called it." He held up his prize.

"Ave never seen an apple like that," queried Jack.

"Wat sort of tree does it grow on?" injected John.

"Well … it's an African apple … it grows on an African tree … 'appen a big un," explained Bill.

"Ave seen coco-nuts on the shy at fair, but never African apples," countered John.

Bill was becoming deflated. His moment of triumph was slipping away. "It's a bloody apple not a nut!"

"Well 'ow do we peel it?" quizzed John.

"Don't rightly know."

For a few moments there was a puzzled silence as the friends studied the tough, prickly, segmented skin and the leathery green foliage. No one knew how to tackle this apple. Suddenly Bill drew his bayonet from its scabbard and thrust it into the body of the fruit. He drew it up and down eventually splitting the fruit in two. Using both hands he picked up a segment and gnawed the moist, fleshy inner - sweet, sticky juice ran down his chin onto his tunic.

"'Ow's it taste?" enquired John cautiously.

"Champion! Champion!" spluttered Bill, his mouth full.

Jack similarly took his bayonet and attacked the remaining half. He shared it with John; eagerly they sucked the juice and devoured the unfamiliar fruit.

It was to prove a long, cold, uncomfortable night. They huddled in their greatcoats, exposed to the elements and shaken relentlessly in the wooden tubs as they rattled through the countryside. Soot and grit from the engine blew into their eyes and trickled down their backs. Late in the depth of the black night the train halted at a station platform. By the shadowy light of a gas lamp Jack read the sign: "Pietermaritzburg".

"Wer are we?" grumbled John reluctant to wake from his fitful sleep.

"Peter … Mary … Burg … or sommat" offered Jack.

"Hi, that's the capital of this place – like London," Bill's voice rose from the bottom of the tub.

Soon studded footsteps clattered down the platform. Voices swirled through the night getting ever closer. Eventually two orderlies, resentful of being denied their beds, bad temperedly thrust a canteen of tea and a pile of slices of bread and butter towards them: "Share that between yer." And with that they were gone.

Jack took charge of the distribution: two sandwiches for each of them. They swigged from the canteen and passed it around. Shortly, with a violent shake as couplings took up the slack, the hooting train dragged the tubs once more into the wilderness. It was so crammed that no one could properly lie down. The quest for sleep resumed.

"Dismount! Dismount!"

It was Christmas Eve morning. In the hazy light of dawn, stiff with cold and aching from prolonged, cramped postures, Jack and the others clambered over the sides of the trucks. Desperate men lined up to urinate against the sides of the tubs; bladders swollen and painful.

"By gum I needed that!" gasped Bill. "Thought I wer goin' to burst."

"Fall in! Fall in!"

Jack looked at his friends, their eyes peering out of blackened faces, "Tha looks like the Coloured Coone," he joked.

"An' you a bloody sweep!" retorted John tired and bad tempered.

"Shut up in the ranks! Cover off! Cover off!" NCOs circled the milling troops like erstwhile sheep-dogs snapping at their charges.

The Battalion formed by companies into column of fours at the side of the railway track. The Company Sergeant-Major gave the executive word of command: "By the right … quick march!"

"Wer are we?" asked John.

"Timbuktu!" offered Bill irritably, lack of sleep and aching bones briefly subduing his spirit.

"Wer's that?" persisted John. Bill hid his ignorance behind a sullen silence.

Grindrod, who was marching by their side, overheard the exchange, "This 'ere is Estcourt, lads", he affirmed. "It's wer Division's assemblin' afore setting off for Ladysmith."

Not much of a town, thought Jack as he plodded wearily down a single, broad street lined with detached houses of stone walls roofed with corrugated-iron. But he couldn't help noticing that despite the war, the shops were full of all kinds of goods.

They marched out of the town a few miles to the north into a slight depression surrounded by gentle hills. There they gratefully collapsed into white bell-tents which were awaiting them; the three friends shared accommodation.

…………………………………………………………………

Estcourt – Natal

The towering, saw-edged mountains emerged from the shadows of dawn with their cascading waterfalls glistening in the strengthening sunlight. Jack marvelled as he looked across the fresh-grassed hills and valleys to the massive, striking ramparts of the Drakensberg Mountains. He had never seen anything so breath-taking before. He had never really gone in for this God-thing, but someone or something must have created this beauty. These thoughts idly tumbled around his mind as he stood in the front rank of a hollow square waiting for the Battalion church service to begin. He watched as drummers marched to the open side of the square and placed their side-drums close together on the ground. The bass drummer followed and laid his drum flat on the improvised platform. An officer covered the whole with a Union flag to make a temporary alter. Then everyone waited in silence; fidgeting. The minutes crawled by.

"Remove…head dress!" the Regimental Sergeant Major spat out the command.

The chaplain strolled piously to the centre of the open side of the hollow square, clenched hands held before his chest. He took up his appointed position behind the drum-alter. He wore a long, black cassock with a bright-blue stole around his neck; he was middle-aged and portly. His round, waxen face was adorned with severe, metal-rimmed glasses which projected a suitable solemnity. He looked uncomfortable among his congregation of bawdy soldiers, and undoubtedly yearned for his rural parish church from which he had been dragged reluctantly by his pernicious bishop, for whom he held little affection. He uttered the opening prayers before moving on to his sermon.

Lately Jack had become conscious of an unsettling unease which welled up inside him; a growing sense of vulnerability; an unfamiliar, unwelcome feeling. As he neared the front, life seemed increasingly precarious despite the beautiful, sun-blessed landscape – or was it because of it. Death was becoming a real and stark possibility. For the very first time he was seeking answers about life. What was it all for? Was there really a life after death? What was the significance of Christmas? He had never been a church-goer. Yes, he had enjoyed watching the annual Whit Walks with their parading Sunday school scholars, bands and colourful banners; he had readily joined in the sports and drinking which followed them. But now he felt a need to understand; for reassurance, for comfort, for strength.

"It is with a new promise for the future that we acknowledge this special occasion. For we celebrate God's greatest gift to mankind, His son, Jesus Christ, who was born on this day. He brought with Him the hope of peace on earth and goodwill to all men." The chaplain went on to recount the story of Christmas: of the journey of Joseph and Mary to Bethlehem, of the birth in a stable, of the angels appearing to the shepherds, of the visit of the wise men. "This was the greatest event in history. The good news about Jesus is that he comes to all, including you and me. He comes to anyone with a heart humble enough to accept him.

You can have Jesus in your life. He offers us a new heart that will last for eternity…"

The sermon finished. The chaplain led the soldiers in a discordant rendering of *Hark! The Herald Angels Sing.* Jack groped for the words, trying to recall them from school assemblies which now seemed such a distant memory - was it really barely seven years ago?

The Commanding Officer of the Lancashire Fusiliers, Lieutenant Colonel Blomfield, mounted his bay Arabian horse and moved to occupy the central place by the drums. From his heightened aspect he could see all his officers and soldiers. He had had a long and distinguished career in the Lancashire Fusiliers, most recently during the Sudan Campaign where his gallantry had been acknowledged with the award of the Distinguished Service Order. He had subsequently been promoted to command the Battalion. He was looking conspicuously clean and smart; his bushy, handle-bar moustache immaculately groomed. It was now his opportunity to address his Battalion and to give the traditional greetings:

"Jesus said: "Blessed are the peacemakers for they shall be called the children of God." And that is our mission today; that is why we are here; to bring peace to this Continent that all men will live together in goodwill. I profoundly believe that so long as we are faithful to the noblest call of duty and to the highest instincts which are in us as a race, we are helping the cause of peace which is the cause of God. There is much work to be done and we have a ruthless, brutal enemy to defeat, but I am confident that you are up to the task. Whatever checks, whatever vicissitudes, whatever disappointments may befall, we march to victory. Our cause is the cause of liberty and of the right. Take heart and do your duty for your God, your Queen, your Country and your Regiment, for surely you will be called peacemakers."

He paused to allow the gravity of his words to sink in before making an announcement. "Her Majesty Queen Victoria has sent a gift for each of her soldiers here in South Africa. You will be issued with a tin bearing her portrait and containing chocolate cakes. Merry Christmas, and may God bless you all." With that he trotted away.

"Fall out the officers!" ordered the Adjutant. "Carry on Regimental Sergeant Major!"

"Yes sir! Company Sergeant Majors, detail yer men for fatigues!"

"A bloody miserable Christmas this is," declared John as he picked up his allotted shovel and trudged off to the place where they were to dig trenches as part of the defences against marauding Boers. "They say this used to be a grand day in the Battalion, with a special dinner, rum in tea and a camp concert. All we get is the chance to dig bloody 'oles. Now if this was 'ome, we'd be rollin' back from Spinners' Arms, tight as a kite, with a meal to be 'ad in front of a blazin' fire. Instead it's bully beef and soddin' biscuits again."

"Now don't be forgettin' yer tin from Queen," reminded Bill mischievously.

They laboured through the afternoon and into the evening, digging trenches and building sangars. As the hours passed the humidity rose oppressively and clouds gathered obliterating the sun. At the day's end they watched as a black, angry storm rolled in from the mountains like a wafting curtain; thunder roared like an artillery barrage and barbed bolts of lightening thrust downwards with frightening intensity, momentarily illuminating the gloom. The rain cut through the still air with the force of a high pressure hose-pipe.

....

Rochdale - Lancashire

Mary ran upstairs to her bedroom, shut the door and sat on the edge of her bed. She nervously fingered the letter. It was from Jack - no one else wrote to her. Although a little heat penetrated the room through the gaps in the floor-boards from the kitchen below, it was cold. She drew her shawl around her shoulders before bursting into a hacking cough; her chest was tight and painful.

She hesitated to open the letter, savouring the anticipation. She looked across at the photograph of Jack enclosed in its cheap frame and hanging on the plaster-peeling wall. It had been a struggle to persuade him to visit the portrait studio on Drake Street, but after her pleading he had finally relented. He had sat stiffly, frozen, only to splutter following the magnesium flash and irritating smoke. But he looked brave and handsome.

She smiled contentedly as she recalled his last short leave - him in his smart uniform of red jacket and blue trousers. She remembered thinking how healthy he had seemed with his ruddy face boasting a trimmed, black moustache: "From wind on moors and good grub," he had explained. He was no taller than his dad - same slight build - but he had put on weight; not that he was fat; no, he was sturdy and strong. She had to admit that he was thriving on the army life. He had walked with a swank, his swagger-stick tucked under his left arm, accompanied by the "clip-clip" from the metal studs of his shiny boots on cobbles – a few times he had inadvertently stood in the horse muck which littered the streets, he had been furious and too serious to be amused by her giggles. In fact, he had been a bit superior, or maybe she was just not used to his new confidence and self-assured manner. One thing was for certain, he was no longer despondent and unsettled, but rather, full of life, expectation and excitement - fun to be with.

"Tomorrow's Sunday," Jack had said, "let's go up to 'ollingworth lake."

She recalled how she had put on her best dress, the one made by Aunty Joan, and the bonnet normally reserved for the Whit Walks or family celebrations such as weddings and christenings. They waited at the tram-stop opposite the Townhall - civic pride required a grand municipal building, and this was one of the best in the north-west. She remembered feeling uneasy under the scrutiny of the four gold lions which stand sentinel over this neo-gothic monument. A monument to reflect the wealth of this cotton town born of raw, hard work – but a wealth, she often thought, unequally shared. Occasionally she would pass the large houses of the mill owners discreetly sited on the edges of the moors aloof from the dirt, squalor and misery which encircled their factories. She saw how they detached themselves from their workers who were confined to the cramped, cold, damp cottages which extended in long terraces like spokes emanating from the hub of a wheel. The hubs being the mills which loitered at street-ends, overshadowing the tiny two-up, two-down slums. The mills, she thought, were both the life-blood and the damnation of the town.

On the rise behind the Townhall the bells of Saint Chad's Church rang out across the town, calling sinners to salvation. She looked across at the many worn, flagged steps which climbed the hill and cut through the ornamental gardens to reach the imposing medieval structure; how many were there … seventy, eighty? So many times she had counted them, and now couldn't remember precisely. With the Joseph's Court gang she had often scampered up them to the ancient stocks at the top – a place where once rough justice had been meted out to the petty criminals of the town. There too was the graveyard full of tall, weathered gravestones and tombs; a veritable stone maze ideal for playing "hide and seek" - that was until some angry adult inevitably chased them away. She snuggled in against Jack, trying to ignore the condemning sound of the bells and the unnerving glare of the lions. When the tram arrived, they rushed up the circular stairs laughing and teasing. At Smallbridge they connected with the horse-drawn omnibus and eventually arrived at the local beauty spot in the foothills of the Pennines. Everyone knew that it wasn't a real lake.

"'Ave yer ever seen the tower of the church?" asked Jack.

"No one 'as!" countered Mary. The reservoir served the needs of the expanding urban population and industries, and it was said that when the water level was low, the church tower and roofs of an inundated village were visible, but Mary had never seen them.

"I 'ave."

"Yer 'aven't ! Wen?"

"Now if I told yer lass, yer'd be as wise as me," he teased with a warm grin. "Cum on, let's walk round to the café on the other side, and we'll get the boat back." He took her hand and tugged gently.

It was quiet with only a few promenading couples about; a contrast with the town wakes and summer weekends, she thought. Then the place was bulging with people enjoying the fresh air and the plethora of amusements: fairground entertainments; sticky peppermint rock with writing right through the centre; toffee apples. Best of all, she enjoyed the little red peddle-boats in the cordoned area of the lake, where everyone mischievously bumped each other in the hope of spilling friends into the water. Invariably there would be a brass band – often from the Salvation Army - to thrill and inspire the crowds. But on that day only the pleasure-steamer plied the calm waters.

They set off walking; it seemed quite natural to link arms. These past months had seen a new intimacy drawing them together with an unfamiliar intensity. How proud she felt as they strolled on that bright autumnal day. As other couples approached and passed them she felt possessive and leaned into Jack as if to say: "He's mine; I'm so lucky." The sky was cloudy; the sun manoeuvred eagerly in an attempt to break through, and when it did the brightness brought feeble but welcome warmth. They nervously glanced at each other with slight embarrassment, then looked at the surrounding hills and thought the day to be perfect. They chatted lightly and frivolously, but the question of his imminent departure was always looming in the background. Finally she brought herself to ask the inevitable: "Why must you go?"

Jack hesitated before smiling with laboured resignation, "Yer always knew that I was bound to go somewhere lass. That's wat I want; so I'm off to sort out Boers." They walked on a few steps. "The trouble with the Boers 'as been brewin' for a long time. For ages yon Dutch farmers 'ave been treatin' our people badly. Englishmen are workin' in mines, bringin' prosperity to the country, and bein' unfairly taxed. Why, not long ago they shot a British miner in 'is own 'ouse. Business contracts are goin' to their own, and our people aren't even allowed the vote. It's a downright disgrace. Englishmen treated worse than natives. When our government tells the Boers to behave properly, wat do they do? But invade our colonies. They've bitten off more than they can chew. General Buller needs more troops to get the job done quickly. A few farmers can't 'old out long agin the British Army. Any roads, it could all be over by Christmas …though I'd like to see a bit of fightin' first."

They reached the green, wooden tea-shop on the far shore. “Save us a table lass and I’ll get tea.” And so she chose a place by the window, sat down and looked through the dirty glass back across the lake. The steamer was pulling away from the nearby jetty with just a handful of passengers aboard. The breeze was strengthening as it funnelled down the valley from the Saddleworth Moors; passengers turned up their collars and huddled together for protection from the chill. The choppy waters slapped against the hull causing the boat to rock gently. Soon Jack would be leaving in a big ship to cross the sea; how long before she would see him again … would she see him again?

“Penny for yer thoughts lass.” Jack arrived carrying a tray with a teapot, crockery and scones.

“Nowt…there’s nowt that matters.” She poured out the tea.

“Next week am off to join the Second Battalion in Chatham.”

“Is that in South Africa?”

“Nay lass, that’s down south. That’s were we’ll gather and receive new equipment and prepare. We’ll get new uniforms – khaki, like dusty plains so we can’t be easily seen.”

“’Ow long afore yer leaves for South Africa?”

“Don’t know. Bet we’ll leave as soon as we can.”

“Will yer write?” she asked.

“Course I will.”

“How ofen?”

“Wen I can,” he replied soothingly.

Their eyes met, not staring but lingering gently, exploring a new warmth and familiarity - no more the mucky, shoeless urchins running wildly through the streets, or friends casually sharing an evening’s entertainment at the Circus. The barracks in Bury was only a few miles down the road, but Jack’s leaves had been infrequent and short. Through the enforced absences had grown a swelling affection between them, a desire just to be close, an all consuming ache to be together. She smiled as Jack spilled tea into his saucer; he sheepishly tipped the liquid back into his cup knowing how that lack of table manners would have excited his fastidious mother.

"It's still fine; cum on; let's walk on moors a bit." With Jack's proposal they left the tea shop and took the footpath to the rear; it wound into the hills degenerating into little more than a sheep's track and followed the side of a dry-stone wall. The wall neatly demarcated a meagre hay field from the rough jumble of brownish-green moorlands. They brushed against the withered, rust-bronze bracken and clumps of aggressive, thorny gorse.

"The gorse don't flower wen kissin' is out of fashion."

She looked at him, "Wat's that mean?"

"It's a sayin'." He pointed, "The gorse 'as flowers all year round."

She could see just a few yellow flowers, not the expansive bloom of warmer months.

"I suppose wat it means is that if the gorse 'as no flowers then luv ends." He blushed. He had never spoken of love before; it's not something a Rochdale Masher did.

"An' 'ave yer got luv?"

"'Appen I 'ave." His face broke into an embarrassed smile; cheeky, boyish she thought, and held his hand tighter.

The clouds grew heavy and it started to drizzle. They approached a field barn tucked away in a corner where two walls met at right angles: a dumpy, stone building without windows, only ventilation slits set high in the walls, and a large wooden door to provide access for the hay carts. Inset in this large door was a smaller one. Jack released her hand and cautiously turned the large, rusty ring-latch on the small door; surprisingly it swung open with a laboured creaking noise. Jack disappeared inside. She was filled with a sudden panic as she stood alone on the muddy track; she experienced a mixture of confusing emotions: pangs of fear; the exciting glow of anticipation; inevitable guilt. She was frightened by the rising strength of her own passion – she was in turmoil. Jack appeared smiling gently, "Cum on lass." He held out his hand. She hesitated. "Cum on lass," he repeated with a little more assertion. She took his outstretched hand and allowed herself to be coaxed into the gloom. She smelt the warm, pungent, enticing aroma of newly-mowed, damp hay.

"Lie with me 'ere lass."

She opened the letter, again paused as she pictured Jack's face. Strangely, the room was filled with the evocative smell of hay. She read:

"My Dearest Mary,

Sorry it's taken me so long to write lass, but since my last leave we've been on the go with barely a moment to ourselves. And tomorrow we're off to catch a boat in Southampton for South Africa. Your brothers have just nipped down the canteen for a quick pint, but I've hung on to drop you a line. I'm sat on my bunk and for once the room's quiet.

I think of you a lot. You're always on my mind. When I collapse on my bed at the end of busy days it's you I imagine and wish you we were laying together. I see your bonnie smile which fills your face, and your bright eyes, and hear your laughter. I even smile as I think of your bossiness. What I'm trying to say is that I miss our being together.

You know that I couldn't stay forever in the mill, but I've come to realise that perhaps the only thing I didn't want to leave was you, but that's only dawned on me recently. We've always been good friends, but after that day at Hollingworth Lake it's different. Now I know that we've grown up and that I have a real love for you. This caper won't last for long, and then I'll come back for you.

As I mentioned, we've been very busy since our arrival here. There's been lots of marching, musketry practice and bayonet fighting. We've spent a lot of time dyeing all our belts, haversacks and new straps in permanganate of potash to make them khaki as well. It's been all bustle and hard work. Yesterday we had a grand parade and inspection by the General here in Chatham. We were all in our new linen khaki ready for the grasslands of South Africa – it were a bit cold. He was very pleased with our turnout and marching, and wished us all success and a speedy and safe return. The Colours were handed over to the General for safe keeping until we get back. It was a marvellous ceremony; made the hairs stand up on my back.

We are about two hundred recruits from the depot in Bury, but we've been joined by plenty of reservists who have been called up. They've left their jobs, and some small businesses; most have wives and children. They had thought their soldiering days behind them, so you can imagine that many are not pleased to be here. For me, I think it's good to have experienced men amongst us. Now we are a battalion unbeatable by any foe.

Well, the bugler will soon be sounding "lights out" so I'm just off to join Bill and John for a quick one - this southern beer is not as good as Thwaite's. You'll get this letter when I'm already on the high seas and the adventure's begun. I'll write again when I arrive in South Africa.

Your very own,

Jack"

CHAPTER 5

The Advance - Lancashire Fusiliers (LFs)

(Natal - 9 to 13 January 1899)

Jack fastened his belt and tugged on the straps of his equipment. He liked his pack and pouches to be good and taut to prevent movement and possible chaffing of the skin. Reveille had been at 3 a.m., it was now 5 a.m. For two hours he had been busy in the incessant rain striking the tent and packing the company wagons. His only respite had been a brief break to eat breakfast prepared by the company cooks: beans, tinned bacon, bread and hot tea. He was glad to be on the move and fed up of this awful weather - it had been raining for weeks. Since he had arrived in Estcourt his main preoccupations had been the digging of channels in a vain attempt to drain the squelching marsh which had become home, or alternatively running about practising the General's new idea of skirmishing for attacking the enemy. John stood beside him, "I just wish we 'ad a change of clothes. Tents are wet, blankets are wet, uniforms soaked. Even ducks would complain. Thank God we're leaving this shit 'ole!"

So often Jack could find the funny side of John's bellyaching, but not right now. He was right; the white bell-tents were so wet that the canvass no longer offered protection against the rain. They'd been working and sleeping in soaked clothes, and at night shivering under damp blankets. We've been rotting instead of fighting simmered Jack angrily. Everyone was low and disheartened.

"Fall in!" the Company Sergeant-Major summoned them. They fell in by platoons in columns of four. "Today we're marchin' to Frere, a small town about thirteen miles away. At last we're off to fight the Boer. Make sure yer keep up … I'll give 'ell to those wat fall out." He paused before shouting the executive order, "By the right … quick march!"

The rain hissed down mercilessly; the thunder rolled around the leaden sky; the lightening slashed through the gloom with alarming ferocity. The road was occupied by the wagons; it was a mere cattle track full of holes, boulders and ant-hills. The infantry marched in parallel on both sides. Jack trudged forward pulling his feet from the sucking, clinging, black mud, one heavy footstep after another. Oilskins were useless. The rain exploited every chink, every gap, to beat its way through. The clouds hovered above the ground, reducing visibility. The earth was pummelled into liquid mud and churned by tramping feet and rolling wheels.

The infantry column flowed past floundering horses and wagons which lurched axle deep into swamps; teams of oxen, doubled or trebled in number, struggled to free their sinking loads. The whole of the Fifth Division slogged through this quagmire. More than five thousand men and three hundred carts and wagons drawn by mules and oxen extended for many miles. This unwieldy caravan contained everything needed for modern warfare: artillery with their guns, balloon troops, engineers, a field hospital with its sixty plus tents and marquis, ambulances, food, clothes, ammunition, water, and more.

Jack was surprised to pass a series of curiously proportioned guns with tiny wheels and thin elongated barrels, each tied to the tail of a wagon drawn by twenty oxen. "What d'yer think those are?" he asked Bill.

"Those is naval guns; 12 pounders I think," replied Bill. "I 'eard they took 'em off the ships in Durban. Look, there's Jack Tar!"

Jack could see them now in the grey light: straw-hatted, blue jackets, pipes in mouth, moving among the guns. "Thank God for Navy, eh!"

After several hours of mindless plodding Jack was brought up sharply from his sodden stupor: "Halt!" He reacted instinctively; before him he could see a drift. It crossed an angry stream. Engineers and Battalion Pioneers had obviously worked to cut sloping ramps through the river banks to the water, but ahead he could see that there was a wagon in trouble. It had been overturned by the strong current and panic-stricken animals were thrashing wildly. Mules were knotted in their harnesses; they writhed in terror as their heads were forced down under the water. The black drivers desperately fought to free the frenzied animals. They waded chest deep into the water to cut straps and to pull and cajole the mules to safety. It was hazardous, almost suicidal work, but finally the shrieking, kicking mules were released. They careered and fled up the far bank, whilst the drivers collapsed with exhaustion and relief on dry ground. The wagon tumbled downstream pushed by the angry waters.

It was now the turn of the Fusiliers to cross. Colonel Blomfield surveyed the scene as the waters continued to rise with the unremitting rains. A rope had already been secured across the stream as a hand-rail. With the waters in full spate, wading looked like a shrinking option. However, he was determined to test the feasibility and to conduct a trial. After a quick meeting with a small group of officers, orders percolated down.

Grindrod approached to where Jack was standing, “Alright Clegg, Murphy, Jackson and Ward.” Jack’s stomach turned at the sound of his name. He dreaded what might come next. “Yer’ve been selected to represent the Battalion; a great ‘onour. Yer goin’ to wade across the river and show us all ‘ow its done.”

The volunteers were stunned into silence; Jack eventually spoke, “But I can’t swim sergeant!”

“Well Clegg, if yer wer born to be ‘anged then you’ll never be drowned.”

The four fusiliers held their rifles aloft in their left hands and gripped the guide rope with their right. Tentatively they edged into the water. The torrent covered their thighs, waists, chests; Jack began to wobble as he was pounded by the forceful current. It was strongest mid-stream and the line began to curve. He found it difficult to keep his footing on the uneven bottom; momentarily his feet were held by the mud. He tripped forward disappearing under the brown, boiling waters. He thrashed his arms frantically, desperately trying to stand and to move to the bank. The rushing water assaulted his face filling his mouth and nostrils; he couldn’t breath; he needed air. The weight of his sodden equipment was pulling him down, he was growing weak, toppling helplessly and out of control, being carried by an insuperable force - he felt hands grasping his straps. He was dragged onto the muddy bank, gasping and terrified. He lay there twitching involuntarily like a beached fish

Grindrod stared down at him, "So lad, looks like 'angin' after all … eh."

No one was drowned, but four rifles were lost. The men of the Battalion stood in the drenching rain, stamping their feet in the sloshing mud to keep warm and awaited a divine solution to their onward movement. The next plan was born. Grindrod explained, "Right me lucky lads, I want tha' to empty these 'ere wagons. We'll wait 'til the waters drop and then we'll push them into stream to make a bridge. Alright, get goin'."

Jack lay on the ground exhausted, oblivious to the wet and mud; now an observer. He watched the rest of the Company make a human chain as they unloaded the stores from two baggage wagons. From one to another they passed great-coats, blankets, tents, boxes and cooking utensils. These were piled high and then protected from the rain by a tarpaulin. He pulled out his tin of Wild Woodbines only to find that the contents were a soggy mess. A smoke was impossible – no one would have a dry match. He looked at his friends and wider at his fellow fusiliers. All were unshaven and filthy in their clothes, a far cry, he thought, from the parades in Bury and Chatham when every button had to gleam, boot-toes reflect your face, and tunics and trousers have razor-sharp creases. Now everyone looked like midden-men on a bad day.

The wagons were unloaded. Everyone waited impatiently, cursing the weather. After a couple of hours the rain ceased and gradually the water level began to subside discernibly. The black drivers of the first wagon led the oxen into the rushing waters; it came to their shoulders. When the front of the wagon touched the far bank it halted; the oxen were outspanned and the drivers led them away. "Right me lads, now it's our turn," announced Grindrod. "Shoulders agin the wagon, an' lets push it into stream." The second wagon was without oxen and reversed. Watched by their officers, the soldiers heaved and pushed and slithered; at one point the wagon jumped forward unexpectedly and John and Bill found themselves flat on their faces.

"Tha's no time to sleep on job, get off yer arses and keep pushin'!" encouraged Grindrod.

Slowly, very slowly, the wheels turned and the wagon nudged to the top of the slope. It gathered momentum as it descended; the men were almost running alongside. It splashed into the water and with much straining and shouting it was pushed forward rocking in the surging torrent - almost floating. With the crashing of timbers it locked onto the first; it was firm. Cheers arose from the watching throng. Quickly, two pioneers mounted the improvised bridge and lashed the wagons together.

Jack pulled on his equipment and moved to join his friends; he almost fell, his legs were barely functioning, his limbs were stiff with cold and damp. "Let's give yer an 'and." Bill and John helped him, and together they cautiously clambered across the slippery boards. Once again the mud-caked, khaki mass clomped onwards, heads down as if searching the ground.

Another wagon stuck. Lazily Jack raised his sunken head and peered through the renewed deluge as the column circumvented the vehicle. A group of soldiers and blacks were heaving and labouring to release the ox-wagon sunk to its axles. The native driver flicked his vicious, long whip causing the whirling lash to strike the quivering flanks and quarters of the animals. "All together now, heave! heave!" The oxen were encouraged to samsonian efforts.

"John, Bill; what d' yer make of that?" asked Jack. They half looked.

"Nowt."

"What'd' yer mean, nowt?" demanded Jack. "Isn't that an officer pushin' that wagon?"

A young officer stood near the stricken vehicle holding the reins of two chestnut horses. He looked awkward and nervous, as if embarrassed. Among the group slithering in the mud and man-handling the wagon was an older, trim, grey-haired man, obviously someone of authority. Extra spans of oxen were harnessed to the original number making twenty plus, and gradually the faltering wagon emerged from the glutinous mud accompanied by triumphant shouts. With this success, the greying officer moved to the horses; he tried in vain to brush the filth from his trousers and shirt. He gave up, accepted his tunic from the one holding his horse, mounted, and together they trotted away up the line of march.

"That were the General," exclaimed Jack. "The Divisional Commander, General Warren. 'I've seen 'im afore."

"Yer sure?" questioned Bill.

"Aye, 'am sure. New Year's Day, he greeted me and shook me 'and," affirmed Jack.

"Nay, pushin' wagons in muck ain't an officer sport!" observed Bill.

"Well I 'eard sommat from a corporal," added John. "He'd been in Aldershot a few years ago. Apparently, durin' march to the exercising area there was a lot of droppin' out. Lads were moanin' about the weight of the kit. Yon General borrowed kit from a sick soldier and led the march back to barracks."

"Aye; well he can carry me pack if he wants," offered Bill in disbelief.

Late in the afternoon the Battalion reached the camp at Frere, bone-weary and with spirits low after being on the go for nearly thirteen hours in atrocious conditions. Jack and friends slumped into a leaking tent, their clothes still soaking wet, now becoming cold from the raw night.

"'Ere; 'ave a swig." Bill offered his water-bottle to the other two.

"'Ave got some. Filled up from a pool a few miles back; bit muddy," frowned Jack. "Yours cleaner?"

"Yer could say that … 'ere, have a swig."

Jack took the bottle somewhat intrigued and sipped cautiously, allowing just a drop to pass his lips. He spluttered as the burning liquid assaulted his taste buds. He drank again, this time a goodly amount; inwardly his body glowed. He stared at Bill quizzically; "Brandy?"

"Hi; were short of nowt we've got," grinned Bill. "When we was unloadin' wagons I noticed certain letterin' on a box. Yer see, each box 'as a code to tell yer contents. I knew that wer brandy. Cum across it before wen I was on fatigues at railway station."

"But that's for the 'ospitals," protested Jack.

"Nay; for the officers. Enjoy it."

Jack buried his qualms and gratefully took another swig, before passing it to John. Together they emptied the bottle, and anesthetised from the cold and discomfort soon lapsed into an uneasy doze.

....

Jack was not used to the sensual feeling of the sun and the breeze on his naked body. But like those around him he had stripped off in the morning sunshine and laid out his clothes to dry. He basked in the warmth, dozing, trying to make up for lost sleep. Some around him were noisy, jumping about like cattle released into spring sunshine following a long winter confinement. Others romped about in the sun; the more energetic kicked a rough, home-made ball. There was much ribaldry as they joked, laughed and ran about uninhibited. Morale rose.

But the rest was short lived. By mid-day the Fusiliers were on the march again, as was the rest of the Division, heading north towards besieged Ladysmith. Buller's Corps had tramped down from Chieveley and the two creeping columns merged as if converging rivers, swelling the khaki armada to more than twenty thousand. The heat of the tropical sun quickly changed the mud into brick-red dust. It was kicked-up by marching men and animals. Jack didn't know which was worst, the rain or the swirling dust which filled his eyes, ears and mouth. The sweat ran from beneath his helmet, stinging his eyes and creating dirty streaks down his face. His boots began to fill with dust despite wearing puttees. He found that his socks were clogging and rubbing; the friction caused painful blisters. He limped along. His mouth and eyes were parched; his exposed skin became inflamed and painful to touch. His friends suffered similarly; momentarily he was amused by their terracotta-like appearance. Fresh water was not available. Jack scooped what he could from shallow, stagnant puddles which imaged the sun. Halts were infrequent and short allowing just enough time to eat warm, slightly rancid bully beef and hard biscuits. He was almost relieved when in the evening the oppressive humid atmosphere was rent by crashing lightening bolts, deafening thunder and violent rain.

Men and animals were utterly exhausted, but the march continued. Now Jack's clothes were wet again; his trousers rubbed his inner thighs raw making each stride ever more painful. Straps and belts chafed leaving his skin sore and sensitive; now saturated socks in unyielding boots caused blisters to burst. He looked around; men staggered virtually asleep on their feet, others were dizzy from hunger and fatigue; some simply moved as if automatons, devoid of thought, plodding mechanically, stumbling, sliding in a vain attempt to dig their heels into the oozing mud.

Jack could see that John was having problems even greater than his own. "'Ere, let me carry that." He took his friend's rifle and slung it over his own shoulder - his had yet to be replaced.

"Got pains in me guts." With that John broke from the ranks, ran a few yards to the flank, pulled down his trousers and defecated. He staggered back and eventually caught up. As they went on he bent forward holding his stomach; a little later he again rushed to one side to defecate. He vomited and crumpled to his knees. Jack and Bill went to recover him. They placed him between them and threw an arm over each shoulder to help him along. John was looking drained and grey. Periodically they waited for him as he relieved himself or was sick. They lost their place in the column and slipped further and further back, soon they were bringing up the rear with others in a similar wretched state. Evening passed into night with no opportunity to sleep, and again into day. Torturously, they advanced; the column extended and ragged.

....

Warren sat on his horse apparently oblivious to the rain and watched as his Division crawled by in the dark. "As far as I'm concerned this is a special blessing of Providence." He was speaking to his aide-de-camp, Lieutenant Patton. "It's for our good and for the making of our Force. This trial is preparing us for the beginning of active work. It is binding us together as a team." He paused reflectively, "I began this march an unknown man in my command and will come out well known to all my soldiers."

He dismounted, tied his horse to a bush and removed the saddle. "Wake me in three hours." With that he lay down on the soaked ground still wearing his Macintosh, rolled up in a waterproof sheet, and with his head on his saddle he slept in his wet clothes.

………………………………………………………………

The destination was Springfield. This marked the crossing place of the Little Tugela, a tributary of the Great Tugela. Inexplicably, the Boers had left the bridge intact. Jack didn't think much of these so called towns; this one was even smaller than Estcourt and comprised of a hand-full of miserable, tin-roofed buildings and a few scattered farms. "Keep marching!" came the order, and on they went, three or four miles beyond the town to the outskirts of a Farm. They flopped onto the sodden ground and waited stoically in the gathering dusk for the transport wagons to arrive and for tents to be issued. Wearily the fusiliers pitched camp and slumped down to sleep.

The bugler sounded the cheery notes of "reveille" and the camp reluctantly stirred into life. The friends joined the breakfast queue with mess tins at the ready.

"Is that it?" challenged Bill of the cooks. "Bloody bully-beef agin!" He turned to Jack, "Yer know summat? They reckon the 'ardest course in the army is the cooks' course."

"'Ows that?" queried Jack.

"Cos no bastard's ever passed it!" He stormed off to find a quiet corner.

Later that morning, dishevelled and aching, the Battalion paraded in the customary hollow square before the Commanding Officer. He sat on his mount and scrutinized his filthy, tired soldiers. He began by congratulating everyone on their endurance and fortitude, and he reminded them that they were now within sight of the enemy. "The River Tugela is in front of us. The Boers hold the range of hills across the river and dominate that natural obstacle. From those heights they can now observe us. In order to reach our brave comrades in Ladysmith, we must break through the Boer defences. Soon battle will be joined. General Sir Redvers Buller, Commander- in-Chief of the Natal Force, has issued a Field Order which is to be known by every man." Colonel Blomfield consulted the document in his hands and read aloud:

> *"The Field Force is now advancing to the relief of Ladysmith, where, surrounded by superior forces, our comrades have gallantly defended themselves for the past ten weeks. The General Commanding knows that everyone in this Force feels, as he does, we must be successful. We shall be stoutly opposed by a clever and unscrupulous enemy. Let no man allow himself to be deceived by them. If a white flag is displayed, it means nothing unless the force displaying it halt, throw down their arms, and throw up their hands at the same time……… Above all, if any are ever surprised by a sudden volley at close quarters, let there be no hesitation; do not turn from it, but rush at it – that is the road to victory and safety. A retreat is fatal……… We are fighting for the health and safety of our comrades; we are fighting in defence of our flag against an enemy who has forced war upon us for the worst and lowest motives, by treachery, conspiracy and deceit. Let us bear ourselves as our cause deserves."*

………………………………………………………………

The brown-clad doves erupted from the mimosa trees which clung to the banks of the Little Tugela, unhappy at the invasion of their habitat. Jack sat with his back against a tree enjoying the shade of the flat canopy with its profusion of small, yellow flowers. For days the spectacular peaks of the Drakensberg Mountains had been hidden by the low clouds and mist, but now, in the sunshine, they presented an awe-inspiring, brooding backdrop to all that was unfurling in the rolling foothills. As he stared at the mountains he wondered how the Boers had managed to drag their wagons over them some sixty years or so ago. Must be a hardy lot, he thought, with a growing sense of admiration; and a tough enemy. His clothes were scattered on the grass around him, drying in the hot sun. He had washed them as best he could in the river, but there was no soap - he couldn't shave and he was finding it difficult to keep his body and uniform clean. He watched as friends and comrades splashed naked in the turgid, brown waters or slept on the grass around him. He was pleased to have the opportunity to relax; although every day some time was spent perfecting the new method of skirmishing about which the Divisional Commander seemed obsessed. No more firing in volleys and then advancing in straight lines with bayonets fixed, but instead rushing forward by half companies; tiring and sweaty work. Like everyone else, he was sure that the battle could not be long now; he was anxious to seize the opportunity to write to Mary. He took his pencil:

"My Dearest Mary,

I know you'll have written, but post hasn't caught up with us yet. I'm really looking forward to hearing from you. Doesn't have to be exciting; but as I read it I can imagine you saying the words. I'm missing you lots. I wish I'd got you to have your photograph taken that time we were together. Some of the lads carry pictures of their loved ones. Please have one taken and send it to me; and without your bonnet so I can see your face proper.

I hope that you've received my letter which I sent from Cape Town. I wrote it on the ship and gave it to a sailor who promised to post it when he returned to Southampton. We saw nowt of Cape Town. As soon as we arrived they bunged us on another ship and sent us at full speed up the coast to Natal. Since then things have been pretty stiff here. We've been marching for days mostly in heavy rains and we only have one suit of khaki; when you get rained on all day you have to sleep in them to dry them. You feel pretty lively I can tell you with all the bugs about.

Then the food we have – mostly tins of corned beef and biscuits. I would give a week's wages for a bowl of my mam's hot-pot, or even just a couple of slices of bread and butter. Tea comes like a hard, packed cake and you have to pour water over it to loosen it; then it becomes a mushy mess and you have to throw most away as we have nothing to keep it in. On the march we found water where we could and now some of the lads have dysentery and are really poorly, including your brother John. But don't worry, while we're at rest he's getting better quickly – soon be fit as a flea. Talking about fleas, we're out of soap and almost out of bacca. As you can see it's not the life of a toff!

At the moment it's very hot during the day and becomes very humid – like in the mill only we're outside. At night, after the sun sets, the storms come; they're tremendous. The thunder comes first and rolls around the sky, then there's flash after flash of lightening shooting downwards, and some times you think it's coming at you. Then the rain. One day when the storm rose, hail came down as big as large plums.

We are resting at the moment before our battle with the Boer, which can't be long now. He sits on the hills only a few miles to our front, and we shall have to chase him off. You would think that being so close to the enemy we would get some information of what we were going to do, but it's just the reverse – we know no more than the man in the moon, where we attack, when or anything. I suppose you will have read in the papers about our exploits before you get this letter.

It's the thought of you which keeps me going. I imagine our future together when all this is over. We'll get married, have a family. I won't go back to the mill when my soldiering's done. How would you fancy us opening a small shop together? In the meantime you mustn't fret about me or your brothers. We are fighting for Queen and Country and it has to be done by somebody's lads.

Give my regards to your mum and dad.

Well, I think that's all for now. I'll write when I can.

Your very own love,

Jack"

CHAPTER 6

Around Ladysmith

(January 1900)

Jan balanced the rocking chair precariously as he spurred on his pony. His cousins carried blankets and useful cooking utensils, while Henry had two sandbags, one slung either side of his saddle; the first contained fruit and vegetables, the other five terrified hens. It had been a fairly successful foraging expedition - the booty taken from abandoned English farms made the life of waiting more comfortable and tolerable, although with everyone scouring the countryside, outings were becoming less profitable. As they crested the hill they came in sight of the burgeoning laagers which encircled the besieged town of Ladysmith. They paused to survey the scene. Groups of wagons were arranged end-on in the form of an oblong with thorn-bush stuffed between the wheels and gaps - the traditional defensive posture. Within the perimeters were clusters of tents and tethered horses. Normally the oxen would also be within the safety of the wagons, but today they were grazing nearby in the care of black servants. Horse riders and pedestrians moved casually between locations as social intercourse flourished. Others were milling around their wagons and shelters busy with domestic chores: clothes were being washed and laid to dry; smoke spiralled upwards as stews cooked over open fires. As they watched silently they were all too aware that since the arrival of many wives and families, who had trekked in from the farms, the war-like atmosphere had metamorphosed into something akin to a carnival.

Henry's horse shied slightly as the still, humid, evening air was ruffled by the boom of the 155 mm Creusot siege gun entrenched on the hill above their encampment; the noise rumbled around the hills and plains. They could clearly see a crowd of men and women gathered around the "Long Tom", obviously entertained by the spectacle of the ninety-four pound shell wrecking havoc amongst the flimsy buildings of the town. Jan thought how his father was so scathing of these developments: “This is not a proper way to fight a war. It encourages a spirit of inactivity and indiscipline.” But no edicts had been issued by the leadership to stop the trend. Sure enough, Jan had noticed some burghers opting out of duties as a sense of lethargy and inertia began to permeate the besiegers.

“Come on, it’ll soon be dark!” urged Hans galloping off down the hill. With a tug on the reins the others followed in hot pursuit. They burst noisily into their laager, dismounting hurriedly and laughing loudly. The sandbags were thrown to a black servant to supplement the evening meal, while Jan carefully sited his chair by the entrance to his tent.

It was Henry who saw her - at first he wasn’t too sure. He stared unbelievingly, but as the wagon entered the gap into the laager and drew closer she was unmistakable. Involuntarily his whole body tingled; he felt goose pimples surging up his back; it was Ruth. He realised that he was excited to see her, “She’s here! It’s Ruth! She’s here!” He turned his head towards the tent and shouted, “Jan, we have a visitor!” As Jan struggled to emerge through the flaps, Ruth drew level and yanked back on the reins to halt the lumbering oxen. Bantu servants on foot held the harness one each side of the leading span; her pony was tethered to the rear of the wagon.

“What are you doing here?” exclaimed Jan, confused, pleased to see her, but uneasy as he anticipated his father’s disapproval.

Ruth jumped down to the ground grinning broadly, and casually adjusted the bandoleer which was slung around her chest. “We heard that our neighbours had sent their wagon, and that others were planning to do the same, so I persuaded Grandfather that I should bring you some fresh supplies and clothes.” She almost laughed, “Actually, it took me a little longer to convince Mother, but here I am.”

“How did you find us?” asked Henry. “And the natives?”

“Easy!” she responded revelling in his obvious admiration, “simply followed the deep wheel ruts of the wagons which had gone before. At night we all laagered together for protection … taken me two weeks.”

The young men were thrilled to see her and grateful for the items brought: blankets, change of clothes, spare boots, food, tobacco. But her father and uncle Hendrick were not so openly welcoming. Jacobus gave her a long, loving hug and then held her firmly by the shoulders and looked directly into her eyes, “Daughter, I thank God for your safe arrival, and yes I appreciate the stores that you’ve brought, but your very presence is awkward for me and your uncle; it’s an embarrassment. We don’t approve of families on commando and have said so publicly. Women and children are placed in danger and the men lose their sense of purpose. Now I have to explain your presence among us. I feel like a hypocrite.” He paused as if allowing her to absorb his words, then continued, “Let me be very clear. You rest for one week and then return to the farm.” He was determined that there would be no compromise.

That evening, as usual, scores of lights flickered across the plain as meals were cooked on open fires. It was not the turn of Hendricks’s corporalship to mount night picket and so everyone could enjoy the presence of their unexpected guest. As had become customary, Henry joined the van den Bergs for the main meal; tonight it was freshly liberated chicken and vegetables. They sat around the fire on up-turned boxes and saddles; Jan rocked conspicuously in his newly-acquired chair. In her confident, slightly tom-boyish manner, Ruth was enjoying the male warmth of family. She had a hungry curiosity.

“What happened on the way to Ladysmith? What of the fighting at Talana Hill and Elandslaagte Station? When will the siege be over?”

“You ask too many questions,” retorted her father with undisguised annoyance. He was still smarting at the awkwardness of her presence.

She ignored his grumpiness and pleadingly justified her inquisitiveness. “Back home accurate information isn’t easy to get. For so long I’ve been living on rumour and speculation. Can you blame me for wanting to know what’s really been going on?”

Jacobus sighed and explained, “After the battles at Talana Hill and Elandslaagte the English fell back into Ladysmith; here we’ve encircled and trapped them. They tried to break out with a night attack over the high ground at Pepworth Hill and Nicholson's Nek," he pointed to the north, "but with daylight we found them confused and exposed on the plain and there they suffered terribly at our hands before eventually scurrying back into the town." He paused reflectively, "Then we attempted to break into Ladysmith by first capturing the English strongpoint on Wagon Hill … this failed." His voice trailed away as he visualised the bodies of his friends and neighbours littering the hillside. "There was much courage and sacrifice … the battle flowed backwards and forwards, until the fighting ended under a sudden, torrential storm. Under a truce we recovered about three hundred of our dead and wounded. For the moment it seems that the English can't break out, and we can't break in. So now we wait impatiently for the enemy to die of starvation and disease."

"But what about Buller?" she persisted. "Will he try again after Colenso?"

"Buller is licking his wounds, but we know him from the native wars. He's brave and stubborn and will attack again – fortunately, he's ponderous and predictable; we'll see him coming and then concentrate to defeat him."

"What I don't understand," added Ruth, "is why we didn't sweep south when the English were so weak? What about the boasts that you'd eat fish in Durban?"

There was an uncomfortable silence. Jan placed a log on the fire throwing crackling sparks into the blackness.

Hendrick, as the leader, felt the question as a personal criticism; he spoke, "As the corporal I attended the kriegsraad – council of war. Joubert offered three options: to attack Ladysmith, to besiege Ladysmith, or to ride south for Durban. Prinsloo, the Commandant-General of the Orange Free State, wouldn't move south; he thought it too risky with reports of English reinforcements arriving, and many others were disheartened by our heavy losses, particularly at Elandslaagte. In the end only the young Commandant of the Vryhied Commando, Louis Botha, was for driving south. Eventually he was allowed to advance, but barely two thousand burghers volunteered to join him; Joubert insisted on accompanying him - no doubt to restrain his exuberance. Following the first skirmish with the English, Joubert was unnerved and ordered a retreat behind the river

Tugela. From that moment we have sacrificed both momentum and initiative." His tone and body language exuded disapproval.

"But didn't Botha defeat Buller at Colenso?"

"Yes," added Hendrick, "he did. Joubert fell from his horse – he's an old man – and Botha has taken over."

Henry was silent. He watched Ruth through the flames and shimmering smoke as she conversed earnestly. He was unaware that he was staring intensely. She could be so serious, quite irrepressible; and yet alternatively so vivacious, so appealing. The flickering light accentuated her attractive almost sultry face. He was enthralled by her: her self-assurance, her beguiling green eyes, her compelling smile. She was feminine yet strong – he found it an attractive contradiction. She sensed his attention and turned to him with a wry look. She switched effortlessly from being grave to frivolous.

"I hope, Mr Barnham that you're not finding life on the veld too hard having come from the rigours of your Boston office?"

"I do miss my morning newspaper, lunchtime cigar and evening bourbon," he fenced, "but I'm learning to live with my new rustic friends and to appreciate the simpler things of life."

"And when this is all over, will you join your rustic friends and become a farmer?" she asked mischievously.

"At the moment, Miss van den Berg, it's sufficient to live a day at a time; but who knows what the future holds?" he parried with an impish grin.

"And you'll call me Ruth?" she smiled.

He nodded, "Henry."

They all talked and laughed into the night. About midnight Hendrick and Jacobus made to withdraw. Ruth saw the meaningful look from her father as he rose, and understood that propriety demanded that she too leave. Having bid good-night, she crawled under a canvas which stretched from the side of the wagon to make a tent – the traditional shelter on the veld. Away from the fire there was a chill and she wasted no time in snuggling between the warm blankets; her coat served as a pillow. In the excitement she had brushed aside her fatigue, but now, as she relaxed, the tiredness swept over her. She lay warm and content in a foetal position, smiling inwardly, inviting the embracing sleep. She pictured Henry handsome with his fulsome moustache which now adorning his bronzed face; his broad-shouldered but supple body; his luring smile; his dry sense of humour, but intelligent and sharp wit. He was a little earnest; but very appealing.

Over the next few days Henry contrived to find the opportunity to be alone with Ruth; it was difficult in the confines of the laager and with the immediacy of her family. But then she was given permission by her father to visit an uncle on her mother's side who was with the Pretoria Commando. He assumed her return route and estimated that she would stay as long as possible, arriving back just before dusk. He lay in wait by the drift across the river Klip.

There were a couple of false alarms, but then he spotted her. She disappeared into the drift and as she emerged he drew alongside her, "Hi Ruth!"

Her face was bright with smiles as she trotted towards him, "Well, what a coincidence!" She grinned with mock surprise, "The whole of Natal and we meet here!"

"A good thing too! I was a little disorientated, and now you can guide me home."

"Of course! This way!" And with that she kicked her little pony into a gallop. His short legs thrashed frantically, throwing up dust in his wake. Henry was taken aback by this sudden departure. He turned his horse and gave chase at a more measured pace. They headed away from the laagers and towards the adjacent heights. When he finally caught up with her she had already dismounted, her pony stood obediently, waiting untethered. She was sitting on a large flat rock looking westward. He tied his horse to a scraggy bush and sat beside her. She didn't look at him. Her body was tense. She seemed pensive, sad; how quickly her mood had changed. "What do you see?" she challenged.

"In the distance the Drakensberg Mountains; to the north I can see roofs in Ladysmith reflecting the sun; the lush green grasslands; below …the laagers."

She became serious, introspective, "I see my people … farmers; forced to fight and die to secure God-given rights and inheritance. We're driven by the simple desire for space and freedom. We want to be left alone to live a quiet, rural existence. But I fear for the future, even if we win this war…this Continent is changing. There's a ruthless struggle for diamonds, gold, land, power - my people are so naïve. How can these opposing forces of good and evil ever be reconciled? My grandfather and his generation trekked into a wilderness to escape oppression and injustice, just like the tribes of Israel out of Egypt; but can it ever be?"

"Tell me about the Voortrekkers."

"The Voortrekkers? My grandfather, Joubert, Kruger … these are the people who made our country. The English wrested the Cape Settlement from the legitimate Dutch government. They were no better at administering the colony; in fact they were obsessed with the rights of the blacks whilst neglecting the security of the outlying and vulnerable farmers. A Boer revolt against the colonial government was ruthlessly extinguished and the leaders hanged. During the frontier wars with the Kaffirs hundreds of homesteads were burnt and pillaged, thousands of head of cattle were stolen, whilst the colonial government cowered smugly and secure in Cape Town." She hardened as she spoke. He found this a new and slightly disturbing side to her character. "The ending of slavery brought many practical difficulties on the land, and the English insistence on paying pitiful levels of compensation - and that only in London - deprived most Boers of any financial return for their loss. The English equate a Kaffir with a white man; it's ridiculous! Isn't it written in the Book of Genesis: "A slave of slaves shall he be unto his brethren" Didn't the children of Israel have slaves?"

Henry suddenly felt uncomfortable, even shocked. His father had been wounded whilst fighting in the Union Army at Gettysburg. He realised that unconsciously he carried the raw feelings of a country which had so recently torn itself apart to bring freedom to slaves; to belatedly acknowledge the equality of man. He felt unsettled by her vehement racism.

Ruth was now emotionally fired as she related the story with a renewed passion, "The final straw came for my grandfather's parents with the theft of fifty cattle by Bantu raiders; they killed two black herders in the process. The family pursued the raiders and found that they had been intercepted by an English military patrol and the cattle impounded. When they asked for the cattle back they were told that they must bid for them at auction as they were now the property of the colonial government; and this despite the fact that they bore the family brand! Can you see why people had had enough? It was early in 1837 that my grandfather and his family joined others, mainly Dutch, German and French Huguenots, and headed north into the wilderness; they abandoned their steads and generations of work. The wagons were pulled by oxen and loaded with all possible belongings; they could only travel at the pace of the accompanying cattle and sheep. Families, friends and strangers on the move grouped together for security, and after several months crossed the Orange River outside the limit of English jurisdiction." Again she paused before continuing with a sense of justification, "We are a turbulent people by nature, a strong spirited, independent people. Who can blame us for trekking – the English stealing our slaves and the Kaffirs our cattle."

"And so they headed for the land stretching from the Orange River to the Limpopo?" assumed Henry.

"No … not at first. They all waited in a vast laager while the leaders and prominent men discussed the way forward. Not surprisingly, large numbers of people, and even larger numbers of cattle, sheep and horses, created a health hazard and hygiene broke down. The community was scourged by enteric fever. Many died, including grandfather's mother and two siblings; he was fifteen. Eventually, the family, with others, decided to cross the great barrier of the Drakensberg Mountains – the ones you see in the far distance." She pointed to the nearer line of hills. "You see the hills where we hold the English?"

Henry was familiar with the sight of the hill range about twenty miles to the south. With the setting sun behind them, the hills stood black and silhouetted.

"You see the one which stands most prominent? … first the two peaks and then the higher flat-topped one; that's where the leader of the Voortrekkers, Piet Retief, stood to gaze down on the promised land. We call the hill Spion Kop – Spy Hill. The Basuto call it Thaba Emunyama – the Black Mountain. Before the Voortrekkers came over the mountains there were no white men in Natal. Our grandmothers and grandfathers were the first settlers here; they tamed the land, defeated the savage Zulus and laid out their first town, Pietermaritzberg. They built other towns too like Weenen – in Afrikaans it means weeping - in perpetual mourning for those Voortrekkers and their wives and children massacred by the Zulus in their laagers on the banks of the Bushman's River.

"I don't understand; why didn't they stay?"

"Because the English said that the land was theirs – they had a trading post at Durban and claimed the hinterland. So the second trek began, only this time the Voortrekkers kept going beyond the Vaal River as far as the Limpopo, en route fighting the Bantu tribes. Of the family group only grandfather and his father survived. But from this trial emerged the two independent Boer Republics of Transvaal and the Orange Free State. Now we're taking back this land that was once ours."

Silence descended. They both watched the sun, a glowing red ball, as it slipped behind the Drakensberg Mountains. For the very first time Henry realised that despite himself, he was developing an affinity to this dynamic people and their lands.

"Why are you here, Henry?" She brusquely invaded his thoughts. "Gerrit thinks you're just an adventurer without any deep commitment; you fight for us today, could be the English tomorrow like your compatriots. You know the Americans sell horses, mules and tinned beef to the English Army? They make money out of our struggle."

Henry felt challenged. He was being forced to confront himself, to solidify a myriad of thoughts and emotions which flowed through him. Yes, he had wanted to escape the confines of his job and the shallowness of relationships. But was he prepared to die for this alternative: for farmers with an unrealisable dream; a people about to be smothered under the weight of an unstoppable imperialism. He'd had plenty of time to think lately. In his mental wanderings he had sometimes visualised himself as a successful lawyer working in Pretoria or even Johannesburg. Or perhaps even a farmer drawing his livelihood from the unforgiving veld – not that he knew anything about farming; but with Ruth by his side? He couldn't verbalise how he felt.

"It's going to be dark very soon and father will worry about me; let's go!" Henry offered his hand; she took it, mellowing at his touch; her anger and frustrations melting away. She felt a strength and reassurance flowing from him – she was surprised by a momentary sense of vulnerability. She allowed him to lead her to their mounts.

....

As dusk approached, the hot, sultry day gave way to the ubiquitous thunder storm; it passed, but the drizzle and sagging clouds thickened the night. There was some anxiety as Hendrick and his corporalship trudged forward in single file to the customary picket location. Hendrick led and Jacobus brought up the rear. Only two nights previous the Khakis had sallied forth from Ladysmith to successfully attack and spike a gun on a neighbouring height. It was always possible that, buoyed up with their success, they might soon try the tactic elsewhere.

Every night the Boers established pickets on the plains between the hills; this was to prevent penetration of their positions and attack by the Khakis. Each morning the watchers withdrew to their laagers leaving observation and warnings to the permanent hill garrisons. Tonight it was the turn of Hendrick's corporalship.

Henry was irritated by the rain which ran down the high collar of his oilskin and trickled down his back. He wasn't too sure which he least preferred, the stifling heat of the day or the damp chill of the night; still, he was almost there now. After half an hour the group stopped. The corporalship was under-strength as eight of them had been despatched to unload newly arrived stores for the commando, and others were on leave or sick. Only fourteen were available for duty. Two men went forward a further twenty yards, while Henry and the remainder rolled up in their waterproof capes for what would undoubtedly be a patchy sleep. Every two hours the sentries would change.

It was only a short time before Henry heard a muted commotion in the direction from which they had come. He thought he heard a woman's voice. Reluctantly he rose to investigate. It was Ruth and Jacobus. Apparently, she had followed the picket at a discreet distance and was now being angrily accosted by her father. He was gesticulating furiously, trying to contain his anger whilst remaining silent – an almost impossible task. Grudgingly he conceded that he could not send her off into the black night alone and that she would have to stay. "Lie there!" He pointed to where his oilskin was spread on the ground. "I need to watch over you." His sharp tone and seething frame clearly displayed his unhappiness at the turn of events. Word of the new arrival quickly circulated within the small group of men. Henry, whilst feeling concern for her safety, felt a resurgence of excitement at the knowledge of her close proximity.

Henry and Jan shared a shift on sentry. Lying on the wet ground straining to see into the ink-black night and listening intently for human noise was both tedious and unnerving. It wasn't long before the night developed a life of its own: bushes took on human form; the rustle of swaying grass became the sound of advancing Khakis. Nonetheless, at times heads nodded and they fought to stay awake. Henry struggled to see his watch, the hands now just visible in a lightened sky as the moon finally parted the clouds and the persistent drizzle stopped - just half an hour to go.

There was movement behind and without ceremony a body flopped between Jan and Henry; it filled the intervening space. The hood of an oilskin was pulled back to reveal Ruth's beaming face. She was clearly pleased with herself.

"You shouldn't be here," whispered Henry, experiencing the conflicting emotions of discomfort and arousal at her physical closeness.

"But I am, and I want to share the night with you all before I return home tomorrow."

"And your father; he's furious with you. He shouldn't find you with us."

"He's a gentle lion. Anyway he's sleeping … he loves me too much to stay angry for long," she whispered, putting her mouth close to his ear. He felt her breath on his cheek and was excited by her sensuous, feminine smell. Surreptitiously she sought out his hand and held it gently. Emboldened, they looked at each other with knowing smiles; they lay quietly enjoying the intimacy of the moment. She snuggled closer, exhilarated by the merging warmth of their bodies.

The stillness of the night was ruptured by a volley of shots immediately followed by wild shouting. It was coming from the site of the Creusot gun and its small garrison on the hill about eight hundred yards to the right. Everyone was awake staring intently at the flashes and trying to make sense of the fighting - for that is what it was. Hendrick was the first to enunciate everyone's fears, "The Khakis are attacking the gun. Their approach must have been masked by the rain and mist." The night suddenly grew quiet. "The silence tells me that they have taken the hill." He was now stirred to action. He had no idea how many soldiers might be involved, but they must help the small garrison or what was left of it.

"We'll move quickly to the base of the hill and then climb quietly. Make sure you have a round in the chamber. Follow me!"

Oilskins were forgotten as Hendrick led the way at a steady trot with the others straggling behind. It was lighter now with the moon more prominent making the gloomy shadow of their objective visible. Jan and his two cousins were in a gaggle around Hendrick. Henry followed closely behind with Ruth; Jacobus, as usual, brought up the rear. After the cold of the long night Henry was soon sweating as he pounded towards the enemy. He held his rifle across his chest as he ran; a bullet in the breach, his finger around the trigger, thumb placed to quickly release the safety catch. He wondered what the next moments would hold.

An enormous explosion rent the air, and as the thunderous noise dissipated it was replaced with a raucous cheer. That's the end of the gun, thought Henry.

Breathless and sweating they reached the base of the hill. Hendrick gathered them in, "They'll descend any time now puffed-up with success and throwing caution to the wind, only too eager to get back to Ladysmith. We'll go up until we find a suitable place to lie in wait for them. We'll try and lie across their escape route. Once in position let them come towards you.

I'll fire first." Hendrick searched the serious faces for understanding, "Right then."

He moved off slowly, crouched, carefully placing his feet to lessen the noise. The breeze brought the laughter and shouting of the Khakis as without inhibition they celebrated their easy victory. The noise grew louder; they were coming down the hill reckless with relief believing that the job was done and that rum and a warm bed beckoned. Hendrick found a shallow spruit running ankle deep with the latest rain; cautiously they sloshed uphill through the mud.

"Halt! Who goes there? Friend or foe?"

A figure loomed large above them on the bank, rifle and bayonet in hand. Pre-emptively Hendrick fired at point blank range; there was a muffled cry, almost of surprise: "God!" and a body tumbled heavily into the bottom of the spruit. The noise of retreating footsteps was clearly discernable.

The party closed up; Hendrick explained, "This would be a picket guarding the escape route. We'll move up a little way and then spread out."

Jan tried to squeeze past the fallen soldier as he hurried after Hendrick, but it was impossible not to stand on him in the confined space. He closed his mind to the pitiful moan emanating from the wounded Khaki, and consoled himself that there was nothing that he could do to help him. After about fifty yards Hendrick stopped and signalled for them to spread out. They knelt in the muddy trickle and took up firing positions along the bank about three yards apart - their linear position stretching for nearly forty yards. The moon flitted between the clouds, sometimes it was translucent, sometimes clearly seen, but at best it gave a visibility of about twenty-five yards. Jan waited with the others, tense but unafraid. His weapon was in his shoulder; it was too dark to allow alignment of the foresight and rear aperture on his rifle in the normal manner; he realised that he could only point in the general direction of his target without the usual precision. Still, he thought, who could possible miss at this range?

Henry glanced to his left to check that Ruth was alright. Instinctively she felt his look and turned; she smiled reassuringly and released her safety catch.

A laughing group of soldiers scrambled noisily down the hill, incautious and ignorant of the presence of their enemy. Hendrick waited until they were about fifteen yards distant before opening fire; the others followed instantly. Shot after shot was poured into the black mass. Only the speed at which the rifle bolt could be operated and the magazine re-filled limited the torrent of metal. Soldiers shrieked and collapsed, some tumbled forward unable to stop, carried by their own momentum and the downward slope. A Khaki body rolled to a halt in front of Henry. His line of fire was blocked so he moved to his left; he came shoulder to shoulder with Ruth. Eventually the movement to the front stopped and the party held their fire. There was a great furore above and the hurried, anxious voices of the Khakis drifted away suggesting that they were escaping further to the left. But there was much confusion and renewed shouting, and soon another disorientated group came onto their position. Again the rifle fire crackled in unison and soldiers fell - silence.

Ruth pulled back the rifle bolt to help cool the exposed hot breech. Moments later she reached into her bandoleer and brought out a clip of five rounds. Carefully she placed the clip into the magazine guide and then pressed the rounds home with her thumb. She drove the bolt forward sharply, driving a round into the chamber. The whole action was done automatically and completed in seconds. Now she was ready to continue the fight. She was grateful that Henry had moved close to her; she needed the reassurance of his presence. Everything had happened so quickly that there had been no time to think or feel: the explosion, running, scrambling up the hill, throwing herself down on the bank of the spruit, rushing Khakis and the frantic minutes of ear-splitting din. The shooting had stopped, but the laboured moans of the wounded rose to fill the silent void. She jumped – there was a hideous scream; perhaps the final wail of a dying soldier. She starred at the mounds to her immediate front; in this half-light they could be fallen logs, except that some were twitching - she knew them to be men, dead and dying.

Henry put his arm around her shoulder. She leaned heavily against him. "Are you alright?" he asked.

"Yes ….yes." But her heart was pounding, her stomach churning, her hands shaking. He mustn't see the inner me, she thought desperately.

"Listen!" whispered Henry.

Hushed voices drifted towards them in the breeze; a stern, uncompromising order was heard: "Fix bayonets! Fix bayonets!" followed by the clung of metal on metal.

Henry felt Ruth's body tense. "Don't worry. The English are not sure where we are. They're going to come at us with the bayonet and try and break through to the plain. Get ready. We'll be alright; I'll look after you." He looked into her face; she was frightened. He just wanted to hug her tightly; but not now. He gently released her: "We must be ready."

Henry sensed rather than saw the soldiers as they descended hushed and cautious in a series of extended lines in depth. He heard the scraping of boot-studs on stones, the swish of trousers, the occasional grunt or clearing of throats. Then they struck, but over to the left by Jacobus. Henry fired rapidly into the flank of the surging soldiers; such was the density that every bullet struck home, bodies fell. But the Khakis burst through. They ran tripping and stumbling over corpses and wounded comrades, jabbing and thrusting wildly with their bayonets until they swamped the corporalship and made good their retreat.

Again the firing stopped. There was a forbidding silence. Henry felt inexplicably consumed by a cold uneasiness. A heavy sense of foreboding washed over him. Had the Khakis really gone? Ruth? What about Ruth? He turned in a momentary panic; she was still peering into the night holding her rifle tightly, the barrel hot from the many discharges. He sensed her tautness; she was rigid and pale starring to her front as if mesmerized by the dead and maimed. He reached across and put his arm around her waist; unconsciously, she huddled close. Nothing was said.

"Give a hand over here!" It was Jan shouting excitedly. The spell broke.

"Let's go!" Henry helped Ruth out of the spruit and together they ran towards the voice. They skirted past survivors frantically separating bodies, heaving them apart in the search for friends and family

"Over here! Over here!"

Ruth and Henry zoomed in on Jan's cries.

"It's father; he's been bayoneted several times."

Jacobus was in the bottom of the spruit propped up against the rear bank. Jan was supporting his father's head and offering words of encouragement, "It's alright, father. It's not serious." Henry jumped in and furiously ripped away the clothing to expose ragged flesh; he identified wounds in the shoulder and side. They bled profusely.

"Get the bandages off the Khakis!" he shouted up to Ruth. "Quickly, we must stop this bleeding!" Everyone knew that the English were issued with individual field-dressings containing pads and bandages. "Try their front pockets!"

Soon Ruth dropped down beside him; distraught and with fumbling fingers she tore at a small package, eventually managing to rip out a disinfected pad connected to a bandage. Together they gently bent Jacobus forward, placed the pad on his wound, wrapped the bandage around him and secured it with safety pins. "It's still bleeding ... we must have another!" cried Ruth. Hendrick passed down several dressings and watched as Henry and Ruth worked feverishly to apply them.

"Now the shoulder," Ruth found herself taking control - subliminal instincts kicked in. She worked efficiently, conquering her emotions.

"We must lay him where it's dry," directed Hendrick. He dropped into the spruit and indicated to Jan and Henry, "Lift him carefully onto the side." The three men strained under the weight of Jacobus' bulk, but with a coordinated heave raised him onto the bank. He was carefully laid on an oilskin and covered with a blanket taken from a dead soldier.

Hendrick collected the survivors of his corporalship around him and addressed them to the backdrop of the murmuring wounded, "Jacobus must be moved by stretcher if he is to survive. We'll wait until dawn. The Khakis are no longer a threat – they're long gone." He paused reflectively before continuing, "The Lord says: *"If thine enemy be hungry, give him bread to eat; and if he be thirsty, give him water to drink. For thou shalt heap coals of fire upon his head, and the Lord shall reward thee."*" The farmers took their cue.

Ruth continued to work with Henry. They moved among the enemy wounded taking field-dressings from their tunics and applying them to Mauser wounds. They offered water and soothing words of reassurance. Ruth looked into their strained faces and felt an unexpected sympathy for her enemies; most were young like her brother and cousins.

With the breaking light Pretorius burst upon the scene with fifty men of the Commando. They looked around in astonishment at what they saw. "How many Khakis?" asked Pretorius in disbelief.

"Eighteen dead and thirty two wounded," stated Hendrick flatly.

"And so many of you survived. I thank God for your deliverance."

"Three of our friends are dead. You didn't come to support us." Hendrick's voice could not hide his sense of grievance and condemnation.

"I thought it too dangerous to deploy into darkness and chaos," defended Pretorius, a little sheepishly. He went on to try and redeem himself, "I'll ensure that Commandant-General Joubert hears of your bravery."

Ruth walked by her father's side as he was carried on a stretcher by a relay of bearers. Henry trailed slightly behind. As he passed the members of the Commando, some patted him on the back: "Well done, Yank!" Pretorius observed him coolly and made no gesture. On reaching the ambulance wagon Jacobus was placed gently on a trestle table in the open air. A German doctor tended to his wounds. Jacobus was anaesthetised using chloroform and the dead tissues around the wounds cut away. The wounds were cleaned, stitched and dressed. On learning that Jacobus had a daughter present the doctor gave him into her care: "He has lost much blood and needs rest, but what is most important is that his wounds are kept clean. The dressings must be changed regularly to avoid infection. Give him plenty of water and strong broths as he can take them. He'll recover." With that, Ruth reverted to one of the traditional roles of the rugged Afrikaner women, that of nurse. She would be staying longer.

....

The heavy bulk of the large figure burst out of the night; he was just feet away. She fired, feverishly operated the bolt and fired again. The bullets struck the flesh without effect – passed through him harmlessly. The naked steel of his bayonet glinted in the moonlight as it thrust towards her, seeking her frozen body, drawn as by a sucking magnet. She starred into the blank lifeless eyes of her tormentor – the grey, gaunt face of the dead. In anticipation of the tearing metal blade she screamed – hands grabbed her; she fought to shake free from the imprisoning hold.

"Ruth! Ruth!" Someone was shouting her name. "Ruth, it's alright, it's Henry! It's just a dream, a bad dream!"

Jan stood by his tent entrance and looked across at the stretched tarpaulin sheet which was Ruth's shelter. Henry knelt holding her in his arms. Her body was racked by a torrent of sobs. It was becoming a familiar occurrence. This behaviour had started shortly after the night battle. At the time her courage had drawn praise from everyone; he was proud of her; she had been called a true "Amazon". She had calmly aimed, reloaded and brought down several khakis. Afterwards she had sorted the casualties and tended the wounded, speaking to them tenderly and offering encouragement. She had been a tower of strength winning the reluctant praise of hardened misogynists. But now? What had become of her strident self-confidence? He'd seen her sit for hours on the edge of the laager staring blankly into the distance. She shunned everyone, preferring to withdraw into her shelter. She ignored her appearance; her hair was dirty and matted and she washed irregularly. Most alarming was her neglect of their father. She avoided him, obviously reluctant to be in his presence. Yesterday the German doctor had visited to see how his patient was progressing and had clearly been unhappy and annoyed at what he had found. Jan had overheard the normally stoical, self-controlled practitioner shouting at his sister. He had found dirty dressings and soiled bedding; he couldn't contain his temper. Ruth had been shamed into activity, but today she appeared to have lapsed once again into lethargy and disinterest. Jan watched.

Gently Henry coaxed her to lie down; he covered her with blankets and spoke soothingly to her. Did he kiss her forehead?

Henry came to stand by Jan. He took out a cigarette and offered the packet. “You know I don’t smoke.” Henry didn’t reply. He lit a cigarette and inhaled strongly, deliberately expelling the smoke through his nostrils.

“I don’t know what’s wrong. It’s as if the courage of the fight has evaporated and now she can’t shake of her fears. She keeps reliving the battle.” He paused, “She’s changed.” Resolutely, he threw his barely-smoked cigarette onto the floor and ground it with his boot. He went into the tent and emerged moments later carrying his bedroll.

“Where are you going?” asked Jan.

“I’ll sleep under the wagon. It might help Ruth to know that someone’s close by … and I can respond quicker.”

Jan couldn’t sleep. He slumped into his rocking chair, uneasy, troubled. He sensed that the carnival was over.

CHAPTER 7

Preliminary Moves

(12 – 22 January 1900)

For a few minutes they stood silently together on top of Mount Alice; with their telescopes they scanned the panorama stretching before them. To the left rose the dark, jagged peaks of the Drakensberg Mountains like skeletal fingers silhouetted against the sky. From the precipitous rocks waterfalls cascaded into the green foothills from which emerged the River Tugela. The waters sought their natural course as they meandered in violent twists through the hills and undulating pastures. The brown river, full from the recent unprecedented rains, surged in front of their vantage point and rushed off eastwards to Colenso and on to the Indian Ocean.

On the far bank, spurs and re-entrants probed northwards about two miles before embracing a line of hills which ran west – east and dominated the river. The highest of these was the dark mass of Spion Kop. It acted as a hinge: to its west the hills ran straight, while to its east they curved as a horse-shoe with the hollow facing the Tugela. The centre of the horse-shoe fell away to a low undulating ridge over which ran the road to Ladysmith. Here, the river made a great loop towards Mount Alice like the protruding tongue of a petulant child. At the tip of the tongue was moored the ferry which signified Potgieter's Drift. Close to the river on the far bank were two small kopjes.

"Damn fine job!" Buller broke the studious silence. "The capture of the ferry; members of the South African Light Horse swam the river and hauled back the punt. The Boer marksmen in the kopjes fired but couldn't hit them. Damn fine job!" he repeated.

Warren had already heard of the exploit and let the remarks pass without comment. His thoughts were troubled.

"This is where your Division is to cross. You are to break through the hills using the road to Ladysmith as your axis." Buller pointed with his telescope.

Warren looked across at the heights of the horse-shoe. Visible were dark lines of shelter trenches and redoubts crowning the hills. Tiny black figures were busy entrenching against the skyline; hundreds of horses were grazing in the plain. There was no apparent attempt at concealment.

"Sir Redvers," began Warren, "the Boers have had several weeks in which to perfect their defences; you can see them on the hills. Once across the river my manoeuvre would be confined to the low ground. I would be engaged by an enemy who would dominate me from elevated, prepared defences against which I would be compelled to make frontal attacks. We should be targeted by Boers concealed for three quarters of a circle. The cost would be high; two, three thousand men, and success uncertain. Before advancing through the valley I would propose to take the dominating hills on both sides first.

"We don't have time for such alpine excursions!" interjected Buller. "Our guns will cower the Boer. You will have the concentrated fire of the howitzers and naval batteries to cover your manoeuvres."

Warren remained unconvinced. He was not going to be easily bullied into submission – too many lives were at stake. "General, I've further discussed possible lines of advance with my Brigade Commanders, and we are of one accord. I continue to recommend to you the capture of Hlangwane which is the enemy's weak spot; it's exposed and vulnerable and once taken will allow us to turn the Boer's left flank. To attack into this horse-shoe is too hazardous an operation."

"General," said Buller with a firm deliberation, "this is our best option. I do not shy away from the hazardous. Unlike some I do not seek popularity." He paused, "I understand that you've personally been busy extracting wagons from the mud." Buller had earlier received this information with disbelief and incredulity; these were actions totally unbecoming of an officer, and a senior one at that.

Warren was thrown by this sudden lurch in the conversation. He countered defensively, "The Fifth Division is a new formation; I am its new commander. At first I was not recognised, but within three days the men have come to know me as I joined them in their trials."

Buller was unimpressed by theatrics, neither was he ready to further discuss his orders with a smug, self-assured subordinate. He drew the meeting to a close, "You have much to do in preparation."

Warren took his leave. Full of misgivings he joined his staff in the lee of the hill, mounted, and rode off to his headquarters and assembling troops close to Springfield.

Buller left the vantage point, accompanied by his aide-de-camp, and made his way back down the hill, past the abandoned buildings of Spearman's farm and through the bustling activity which marked the arrival and setting up of Number 4 Field Hospital. As he neared his tent he was approached by a young man in civilian clothes, round faced and bespectacled.

"Good day, General. Could I speak with you?"

Buller stopped. "You are?" he enquired brusquely.

"Leo Amery, chief correspondent of *The Times.*"

"I don't speak to the press." Buller made to leave.

"But I'd just like a few words with you, General, about the coming battle … for the public in England."

Buller turned to his aide-de-camp, "Get rid of him!"

Once in his tent he removed his cork sun-helmet, threw off his equipment and reached for the champagne bottle; he filled his tankard with the tepid, barely-sparkling liquid. He sat down heavily on the straining canvas chair by his table, drank thirstily, and reflected on his discussion with Warren. He was unsettled, uncertain. The prospects for success looked no better than at Colenso, and yet the Government and Field Marshall Roberts were urging him forward; it was an unenviable dilemma. He quaffed the champagne. Perhaps there was an alternative plan. About five miles to the west was Trichardt's farm and by it a drift with another track leading through the Rangeworthy Hills to Ladysmith. There were no horse-shoe heights to negotiate, although the line of hills to the west of Spion Kop would need to be breached. "Orderly! Orderly! Get me Major Gough."

He was worried: if this all went wrong then he would be finished; that ex-policeman would replace him. After Colenso, there was no way that he could afford to fail again. But what if he should delegate the next attack to his second-in-command – the man recommended for his South African expertise? Should Warren succeed then he, Buller, as Commander of the Natal Field Force would receive the accolades. And should it fail, then he could disassociate himself from the disaster. After all, he would not have been directly in command.

"Sir," announced the aide from outside of the tent.

"Yes, come in," shouted Buller.

"Sir, Major Gough to see you."

"Major, I want you to secretly reconnoitre the drift at Trichardt's farm and to report back to me personally. I need to know whether or not it is feasible to cross a considerable force at that point."

....

The water was barely warm, but then on the veld kindling was at a premium. Warren found the tin bath rather constraining for his tall frame, but nonetheless he enjoyed the cleansing ritual. With his knees drawn up he soaped himself vigorously, oblivious to the bustle of orderlies, soldiers and natives as the camp shook off the inertia of the night and prepared for the new day's routine. He looked across to the majestic Drakensberg, still capped with the clinging clouds, and paused to admire the beauty of his surroundings. The rain had stopped and the morning sun had already burnt off the ground mist; it was going to be a hot day.

He was still apprehensive following his meeting with Buller. The coming battle at Potgieter's Drift would be extremely risky; casualties would be high and there was no guarantee of success. He had hurriedly sketched maps of the ground for his staff and commanders and had tried to enthuse them at his council of war. His brigade commanders knew of his misgivings and it had proven difficult to engender any confidence in the approaching fight. Among those who understood the implications of this plan, there was anxiety and foreboding; hardly the ingredients for inspiring the men.

As he mused fretfully, he became aware of the arrival of a horseman who dismounted hurriedly. His aide engaged the newcomer in conversation before escorting him purposefully into his presence. “A rider from General Buller, sir,” he announced.

“The letter is marked “secret” and is for your eyes only sir. I must deliver it to you personally,” explained the courier as he offered the small package.

Warren rose from his bath; naked and without inhibition he accepted the letter. “Have you breakfasted?” he enquired of the startled young officer who tried to avert his eyes whilst addressing the General. “No … Jonathan, see to it that he gets something at the mess tent before he returns.”

Warren took a towel from his orderly, wrapped it around his waist and entered his tent. Standing in a pool of water he took a steel letter-opener from his table and slit the top of the envelope. He read:

> *The enemy's position in front of Potgieter's Drift seems to me to be too strong to be taken by direct attack.*

“At last some sanity; thank God for that!” sighed Warren audibly. He continued to study the contents:

> *I intend to try and turn the Boer right flank by sending a force across the Tugela from near Trichardt's Drift and up to the west of Spion Kop. You will have command of that force. You will of course act as circumstances require, but my idea is that you should continue throughout refusing your right and throwing your left forward until you gain the open plain north of Spion Kop. Once there you will command the rear of the position facing Potgieter's Drift, and I think make it untenable.*

He read further coordinating instructions and noted that the operation was to begin on Wednesday 17th January; it was now the morning of the 15th; but where was Trichardt's Drift?

“Orderly! Orderly!” shouted Warren, “my breakfast, and tell my aide to assemble my staff and colonial scouts … we ride in one hour.”

The reconnaissance party rode carefully, anxious to avoid the barbed wire which had been strewn in the tall grass by the Boers with the aim of disabling the English horses. Warren deducted that as the crow flies the distance to the drift was about five miles, but he needed to select a line of march unobserved by the enemy. It entailed a considerable detour. On arrival his professional engineer's eye and wealth of experience as a surveyor quickly absorbed the terrain. On both sides of the river the banks were steep, rocky and rugged, but negotiable – it would entail a good deal of manhandling of pontoons and wagons. He identified a position where the twist of the river would screen a pontoon bridge from the dominating hills to the north. He marked on his evolving sketch map separate approaches to the river for infantry, pontoons and wagons so that they would not interfere with each other. He knew that once his force appeared at the drift all surprise would be lost – it would then be a race to cross and deploy before the Boers could bring their long range artillery to bear. He would need to strip his wagon train to the essentials, but even that would leave several hundred vehicles stretching over many miles. By European methods he reckoned a full week would be needed to cross, but the colonial way? - perhaps as little as two or three days.

Through his telescope he could plainly see Boers and blacks digging trenches and building sangars on the northern hills. Buller's intelligence staff believed that at least two guns were mounted on Spion Kop. Warren considered; yes, a crossing in the vicinity of Trichardt's Drift was possible, but it would not be without considerable risk. It was a veritable hole to be caught in. He rode to Mount Alice to represent his views to Buller.

"It seems to me that we can throw a pontoon bridge across the Tugela about one hundred yards upstream from the drift and be screened from the view of the distant hills. This would mean that the Boers could not engage us directly with artillery during the crossing. I will leave all non-essentials behind, but I will still have a train of over three hundred wagons. Many of these are drawn by newly acquired oxen unfamiliar with pontoon bridges and inexperienced Kaffir drivers. To cross safely I will need to draw the wagons by horse and swim the oxen. This whole process will take two or three days, and I cannot begin meaningful operations until my supplies are secured on the northern bank. Our secrecy will only buy sufficient time to cross without interference, but once our intentions are known the mobility of the Boer will enable them to concentrate against us. Besides, I don't know the ground north of the river, and cannot make a plan of attack until after a reconnaissance with my commanders."

Buller was irritated by Warren's self-justifying exaggeration of the difficulties, "My intelligence estimates that only four hundred Boers will oppose you compared to the seven thousand against Littleton's Brigade which I shall leave here at Potgieter's. I'll get him to make a feint to hold the Boers on his front and keep them guessing as to the main point of attack." Then Buller quipped almost disdainfully, "It shouldn't be too difficult for you to break through the hills."

Warren ignored the sneer and turned to tactics, "The dominant hill of Spion Kop seems to be the key to unlocking the defences in that area. I would propose to take that as my first objective. It should then allow me to roll up the Boer line from east and west."

"That's not as I see it!" responded Buller sharply. He bent down and picked up a straight stick. He held it horizontally, "This is your line running east – west. Spion Kop is the pivot on which you should hold your right and around which you should swing your left and so break through the lower hills – turn the mountain of Spion Kop…." As he spoke he rotated the stick bringing it to the vertical, "…until your line is north – south." He emphasised, "Do not be drawn too far to the west, but ensure that your right flank remains in contact with and protected by Littleton at Potgieter's."

The imagery is simple, thought Warren, but the reality is that it is still a series of frontal attacks; quite possible, but first he would need to soften up the enemy positions. "I need to be able to prepare the enemy before I attack and to counter the Boers' long range guns. Our field artillery is too light and has too short a range. I need the 12 pounders of the naval detachment and the heavy howitzers."

Buller parried, "I have already given you thirty six field guns. I need the other guns here in reserve. They can provide you with some fire from this location."

"But they are not in the right position to reach out to the Boer guns hidden in the hills. I need something with which to destroy the Creusots and Krupps."

"I must keep something in reserve!" repeated Buller becoming annoyed.

"Yes, General, but not of heavy calibre and long range," countered Warren. But Buller would not budge.

Warren pressed on, "General, I have the majority of the Field Force under my command for this task, yet only the staff of a division for its planning and execution. I have a fairly difficult operation ahead of me: to command a large mixed force, to manage an extensive logistic train, to supervise the crossing of a formidable river, and to execute a tricky tactical operation with untried troops over unreconnoitred terrain. I request the secondment of some of the staff officers from your headquarters who otherwise will be redundant throughout this battle."

Indeed, Buller had deliberately delegated the majority of the Force to Warren, but to give him his headquarters' staff as well would create the impression that he had completely abrogated command; Warren would appear to be the Force Commander. He was not prepared to go that far. "I recall quite clearly that I managed very well before I had my full complement of staff officers. I am sure that you'll be able to cope. Besides, I must retain them to plan for unexpected contingencies." He was becoming increasingly irritated by Warren's unreasonable demands and constant whingeing.

Warren's silence and hostile body language betrayed his unhappiness.

"However," added Buller, "You may take any regimental officers released by their commanding officers."

They both knew that to be a forlorn hope; no commanding officer would willingly deprive himself of his officers on the eve of battle.

As he rode back to Springfield and his waiting Division, Warren was only too aware of the daunting task before him: to lead a column of twenty thousand mostly untried troops across a swirling river, and then to break through unfamiliar hills in the face of a determined enemy. He knew well the difficulties of his mission and the inadequacies of his Force, but he was tenacious and conscientious and would make every effort to succeed. But time was short. His troops must be marching within twenty four hours.

…………………………………………………………………

Grindrod finished briefing the platoon, "Tents aren't to be struck; others 'ave been appointed to stay behind to light fires, play bugle calls, and generally make the Boer believe that we're still 'ere. Be ready to form up at five o'clock."

"We'll soon be at 'em," said Jack sitting on the ground in a circle with John and Bill as they busily gave their rifles a final clean. But beneath the forced bravado he felt his stomach churn – was it excitement or fear? They checked their ammunition, and packed their knapsacks and pouches - greatcoats were loaded onto the company wagon.

In the half-light of dusk the Battalion formed columns of four and marched quickly to the north. Potgieter's Drift here we come, thought Jack. He raised his tunic collar against the raw chill of the night. At first the light of a full moon lit the way, but soon it was lost behind the gathering clouds. It began to rain. There were plenty of unexplained halts.

"Wish we could keep movin'," grumbled John, "or at least 'ave a tab; I'm freezin'."

All lights had been banned. They plodded on accompanied by the muted swish of trousers and the gentle, metallic clinking of swaying equipment. After about four hours they veered off the well-trod, muddy road onto virgin grassland.

"There's summat up with summat! Wer 're we goin'?" demanded John.

"Wat do yer mean?" queried Bill.

"If you'd stop sleepin' on march and pay attention, you'd see that we came off the road and turned left."

"Means we're 'eadin' west away from Potgieters'," interjected Jack.

There was chuntering in the ranks; no one knew what was happening any more; a restless uncertainty permeated the column; but no explanation came. Gradually the plodding soldiers resigned themselves to wait until someone deemed it fit to tell them what was happening. Now the track was barely discernable. The halts continued while shadowy horsemen, silhouetted against silvery skies, rode up and down the column whispering instructions to officers; spasmodically the weary line advanced.

The trio, from their position near the front of the column, were among the first to hear it. Through the murky, misty night an indistinct sound penetrated; it had a certain comforting familiarity. Gradually the noise took on form, solidified, became recognisable. It was the heavy plonking of a piano; voices could be heard in rough accompaniment:

"She's my lady love,
She is my dove, my baby love......."

Jack couldn't believe his hears. Instinctively, he began to hum quietly:

"She's no gal for sitting down to dream,
She's the only queen Laguna knows ..."

He was home; in the familiar Circus. Others joined his lead. The humming swelled to loud singing. Weary heads lifted from chests; hunched shoulders unfurled:

"She is ma Lily of Laguna.
She is ma Lily and ma Rose."

Soon they were tramping through the yard of a prosperous looking farm. There was a single-storey, colonial-style house with a spacious veranda surrounded by numerous corrugated-zinc roofed outbuildings. It was from the house that the music and bellowing voices came - what Jack could not see was the group of young officers gathered around an oiled, walnut piano enjoying the liquid spoils of war. As the column swung by the singing intensified; spirits rose:

"Good-bye Dolly I must leave you,
Though it breaks my heart to go.
Something tells me I am needed,
At the front to fight the foe ......"

The order imposing strict silence was momentarily forgotten or ignored as young officers too joined in the chorus. But then discipline was re-asserted: "Quiet! Quiet!" The command rippled down the line. Once again heads drooped and feet trudged mechanically. The sound dissipated behind them, but for a short period Jack, and others, had been back home among the cobbled streets and terraced houses, the corner pubs and the music halls. Jack stubbornly and sentimentally clung to the familiar images unwilling to let them go, until reality reasserted itself, and once again he was absorbed into the monotony and fatigue of an army on the march.

Shortly afterwards the column halted. "Get some rest!" came the vain order. Tired bodies responded by dropping down on the damp ground. Jack was sorry now that they had not carried their greatcoats; there was nothing to snuggle under. He rested his head on his knapsack and curled up into a ball.

"Jack ... Jack."

He felt a rough pulling of his shoulder. "What do yer want?" he grumbled, annoyed that he should so quickly be roused from his chilled, uneven sleep. He wasn't scheduled for sentry duty.

It was John and Bill, "Psst ... veggies," said the latter quietly.

"Wat d'yer mean, veggies?"

"Ssh....at farm there was veggies. Let's go and get 'em."

"That's lootin'"

"Nay," stressed Bill. "A slice off a cut loaf isn't missed."

Jack allowed himself to be persuaded; after all, there was little chance of a decent sleep. They walked over the hill and headed back in the direction of the farm. Fires indicated the sentry posts and they soon skirted around a couple of them without incident. A short walk and the buildings loomed out of the night. As they approached hesitantly they could hear sounds of laughter and merriment. The piano was silent.

Cautiously they slinked between outbuildings and around to the side of the house. Jack noticed half a dozen or more horses tethered to the veranda - this was officer territory.

"Over 'ere," whispered Bill. With Bill leading the way they passed through an open wooden gate and into an area enclosed by a rough, waist high, wooden fence intertwined with bushes. The scent of peaches pervaded the still air.

"Spuds," announced Bill. He indicated to Jack, "You dig some up, we'll look for sommat else." The two brothers moved further into the vegetable plot; John found onions while Bill located a patch of carrots. They all worked frantically. Jack unfastened his entrenching tool and started to turn the soil. He collected the tubers, scraped off the dirt and stuffed them into his knapsack.

A door on the veranda swung open with a dry creaking sound that seemed to fill the tense darkness. The sound of voices and clinking glasses spilled into the night. A figure stumbled noisily down the stairs and staggered towards the vegetable plot. The three froze. The officer was worse for wear. He stopped by the gate and held on to the post for support; there he wrenched violently vomiting over his boots. "God, what a mess," he muttered. He wrenched again. He wiped his mouth with his sleeve then groped to unfasten his trouser buttons. Again holding the post for support with one hand, he urinated. With an expressive sigh of relief he stood unsteadily and adjusted his clothes. As he was about to leave he caught a glimpse of a shadowy figure. Clumsily he drew his pistol from its holster and lurched through the gate. He confronted Jack with drunken truculence, "Hands up! Who are you? A bloody Boer spy?"

Jack's stomach sank. Looting was a serious crime. For a moment fear pinned his feet to the ground and tied his tongue. What should he do? He could barge the drunken officer and perhaps get away, but that was assault, and if he got off a shot then others would be alerted and the whole situation would blow up. Bluff it; that was the only way out of this. "Just collectin' vegetables for the mess," uttered Jack with as much confidence as he could muster. "Commandin' Officer sent us," he added.

The young officer was momentarily taken aback by this unexpected response. He stood still, visibly struggling to gather his composure. After laboured thought he managed to enquire, "Commanding Officer? Which Commanding Officer?"

"Colonel Blomfield of the Twentieth - the Lancashire Fusiliers. We've just bivouacked over the 'ill." He deliberately pointed in the wrong direction.

"Doesn't your Commanding Officer know that taking vegetables could be construed as looting?" He slurred his words struggling with the pronunciation of "construed."

"He said that if we didn't collect 'em then they would rot in the ground. The farmer bein' on commando and all." Jack needed to reinforce his point. "Colonel Blomfield did say that we might meet officers 'ere who were enjoying what the farm could offer. He said that we wer to ignore that and just get sufficient spuds and things for the mess."

The officer knew that the peach brandy and the whisky that he and his friends were enjoying, were in fact from the cabinet of the absent owner. He was on dodgy ground. He fumbled as he replaced his revolver - the securing strap refused to cooperate. Finally he gave up the attempt and left the pouch- flap dangling. He drew himself up trying to regain an authoritative posture, "You'd better do as ordered." And with that he swayed gently as he returned to the house, mounting the veranda steps with exaggerated caution.

The three grabbed their booty and ran. Their hearts pounded as they sprinted through the grass; about four hundred yards on they stopped, gasping, hanging on to each other and laughing.

"That wer close!" panted John. "Quick thinkin' Jack; quick thinkin'. I though we wer' for the 'igh-jump."

Jack was pleased by his own boldness and with his friends' compliments. He had never confronted an officer like that before. It so easily could have been a disaster. "Aye, well," he said, "'aven't we been learnin' that attack is the best form of defence?"

Still chuckling they wandered off to find the Battalion. They had plenty of vegetables for the next few days. But then Jack realised that he had left his entrenching tool behind. Hope Sergeant Grindrod doesn't notice, he thought.

"Cum on, ger up!"

Jack pretended not to hear. The harsh voice cut jarringly through his chaotic dreams, "Cum on, ger up! For God's sake, damn yer! ger up!"

Jack joined the general confusion as men began to stir in the emerging daylight. Groans and oaths resounded throughout the bivouac as half-conscious men staggered to their feet, and with clumsy fingers fumbled with their kit. In truth, he was glad to be on the move again. During the couple of hours since the foraging expedition proper sleep had proved to be illusive and his limbs were chilled and stiff. What he wouldn't give for a hot brew of tea, but there was no time. He fell in with his Company and marched towards the drift. Field guns opened fire from the high ground behind them onto the hills and farms across the river; the shells whooshed overhead. Unexpectedly, they halted short of the river.

"Bridge ain't built yet," announced Grindrod. "Should 'ave been ready by now, but sappers is only just startin'. We've a couple of 'ours to wait ….get yer breakfasts."

Jack broke ranks with the others and immediately claimed a nearby thorn bush. Bill and John hacked at it with their entrenching tools, and together they gathered the tough branches for fuel. They divided responsibilities: Bill would make the tea, John open the tins of Fray Bentos corned beef and boil some vegetables, and Jack would prepare the first course – porridge. Jack lit some kindling between two stones, and once burning well, balanced his mess-tin, almost filled with water, over the fire. Once boiling he crumbled in hard-tack biscuits stirring with his spoon until he achieved the consistency of a paste. He added issued plum jam from a tin. "Are yer right? Am ready with first course."

They ate well and then lay on the ground, dozing and gratefully absorbing the warmth of the rising sun. In the meantime, the engineers strained to build a pontoon bridge.

"Right, off yer arses; there's a war to win!" Grindrod roused the platoon. The column trudged the short distance to the river where Jack saw what looked like a series of small boats stretching between the banks and overlaid by a platform of planks Despite obvious lashings and ties, the structure didn't appear too robust as it rode the strong current. "Single file!" And with that Jack tentatively negotiated the eighty-five yards of swaying timber. He then waited for the remainder of the Battalion to cross.

About three or four hundred yards down stream he could see the cavalry wading and swimming their mounts through the fast-flowing, swollen waters. He noticed that the large horses had little difficulty, but the ponies of the Light Cavalry and Mounted Infantry struggled - there were many duckings. He laughed loudly with the other amused spectators. But then came excited, panicky shouts. He could see a trooper thrashing desperately in the water before he disappeared from sight. An officer - a Captain he thought - launched himself into the torrent; those on the bank screamed encouragement; some waded in waist deep. Eventually, from the melee two limp figures were dragged from the water by anxious comrades. They were pulled up the muddy bank and laid on the grass. Jack fearfully remembered his own awful experience when he had almost drowned. Then the rescuers stood still, heads bowed, shoulders sagging. The word quickly spread: "The trooper's dead." How quickly comedy had given way to tragedy.

Jack trudged northwards for a mile or so, and with the rest of the Battalion occupied a ridge overlooking the pontoon. There they bivouacked, looking down on the ponderous, khaki juggernaut as it manoeuvred ready to attack the silent hills. He watched as the engineers built a second pontoon bridge, and as the frightened, tetchy oxen were unspanned and swum across the river. Horses were limbered to the wagons to drag them across the bridge, where once again they were reunited with the oxen. He could see that it was a slow and tedious business.

"What's that over there, sir?" Jack enquired of his passing platoon officer, Lieutenant Awdry. He was looking at the dominating heights.

"You mean those figures moving about on the hills?" confirmed Awdry. He took his field glasses from around his neck and handed them to Jack. "What do you see?"

Jack wasn't used to manipulating binoculars and struggled to set the focus, but finally he had a clear view, "There's people diggin'...Boers and blacks...makin' trenches ... buildin' sangars."

"That's the enemy Clegg. Whilst we're waiting for hundreds of wagons to cross the river, the Boers are preparing their defensive positions. But don't worry; we'll soon inspect their handiwork."

Jack's puzzlement was apparent.

"Soon we'll be attacking their defensive positions," clarified the Lieutenant. He took back his field glasses and turned to scan the bridge site. "Look Clegg!" he pointed to a group of mounted figures, "Generals Buller and Warren; they're hatching the plot."

....

The guns had been firing on the hills for almost four hours without any response from the Boers, when the signal to advance was given. The Company rose in extended line with men five paces apart. They moved forward aligning by the centre as frequently drilled. With each step they anticipated the enemy fire, ready then to dash forward by half companies - the new tactics introduced and rehearsed during the time at Estcourt and Springfield. No shots came. Jack was unnerved; the pulse in his temple throbbed with excitement. Where were the enemy? Why didn't they fire? Onwards he advanced growing tense and taut; his stomach knotted; his heart pounded. Were the Boers really there? Perhaps they had fled not wanting to face the attack? He didn't want to be shot at, but at least then it would all begin; he could react, could fight; not this eerie walking into the silent unknown ...waiting ... waiting ...

He drew level with a clump of white flowers; the air was suddenly filled with violent cracks, rattling like rain on a tin roof. The man on his right spun like a cork-screw, hitting the ground hard; others screamed. The officers yelled, "Forward! Forward!" Instinctively fusiliers dashed towards the foot of a slight rise and collapsed behind it. Bullets hit the ground all around kicking dust into their faces. Jack looked back; at least half a dozen men lay on the ground behind him, some writhed; others were still.

Bill crawled to him, laughing with nervous fear, "Those flowers," he gasped pointing to the rear. "That was a range marker; clever bastards!"

Close by a fusilier rose to his knee in a classic position to take aim and fire as if on the depot range at Holcombe Brook, but before he could pull the trigger his head burst into a bloody mess as Mauser bullets impacted. His body hesitated as if surprised, and then collapsed like a sack of coal spilling into the cellar hole.

The advance came to a halt. Men pressed themselves to the earth.

The air was thick with fear - officers were not immune. Behind they could see that the supporting lines had stopped, men were bunching making vulnerable targets; they must go forward. The Company Commander looked along the line of men cowering behind skimpy cover. The eyes of those closest bore into him with fear as if willing him not to do the inevitable. There passed a moment of hesitation. He had no wish to confront that deadly maelstrom. He swallowed hard then flung out that terrible, irrevocable order: "Right half company, prepare to advance …Advance!" The order was taken up by the platoon officers and sergeants: "Advance! Advance!"

Jack, Bill, John, the others, left the safety of the undulation and dashed forward. They were to go fifty yards as rehearsed; one, two – crack, crack; ten, eleven – ping as a ricochet bounced off a nearby rock; twenty one, twenty two – a dull thump as a bullet bore into the ground in front of him; forty, forty one – looking for cover. Jack dived behind a small mound on which stood a scraggy thorn bush; bullets cut the air. He lay motionless face downwards finding comfort in this position as if, like a child, he believed that not seeing meant not being seen. He sensed others crashing down beside him. He was now meant to engage the enemy so providing cover for the left-half company to dash forward and come into line. Hesitantly he raised his head, eased slowly forward, poked his rifle through the grass and lower branches, searching the heights above for the enemy. Whack! The rifle flew from his grip as if kicked away by a violent blow; wooden splinters hit his face. He jerked back sharply dropping to cover. He placed his hand on his bleeding cheek, his ears rang loudly. He noticed his rifle lying a few feet away; the wooden stock shattered by a bullet.

"That wer a near do!" offered Bill, lying behind a group of rocks to his left, out of breath, but grinning.

"Aye, yer right there!" Responded Jack straining to hear and trying desperately not to show his fear.

The Boers lifted their fire and engaged those fusiliers now rushing forward. Jack surveyed the frantic race; the losers fell, the winners drew level then collapsed panting, crawling, searching for illusive cover. One fallen soldier raised his head and peered through the grass. Blood seeped from a head wound; it ran down his face in several crazy rivulets. He crawled forward shouting, almost screaming, "Wer 're yer? Wer 're yer? I can't see! God I can't see!"

"This way; over 'ere," encouraged Jack. "Crawl towards me voice."

"Am comin', am comin', I can't see!"

"Over 'ere! Over 'ere!"

Thud! Thud! The blinded fusilier twitched then stiffened as the bullets hit home. Jack lay immobilised, stunned, starring. He knew him; he had been in the group that answered the call that night in the Circus; a Rochdale lad.

"Prepare to advance!"

"'Ere yer are," shouted Bill as he tossed a rifle across to Jack. "See if yer can 'ang on to this un, yer might need it."

"Advance! Advance!"

There was no time to think. Jack staggered to his feet, and tumbled forward almost losing his footing. He ran amid the crack of bullets passing close, propelled by self-preservation and the need to find cover. Men were going to ground, or were they hit? His heart raced; sweat dribbled down his forehead stinging his eyes. He noticed Bill who was ahead of him drop behind an ant-hill. Gratefully he slumped at his side. He was welcomed by a still beaming, dirt-smeared face.

"Not as much fun as the three-legged race on Cronkey Shaw Common," panted Bill.

Jack looked at him. It was as if Bill was enjoying this madness. How could he joke? Still, he was glad to have him by his side.

Each time the "advance" was given, fewer men stood up to offer themselves as targets to an unseen enemy. Each rush forward covered less ground. Enthusiasm waned as fear and a sense of hopelessness grew. But the line advanced slowly up the slope until it was decided to halt and to consolidate the gains. As the fusiliers painfully edged forward, the Boers gave ground and withdrew to alternative defensive positions in accordance with their carefully rehearsed battle plan. Finally, they held the highest crests with open plateaux before them. They knew full well that for the Khakis to attempt to cross this bare ground would be suicidal.

Jack lay behind sparse cover under the blistering sun - the slightest move invited a Mauser bullet. He was thirsty; his parched tongue stuck to the roof of his mouth, but he dared not reach for his water-bottle. Eventually, the sun dropped below the Drakensberg; only now with the failing light did the firing end. The order rippled amongst the survivors: "Dig in!"

"Me entrenchin' tool is back at yon farm, so I'll be ganger," announced Jack.

"Like 'ell yer will!" countered Bill. "We'll share." He threw his tool at Jack, sat on a rock and took out a packet of Woodbines. "Been dying for this all day."

John joined them. During the advance the weight of fire had pushed him to the left; he was relieved to find them again. He threw off his equipment, slumped down and leaned against a rock. He didn't speak.

"Wat's up with yer, yer miserable bugger?" challenged Bill. "Cat got yer tongue?"

"Don't wanna talk ….am knackered…need to rest. He closed his eyes ending further conversation.

"Well Jack, it's you and me."

Together they marked out a trench and cut the turf. They dug into the top-soil which was barely six inches in depth before they struck rock. “It’s bloody ‘opeless,” declared Bill. And by mutual agreement they decided that sleep was a greater priority.

“Fusiliers, wer are yer?”

“Bill! John!” Jack shook his friends awake, “replacements are comin’, I can ‘ear ‘em.” He faced the approaching figures, “Which regiment?” he shouted into the blackness.

“Border Regiment.”

“Over ‘ere mate …it’s all yours.”

And with that the trio happily left the killing ground. As they trudged back down the slope a bright moon flitted between the clouds to illuminate the work of the stretcher bearers now recovering the dead and wounded. It seemed as if the sheer scale of casualties was overwhelming them. They heard a moan to their right. “I’ll take a look,” said Jack, and he moved off to investigate. Soon he summoned the others, “Give us an ‘and.”

They recognised a lad from Wigan. He was delirious and ranting incomprehensively, but thankfully he soon lapsed into unconsciousness. He had been several hours lying in the sun and without water and medical assistance. Jack unbuckled the fusilier’s belt and eased off his harness. He took the field dressing from the casualty’s pocket and then in the poor light sought to identify the wound. It was difficult. He removed the tunic, sticky with coagulated blood, and after close scrutiny identified a neat, pencil-hole entry wound just below the left shoulder bone. He ripped off the waterproof cover and applied the sterile gauze pad and secured the bandage. Concurrently, Bill and John constructed a stretcher by buttoning up the casualty’s tunic and slipping two rifles through the garment. They hailed a fourth soldier and together hauled the make-shift stretcher to the aid post about a mile distance. They placed their charge on the ground with other dark forms, their details indiscernible in the blackness. From some came low, suppressed moans; occasionally an anguished scream rent the now still night. Jack hailed a medical orderly who was moving purposefully among the wounded with a candle-lit lantern, offering reassurance and adjusting inexpertly applied dressings.

"'Eh mate!" Bill attracted the attention of the weary orderly. "We've brought yer another un."

"Right," the orderly hurriedly acknowledged and continued with his consuming task.

Jack observed the ambulance wagons coming and going as they transferred the wounded the five miles to the Field Hospital at Spearman's farm – a torturous journey for many on the unsprung carts. As tensions eased, Jack felt the need to relieve himself. He walked around a stationary wagon opening his buttons as he moved. He stopped abruptly. In front of him in the shadows and on his knees was a figure; the residual light from a nearby campfire was sufficient to recognise him as a Lieutenant from B Company - he was younger than himself. The officer was retching violently and trying unsuccessfully to suppress his crying, his shame; his shoulders heaved uncontrollably. For a moment Jack was transfixed. He was fearful of intruding into this sensitive scene. But then a solid grip on his shoulder suddenly pulled him back around the wagon. "It affects some men like that first time. 'E'll be better for it in the mornin'." It was Grindrod. "Make yer way to the muster area Clegg." His voice was firm, reassuring and unusually sympathetic.

Jack rejoined the others and together they strolled back to the valley in rear of their morning start line. They stood with the rest of the Battalion, grouped together informally, grasping a cup of hot Bovril and responding as the roll was called - one hundred and thirty eight men failed to answer their names.

CHAPTER 8

That Massif

(23 – 24 January 1900)

Warren was pleased with the way the crossing of the Tugela had gone; not in the two to three days as forecast, but under his personal supervision it had been achieved in a timely thirty-seven hours. And his worst fears of the guns on Spion Kop had not materialised; they had been strangely quiet. Once across the river he had addressed the problem of breaching the hill defences to his north. It had been impossible to find anyone with knowledge of the immediate ground, and he learnt that the local farmer, whose land it was, was incarcerated in Ladysmith. For two days he had reconnoitred the area looking for the best way through the hills, all the time painfully aware that the Boers were industriously improving their defences. It was during this time that he found it necessary to constrain the exuberance of the Mounted Brigade under Lord Dundonald. Given the task of guarding the open flank, the cavalry had ridden along the track which passes through the valley to the far west, and just short of the village of Acton Homes had successfully ambushed a party of Free State Boers killing or capturing forty-two for the loss of only two.

"General, the route to the west is open," declared Dundonald. "All I need to exploit the breach is reinforcements."

"You don't know the country. Each of your men has one horse. How can you possibly outflank Boers with two or three horses who do know the country?" countered Warren.

"The valley is clear and there are no signs of the enemy on the hills. I am sure if we move quickly we can get behind them," insisted Dundonald.

Warren was exasperated, "I have considerable experience in fighting both with and against the Boer in similar terrain. Consider; the Boer has the internal lines of communication and can concentrate to block such a manoeuvre. We will be sucked into a cul-de-sac and annihilated by fire from three sides. Indeed, White has signalled from Ladysmith only this morning to say that he can see up to two thousand burghers riding westwards. It's essential not to divide our force, but to keep in touch with the troops at Potgieter's and to remain under the protection of the long-range artillery. Our strength and safety lies in our keeping together."

"Sir, I believe that you are being over-cautious. The opportunity to swiftly relieve Ladysmith is slipping through our fingers." Dundonald made no attempt to conceal his frustration.

Warren, similarly, was becoming heated, and in his fury disregarded the embarrassment of his staff officers as they awkwardly observed what had become a shouting match. "Colonel, let me make myself very clear. I believe that the western route is too far and too dangerous for your cavalry and for my slow moving column. Besides, we are only carrying four days of supplies."

Dundonald remained furious at what he believed to be a failure of boldness and initiative. With desperation in his voice he probed, "Then sir, what would you have me do with my cavalry?"

"Maintain a screen on the western flank, but bring in the bulk to guard the slaughter cattle and wagon train."

"So we are to be herdsmen! Sir, I do not regard this to be the correct use of cavalry." Without waiting for a response Dundonald abruptly turned his horse and galloped away still livid.

Warren had only found one track through the hills which could accommodate the wagons. It ran almost due north from Trichardt's Drift via Ross and Fair View Farms, and skirted around the west flank of Spion Kop. As directed by Buller, he had attempted to pivot on the Mountain and force the adjacent Rangeworthy Hills. Unfortunately, this was proving to be a pretty hard nut to crack. For almost three days his Force had been hammering away at the Boers, and although the lower slopes of the spurs and hills had been captured, albeit at considerable cost, it was proving impossible to dislodge them from the final crests. It was time to examine other options before the attack stalled completely.

As had become his habit, Buller rode across that morning from his own headquarters to offer unsolicited advice. Warren recalled the exchange:

"I think it possible that the enemy may try a counter-stroke; they are concentrated, while your troops are widely extended, and do not support each other. I should be cautious how I attempted any enterprise further to our left at present. In fact I suggest you redeploy some of your guns to cover the threat."

"Thank you for your observation, General. I'll order the move," replied Warren phlegmatically.

"I see that you've made some progress in the foothills. I suggest that you drive home your assault from the left. I understand that we've captured Bastion Hill; it should provide a good jumping-off point."

General Sir Francis Clery was the Commander of the Second Division and in charge of the troops in that sector. Warren had become increasingly concerned about his lack of enthusiasm; he seemed resigned to failure. "General Clery is suffering from painful varicose veins and has become too focused on his personal illness. His heart is not in the fight; he has lost confidence. I request that he be replaced."

Buller was still bearing bruises from his shrapnel wound of a month ago, and Warren? "I recall that during the Transkei War you were badly injured in a native ambush. How long did you continue the fight before being invalided home?"

"Twelve months."

"I thought I remembered correctly. And Clery has varicose veins?" he smiled contemptuously. "He stays … so what are your options for the fight?"

"The hill crests are heavily fortified and I need to bombard them with the howitzers – you have only just released them to me. My preferred plan is to break down their defences with sustained artillery preparation, and then break in with my infantry."

"In the meantime," Buller observed sharply, "your infantry cling to the hillsides exposed to the Boer guns and rifle fire."

Warren chose to ignore this caustic comment and sought to develop his argument, "Even if we break through we can't traverse the pass across the hills until we have neutralised Spion Kop; it dominates the whole area."

Buller seethed inwardly: from the very first Warren had been mesmerized by his perceived need to seize Spion Kop, and now his failure elsewhere left few alternatives. It was take this damned hill or withdraw, and he was not ready to countenance that – not yet. His annoyance was visible, "Of course you must take Spion Kop!" he asserted irritably.

"Then I will lead the attack myself." Warren had felt it right to demonstrate personal leadership.

"No!" Buller insisted. "Your left flank remains open and I have reports from White in Ladysmith of Boer movement around Acton Homes. I continue to be concerned about the enemy threat from that direction. You should not become absorbed in an individual action, but remain free to exercise the wider command. I suggest that you discuss this proposed enterprise with your commanders." He paused, looked at Warren defiantly, and spoke calculatedly, "After your deliberations, should you determine that there is to be no attack, I personally will order a withdrawal back across the Tugela."

....

Warren cast about the tent. Of his commanders and specialist advisors assembling for the council of war, only Clery was absent. At last the tent flaps opened and his portly figure spilled into the interior.

"Take a seat Francis, and let's begin," invited Warren.

Clery limped awkwardly and slumped into the empty canvas chair; he carefully placed his painful, swollen foot. Warren was aware of the troops' nickname for Clery, "Old Blue Whiskers", on account of his bushy buggers'-grips. Now he examined him with a mixture of sympathy and derision: he was ineffective, physically unfit and eccentric. Warren began, "The troops have done extra-ordinarily well, but our casualties are high and we are stagnating on the hill sides. It's time to consider our options if we are to be successful. Francis, what about renewing your attack from the left … from Bastion Hill? Is it possible to roll up the enemy from that flank?"

Clery stiffened; he was visibly unhappy with this proposition. “I can see no advantage to pressing the attack in this area,” he replied emphatically. “Let me summarise the situation: we captured all the Boer first-line defences, but as the action developed the strength of the second defensive line has revealed itself. It runs along the crest of the plateau which rises in a series of smooth, grassy slopes of concave surface forming a glacis for the musketry of the defence to sweep…” He stopped, grasped his lower leg, his face contorted with pain – it passed. “The position consists of earth redoubts and shelter trenches with overhead cover cleverly arranged to command all approaches with fire – often with cross-fire, sometimes converging fire. Six field batteries and four howitzers bombarded the whole day yet failed utterly to silence the rifles, clear trenches or silence the Dutch artillery. Yesterday our casualties were one hundred and thirty for no serious contact with the enemy.” He was determined to make his position absolutely clear, “To take the final crests means assaulting across open ground; casualties would be enormous. Even if successful we are likely to be faced with yet more depth positions. We would have to start the assault all over again and our artillery is proving to be ineffective. It’s too costly an option.” There was no way that he was going to put his neck on the line, “I refuse to bear the consequences of such a plan alone. I insist that any orders to attack come in writing directly from General Buller. Sir, it is my intention to maintain a strictly defensive posture.”

There’s much which is valid in that appreciation, thought Warren, but without determined leadership no plan of attack would succeed, whatever the odds. Clery’s reluctance to resume the offensive reinforced his intended course of action. He would leave Clery to wallow in his own inadequacies and use the newly arrived 10 Brigade commanded by Major General Talbot-Coke for a renewed attack. He addressed the whole group, “As a precursor to any attack I believe that we would need to bombard the enemy positions for at least three days. This would enable my preferred tactic of breaking in and then breaking through. But I fear the guns which would facilitate this – the howitzers – have come too late. The infantry remain exposed on the hillsides, our supplies are rapidly reducing, and we cannot wait. The road north from Trichardt's Drift, Wagon Road Pass, is the only possible axis." As he spoke, he unhurriedly surveyed his audience, fixing their eyes and imposing his surety. At this pivotal point in the battle they were looking to him for a solution. Firm leadership was essential; and Buller's threat of withdrawal with its stigma of failure was unimaginable. With assured confidence he continued, "I believe the answer to our problem is Spion Kop. Once it's in our possession we can establish our guns on its heights to enfilade the Boer defences both to left and right; it would shatter the enemy line and induce a retreat. A considerable advantage is that the hill lies within the range of the naval 12 pounders at Potgieter's which could assist us while attacking."

The meeting was taking place in the shadow of this dark massif. It stood dominant, menacing, like a latent volcano straining to erupt. It was the highest point in the hill range - some 1,470 feet above the Tugela - and although there had been no overt enemy activity from its heights, its intimidating presence aroused a psychological need to posses and control it. Everyone at the council of war could see the advantage of holding this vital ground, and nodded affirmatively.

Warren turned to Talbot- Coke, "I want you to command this attack with your Brigade. The assault will be tonight. Once you've driven off the Boer garrison, you are to entrench and hold against the inevitable counter-attack. Tomorrow night we will reinforce with guns and thereafter sweep the Boers off the crests." He turned to Clery and said pointedly, "Then General Clery, you will be able to advance." He motioned to Talbot-Coke, "Liaise with my staff to ensure that you have everything you need."

Talbot-Coke was recovering from a broken leg and moved stiffly and cautiously, nevertheless, he felt honoured to be given this task. But he didn't know where he was going or what he would find on the top, and nightfall was fast approaching. "Sir Charles, I would like to delay for twenty-four hours and to attack tomorrow night, the 23rd. That will give me time to reconnoitre with the officers commanding regiments."

"That's agreed. Gentlemen, we will take Spion Kop and break through these damned hills to Ladysmith."

The meeting ended with confident smiles and murmurs of approval; they all poured out into the inky night. Talbot-Coke limped into the blackness to make his way back to his own headquarters' wagon. He soon realised that he was disorientated. He blundered about frequently banging his damaged leg against scattered rocks; it hurt like hell! – he sucked in sharply to absorb the pain and smother his shout. He missed his footing and fell. As he pulled himself to his feet he reluctantly acknowledged that he was lost and becoming increasingly tired. It was hopeless. He finally decided to remain where he was and nurse his throbbing leg until dawn came to his rescue. He sat restlessly on a cold stone and fretted about the following night; if he couldn't find his own waggon in the dark, how was he to find his way to the top of Spion Kop?

The following morning Buller made his now habitual visit to Warren. He was surprised and then maddened to learn that the proposed attack on Spion Kop had not yet taken place. He had not been informed of the postponement

"Tomorrow, Sir Redvers; we shall attack tomorrow," defended Warren.

"And who will command?"

"Talbot-Coke; his Brigade is fresh."

"Not a wise choice. The man's lame; send Woodgate!" He hesitated as if thinking deeply, "It will be a hazardous task so you must have tried troops. Lead with the Lancashire Fusiliers; they performed well recently in the Sudan."

Buller took one of his accompanying staff officers aside, Colonel Court, "I want you to stay behind and go with the assaulting troops. Report back to me personally."

"What are they to do once they have seized the summit?" enquired Court.

Buller considered for a few moments; "Hold the hill."

....

Dark clouds hung heavily releasing a fine drizzle; Jack found the rain refreshing after the stupefying heat of the day. He waited impatiently with the remainder of the Battalion in the bivouac area away from the immediate fighting. Earlier they had been addressed by Colonel Blomfield:

"I congratulate you all on your brave conduct and steadiness in the actions of the last few days. General Warren is similarly impressed with your excellent performance and has personally asked me to pass on his gratitude. Tonight we attack Spion Kop which is the key to the Boer defences. The General was clear that he must have the best men for the job and has selected the Lancashire Fusiliers to lead the way. The honour of the Regiment is in your hands. As we march let there be no noise, no talking, no smoking. Its bayonet work only, so ensure that your rifle chambers are empty to prevent an accidental discharge which would alert the enemy. When we reach the summit we will form an extended line, fix bayonets and advance slowly. When challenged by the enemy garrison lie flat and allow them to fire over you. Remember, the Mauser magazine holds five rounds only, so when we hear the sound of bolts clicking on empty chambers that will be our signal to rise and charge. The password is Waterloo."

He went on to make it clear that the Boers would not give up such an important hill lightly, and that a counter attack would surely come with daylight. The Engineers were following, and together they would prepare a defensive position. "I trust every man to do his duty. Good luck."

As dusk fell, Jack took his place with John and Bill in the column as they set off for the rendezvous. After a couple of hours of stumbling over uneven ground, they halted in a rocky ravine. "We're waitin' for the others to arrive …rest." The hushed message trickled down the line.

As he waited, isolated in the dark, Jack couldn't help thinking of other hills closer to home. He visualized the Sunday outings with Fred, Sally and the Naylors. Together they would wander over the moors which confine the industrial towns of Lancashire to the sinuous valleys. Sometimes they would walk over the Syke Hills, or pass through the neighbouring town of Littleborough to explore the Moss Moors. Favourite of all was to take the tram to the Norden terminus and then to strike out for Knowle Hill. This isolated knoll rises up to command the surrounding moorlands, not unlike Spion Kop. The climb is steep, but the reward is always an exhilarating sense of being on top of the world. From its summit is an all-round, uninterrupted view: brown moorlands stretching into the distance; tall red-brick chimneys protruding from smoky dales. The unencumbered space and inevitable bracing wind bring a satisfying sense of freedom from the cramped, intensity of life; from the noise, the crowds, the omnipresent mills; for a few releasing hours all that would seem so far away, so irrelevant. But inevitably reality would intrude. He could see them all now as they laughed, shouted, ran and tumbled down the slopes. Their childish noise was but a loud veneer covering reluctant hearts as they scurried back to the monotonous, dirty greyness of their grim existence. How he had enjoyed those brief carefree hours. How he had relished the opportunity to be with Mary; holding hands would invite loud bawdy jokes and cheesy grins from the other boys, but that hadn't repressed the lively banter between them both. Her very presence had brought a secret intimacy. He smiled inwardly with a warm glow as he pictured her taking off her bonnet; how her long hair swirled enticingly in the wind. He longed once more to see her rosy cheeks and her wide, compelling smile which filled her laughing face. For a moment he felt saddened by her absence. Increasingly he felt a desire to be with her. Was she thinking of him now? Was she still excited by memories of their passion in the barn?

A sharp nudge brought him back to the present; it was John, "They're 'ere! Lads from Lancaster and Warrington. We're off!" The column moved forward slowly, and on reaching the base of the hill adopted single file. The track was an ill-defined sheep path, and in the thick night only the man in front could be seen. The muffled rustling of men moving was all that could be heard; that, and the occasional scraping of metal boot-stud against rock and the clatter of bayonet scabbard. There were frequent and long halts when men stood resigned, leaning on their rifles, or flopped unceremoniously to the ground. Jack assumed that navigation was proving difficult, or perhaps the leaders were stopping to listen for Boer activity. They passed through a group of kraals on the slope - fortunately no dogs barked. “Keep together men; keep together.” The whispered urging came from the darkness: “March as close as you can to the man in front.” Jack quietly passed the warning down the line and anxiously scrambled to close the gap. He was only too aware of the confusion that would ensue should the tenuous line be broken. His mind bubbled with the repeated thought – almost audibly - the line mustn’t be broken …at all costs it mustn’t be broken. “Mind the rock!” Too late; Jack tripped almost losing his footing. He paused momentarily to gather his composure, and then frantically hastened upwards to catch the shadow disappearing to his front. Now it was necessary to scramble on all fours as he clambered up a steep, rocky incline. He slung his rifle across his back to free his hands and so better feel his way forward. During one pause the curtain of clouds parted allowing the moon to peep out hesitantly. Jack looked down into the valley below, and in the grey light could see the flickering of numerous camp fires. He visualised crouching men absorbing the heat whilst tightly grasping a metal mug of soul-warming tea. The moisture dripped from his helmet and ran down his neck: lucky buggers! he thought.

Several hours passed - the pace was slow and erratic. The higher they climbed the thicker the mist until visibility was reduced to a couple of paces - the lights in the valley had long disappeared. At last there was a sense that the narrow shoulder of land was opening into a plateau. Hushed words were passed along the column: “Form extended line.” Jack followed John to the right; they were halted by Grindrod. He pointed with his hand up the slope indicating the direction of assault and whispered, “Fix bayonets.” He moved along the line to instruct others.

There followed an irregular rattle of metal on metal as bayonet rings gripped muzzles and studs found their locking lugs. It’s a good job the breeze is in our faces, thought Jack, otherwise we'd be announcing our arrival to the Boers.

On muted orders the extended line advanced slowly and silently. Instinctively, Jack kept his position by glancing inward to the next man who was just visible. Suddenly there was a terrific clatter behind as two engineers carrying a stretcher full of shovels tripped and spilled their load, they cursed quietly, but surprise was lost.

"Wi com dar! Wi com dar!" challenged a startled, guttural voice from the mist.

"Waterloo!"

A ragged volley of rifle fire filled the night.

Jack dived to the ground as the bullets whizzed high and harmlessly above him. After a few minutes the fire slackened: "click, click".

"Fusiliers Charge! Up the Twentieth!" The line of men bounded forward with a terrifying shout, propelled by pent-up tension and a surge of adrenalin: "Up the Twentieth!" The firing stopped. Jack sensed rather than saw figures fleeing before them. To his front Lieutenant Awdry dashed ahead; this huge, burly, rugby player outrunning his men shouting: "Remember Majuba!" Then came a fearful scream as Awdry bayoneted a sentry who had been slow to make good his escape. Jack jumped over the squirming body in pursuit of his officer. Now he was running downhill. "Stop! Stop!" The charge was brought to a gasping, stuttering halt.

"We're over the brew." It was Bill, almost laughing as he bent forward to gain his breath, "The Boers 'ave gone. It's ours. For days we've been bangin' our 'eads against these bloody 'ills; tonight we've done it!' Easy victory ..eh!" He beamed.

"Fusiliers close in! Close in!" It was Colonel Blomfield. "Well done men! Well done! Now we must convey our victory to General Warren and the rest of the Field Force. The mist is too thick for the oil lamps to penetrate, so we shall raise three hearty cheers....Hip, hip- hooray! Hip, hip - hooray! Hip, hip - hooray!"

Within minutes the sound of triumph was acknowledged from the valley below with a salvo of star shells which drifted among the clouds creating an ominous, silvery shroud.

Jack sat with his friends a little unnerved by the agitated antics of the senior officers as they drifted in and out of the confining mist. Apparently, no-one knew the physical layout of the plateau, the extent of its perimeter, or the nature of the surrounding features; and nothing could be seen. Officers peered anxiously over their compasses. At last a decision was made. Blomfield's voice rang out, "Get the sappers to lay the tape here to demarcate the defensive line; and get the men digging … it'll soon be light and the Boers will come calling."

Jack sweated as he tried furiously, and with little success, to dig his allocated portion of the trench. He had grabbed a shovel from the rueful engineers. His helmet, equipment and jacket lay on the ground behind him with those of the others.

"This is bloody rock! 'Ow can we dig 'ere?" protested John.

Bill soon became bored, "Just goin' to see wat I can find." And with that he disappeared back over the crest.

"Is this best yer can do?" Grindrod emerged from the mist.

"The shovels are next to useless," offered Jack defensively. "Could do wi' some sandbags to 'elp build up parapet."

"Aye, you and everyone else Clegg. But they've been forgotten – still at bottom of the 'ill. Wer's yer brother Naylor? You two stick to each other like shit to a shovel. Wer is 'e?"

John couldn't tell the sergeant that his brother was skiving. He clutched at an excuse, "Gone to privvy, Sergeant."

Grindrod's half-belief was reflected in his body language and biblical mis-quote, "Crap can cover a multitude of sins. He'd best be 'ere wen I return in ten minutes." His attention returned to their meagre diggings, "Need to show a bit of gumption and make a parapet out of rocks … build up if yer can't dig down." He made as if to leave and then suddenly stopped; he pinned Jack with his keen eyes, "Wer's yer issued entrenchin' tool?"

"Lost it," conceded Jack nervously.

"Lost it! Lost it! Yer a waste of bloody rations! Yer'd lose yer balls if they weren't in a bag!" With that he moved of down the line. He was enveloped by the mist, but his gruff words of encouragement to their neighbours drifted back through the night.

Jack and John laboured together, but their strenuous efforts produced disappointing results; their neighbours were faring no better. Rocks there were a plenty, but prising them from the solid ground without proper tools was another story. It seemed to Jack, evidenced by everyone's curses, that this trench construction was futile. After a long night's climb and several hours of heavy work for little reward, everyone was beginning to feel tired. The initial exhilaration of success passed as fatigue set in; their momentum waned. Jack surveyed the finished product: a pathetically shallow trench barely two feet deep, fronted with a parapet of small rocks and turf and lacking any head cover.

"Give us a swig of yer water," demanded John. "Am empty."

"Yer knows the regulations about water discipline - no sharin' of water. Each man's responsible for 'is own."

"Nay, yer know 'ow that bully beef's so salty; am always thirsty."

Jack checked his bottle. Despite the chill of the damp mist, it had been thirsty work and he was conscious that he too had very little water left. "Just one swig, I don't 'ave much."

"Be alright; we should get a resupply in mornin'," soothed John.

"Look wat I found!" Bill blundered on their position grinning and very satisfied with himself. He dropped a bulky load, "Blankets! The buggers wer freetened to death and left in such a rush they forgot their blankets; and their shoes are all over the other side of the 'ill." He gave a blanket to each of them, "Time for a kip!"

Jack stirred from a fitful doze disturbed by a commotion around him. He awoke to a hazy, half light as the sun battled to dissipate the stubborn mist. Suddenly the sun broke through and their position was revealed.

"The rocks in front!" Blomfield was gesticulating and directing Awdry's gaze. "Those rocks are the edge of the plateau; they command dead ground which we must cover. We're too far back!"

Jack roused himself and gazed about; he was on the right edge of a relatively flat area which sloped gently forward - it was about the size of two football pitches. To his front, at about fifty yards, was a girdle of scattered rocks. To his left he could see parties already at the rocky ledge vainly striving to construct new defences. Now he watched as Awdry selected twenty men, including John, and went forward to occupy the nearest boulders. Once again the mist descended enshrouding them in their immediate environment, seemingly isolating them from the rest of the world. He could hear the scraping of shovels and the thudding of picks on stone accompanied by frustrated shouts. He was happy to have been selected to remain with Grindrod in order to provide depth to the position. He slept.

****

The corporalship sat around the fire; it was a damp chilly night. Someone threw wood onto the flames – the remnant of a door taken from an English farm. The wood crackled, spewing sparks into the night. Soon the reinvigorated fire radiated welcome heat.

Hendrick had been summoned to a kriegsraad where the present situation would be reviewed and plans for the future laid. For days the ominous sounds of the guns had carried across the plain from the battle which was raging along the Tugela. Eagerly they had pressed those passing by the laager for news of the fighting: the wounded, those organising supplies, and a few dribbling back home for impromptu leave. It appeared that the Khakis had made some gains along the spurs rising northwards from the river, but had been held along the crest of the hills. However, the reports were of his countrymen becoming exhausted under the constant strain of battle, particularly from the guns, and the lack of sleep and proper nourishment.

At last Hendrick returned to the laager, dismounted and joined his family and friends. They all waited patiently and respectfully until he composed himself and began to explain, “Our spies tell us that fever is rife in Ladysmith. There is little to eat. The cavalry horses are being slaughtered for food. Spirits are low amongst the soldiers. Surrender can’t be far away. As for Buller on the Tugela; he may be across the river, but he can’t get through the hills – he’s bogged down.” He scanned the smiling faces. “However, our countrymen on the Tugela are weary; for many days they laboured to build defences and now have been fighting for three days without respite. The kriegsraad called for volunteers to help our comrades. You should know my friends that we have a reputation since our night battle. It was expected that we would lead the way. I agreed … did I do right?"

"How could it be otherwise?" ventured one of the group. Others murmured with proud consent.

"So be it!" declared Hendrick. "Pack food, water and ammunition. We leave within the hour."

The cousins and Henry rode together. The drizzling rain was persistent, but the twenty miles were covered without mishap. They arrived tired and expectant at the foot of the most imposing feature, Spion Kop.

"Wait for my return," instructed Hendrick as he galloped off towards a farmhouse sited on a low hill about a mile to the north.

The corporalship dismounted and tethered their ponies and horses to scraggy thorn bushes. Branches were gathered to build fires and the task of making coffee began. With the dawn a scorching sun filled a cloudless sky, turning the icy morning into a furnace blast.

Shortly afterwards about seventy burghers of the Carolina Commando galloped onto the scene, their ponies kicking up a coughing dust. They secured their mounts and quickly gathered around their legendary Commandant, Hendrik Prinsloo, who addressed them: "Last night the Khakis rushed the summit of this hill and pushed off the small picket drawn from men of the Vryhied Commando and a few German volunteers. Our new Commandant-General, Louis Botha, has ordered counter moves. Guns are being dragged up the adjacent hills to shoot onto the hilltop. Some of our friends have been ordered to occupy surrounding heights in order to snipe the enemy positions and prevent any forward advance. We are to drive the Khakis off the summit."

The mood was sombre as the Carolinas absorbed this information and anticipated their task. Prinsloo looked into the grave faces of his men, "Burghers, we are going in amongst the enemy and not all of us will return. Do your duty and trust in the Lord."

Jan watched as they disappeared up into the mist which still blanketed the summit. Within minutes others from the Pretoria Commando arrived. They too dismounted and tethered their ponies. There was little conversation; the atmosphere was subdued, strained, determined. Their leader, “Red” Daniel Opperman - a huge man - led the way up the hill in the wake of the Carolinas. The Witbergers were left in a silence, save for the scratching and snorting of the many tethered ponies.

With a flurry Hendrick arrived, dismounting he shouted his news, “We are to follow the Carolinas and Pretorians, and sweep the Khakis off the hill. Follow me!” He set off at a trot.

Jan was near the end of the straggling line; the climb was steep; in places he was reduced to scrambling on all fours. They moved cautiously, slowly, as if stalking dangerous game, stealing unseen from boulder to boulder. They were fearful of closing with an enemy who fixed his hopes on the bayonet.

CHAPTER 9

The Battle for Spion Kop I

(Morning 24 January 1900)

"Look, look yonder!" shouted Bill.

Once again Jack was startled out of a rough sleep; he was finding it difficult to stay awake. As he became conscious of his surroundings he realised that the mist had melted away, and he could feel the growing warmth of the sun set in a vivid, blue sky; the day was sharp and clean with excellent visibility. "Wat 're yer gawping at?" he muttered bad temperedly.

"The reflections … look!"

Jack followed the direction indicated by animated hands; before him was a wide plain with low hills in the distance, and sure enough, there, tucked amid the folds, could be seen glinting sheets of white-metal roofing.

"That's Ladysmith!" shouted Bill, to be echoed by other exuberant voices. "That's Ladysmith, that's wer we're goin'!"

Jack stared at the objective of the Natal Field Force. Surely it couldn't be long now before they reached the beleaguered town, they could see it; it was within their grasp. There was a real sense of exhilaration and expectation. Excitedly Jack looked around him at the expansive panorama and the awe-inspiring view from his hilltop. Then he studied the immediate ground: the main trench extended for about four hundred yards in a semi-circle facing forwards: north he thought. It was approximately one hundred yards in advance of the actual summit behind them. Ahead he could see John and the others among the ragged line of rocks; at that point the ground fell away sharply. To the left were the hills that they had previously attacked unsuccessfully. To his right he could see a gully which separated them from a low hill at about four hundred yards. Beyond that, at perhaps two thousand yards, were two twin peaks slightly lower than the one which they occupied. It was now evident to Jack that the Fusiliers occupied the extreme right sector of the trench. The irregulars of Colonel Thorneycroft's Mounted Infantry were on their immediate left; beyond them he could just make out the lads from the Royal Lancaster Regiment boosted by a couple of companies from the South Lancashire's.

He joined the others, generally milling about around the trench and rocks; some began to produce their breakfast of the inevitable bully beef and hard tack. There was no sign of the enemy.

"Crack!"

Jack saw the ground two yards to his right throw up an angry fountain of dust. Again "crack!" as a bullet whipped by his head. The party atmosphere was rudely shattered. Men hesitated; were confused. Drummer Greig gave out a piercing scream and, clutching his chest, crumbled to the ground. He lay squirming. Realisation dawned; rifle fire was coming from amongst the dense aloe plants on the low hill on their open right flank. There was an undignified scramble for the trench; men grabbed their harnesses discarded during the digging and fumbled to put them on. Rifles were cocked. Another fusilier was hit on the right side of the head as he sought cover. His skull exploded throwing out blood and brains. The impact threw him onto the prostrate bodies of his comrades who were elbowing and shoving to gain the protection of the shallow trench. Alarmed, they unceremoniously pushed his corpse to the rear.

Jack knelt in the now crowded trench, but it gave little protection from the incoming rifle fire. Warily he peered over the stones which formed the parapet. He thought he could see movement on the low hill at four hundred yards, but he wasn't sure. The Boers, he knew, were expert at field-craft and their smokeless cartridges gave no clues as to their position. At that range their marksmanship was unbeatable. "Splat!" the bullet hit the rock and ricocheted into the air with a sharp "ping". A stone splinter struck his helmet. Like an agitated tortoise he instinctively withdrew his head below the parapet.

"That wer close!" He exclaimed to Bill with a tense grin born of fear. "Tha can't even raise tha rifle to take aim; besides, I can't 'it nowt at that distance."

Rapid fire broke out amongst the rocks to their front. There was shouting, yelling and curdling screams. Then wounded began to stagger back, falling over the parapet onto the huddled figures; others didn't halt there, but ran upwards over the summit seeking cover, safety, and medical treatment at the first-aid post. Some failed to cross the open ground and fell from the blows of further bullets.

Jack and Bill seized the harness of a fusilier who collapsed just in front of the trench and dragged him over the parapet into doubtful safety. His bloody hands cupped a wide wound in his stomach; intestines oozed. Jack thrust his hand into the injured man's tunic pocket and located his field dressing. Clumsily, his fingers shaking, he tore off the cover and applied the bandage as best he could. Such a gaping hole could only come from an exploding bullet; dum-dum, thought Jack.

The wounded man lay on his back and sought their gaze through fearful eyes, "There's 'undreds of 'em climbin' up th' hill," he stuttered with difficulty, "'undreds." Suddenly his face contorted with pain and his body arched violently. He spewed blood and began choking on the hot liquid. Then the pain seemed to pass as he relaxed, "We're keepin' the buggers back." He grinned, and then slumped lifelessly.

Jack examined his own bloody hands, fixed, staring; his gaze was held.

"They're fallin' back, give coverin' fire!" shouted Bill. "Cum on!"

Jack was stirred to action. He propped himself up against the parapet and brought his rifle to bear. Fusiliers were rushing back the short distance from the rocks, some moving fast crouched low, some staggering, some leaning on friends, others dragging limp bodies – some lay motionless on the ground . He saw a bearded face below a crumpled hat appear around a rock. He aimed quickly and fired; he noticed the "splat" as the bullet struck the rock. "Bloody missed!" Other heads and shoulders were emerging all along the line of the rocks. Jack and Bill fired furiously.

"Got one! Got one!" screamed Bill.

Bearded men in scruffy jackets bounded forward in pursuit, but several were hit. The others withdrew. The stampede finished.

"'Ave yer seen John?" Bill demanded of Jack with a wild desperation in his eyes. "I 'aven't seen John …wer's John?" Recklessly he rose above the parapet to scrutinise the still, khaki figures among the rocks and lying in the dust of the open space, "'E might be wounded." He made as if to move forward further exposing himself; "thud, ping" – two bullets struck close. Jack grabbed the harness straps on Bill's back with both hands and yanked him into the shallow hole.

"There's nowt yer can do yet, apart from get killed!" shouted Jack. "If he's wounded we'll find 'im later. He might even be a prisoner."

****

By now the sun had broken through and banished the persistent mist. The sky was deep blue and cloudless; the sun's heat growing in intensity. Jan could hear the devastating English volleys amid the backdrop of ragged Boer rifle shots. There was intense shouting and screaming, evidence of the vicious hand-to-hand fighting. But the upward movement didn't falter; relentlessly the burghers pressed on. He followed tense and with knotted stomach. He stepped respectfully over the body of a burgher lying across the track; a gaping head wound spewed innards. A little further and he passed another burgher who lay writhing, holding his chest, others, dead and wounded, littered the slope. He emerged from the undergrowth to witness the primitive struggle; no longer the impersonal, long range Mauser snipes, but instead a savage and individual fight for survival, one on one, strength against strength, ferocious and merciless. He froze, hesitating to become embroiled in that mad, bloody brawl. He had no wish to grapple with bayonets. To his relief the Khakis gave way and began to fall back from a line of scattered rocks. He advanced and peered over them. The soldiers were teetering backwards, dragging their wounded, covered by fire emanating from a low, long sangar of small rocks and stones. Some Boers tried to pursue and cross the open plateau of forty or fifty yards, but fell after a few steps; their bodies augmenting those of the lifeless Khakis. To follow was impossible, but the rocky ledge was theirs.

Jan tucked himself below a sturdy rock; his cousins and Henry were close by. Hendrick moved among his men, sullen, but strong and steadying. The fire from the low sangar was fragmented, but unrelenting. Any movement was met with a deadly response from the defenders. Casualties increased.

Jan could see his fellow country men on Aloe Knoll to his left shooting into the open English flank. They must have perfect targets, he thought, as the soldiers lean forward against the trench exposing themselves from head to foot. Several times the burghers increased their rate of fire to destroy embryonic attacks before they could reach his rocky refuge. He glared into the sun towards the Twin Peaks and observed a team from the Transvaal Artillery hauling their gun into position. Soon there came a "whoosh" as the first shell passed overhead. There was a man just behind him whom he recognised as a teacher, Louis Bothma. He was operating a heliograph; his flickering messages sending corrections to the gunners. On idle days Jan had watched the Long-Toms bombarding Ladysmith, and now he could visualize the gunners responding to the instructions: barrels would be elevated, lines of fire adjusted. Moments later the ground shook violently as the second shell struck the plateau. "On target!" he shouted aloud with approval. Other guns began to fire from nearby hills to north and west. The distinctive "pom-pom" of the maxims played percussion in the manic, orchestral overture. The hilltop rocked and quaked under the pounding.

They were joined in their position by a number of German volunteers who had been redeployed from the Rangeworthy Hills where the English remained inactive. Henry sidled up to Jack and gave him a gentle nudge. Covertly he indicated a tall, athletic, lithe figure whom, despite the grubby circumstances, was neatly dressed and well groomed. His bush uniform was superbly tailored. He had a waxed moustache, short hair and an aristocratic bearing. Henry placed his mouth close to Jan's ear. He was trying to be discreet whilst wanting to make himself heard above the infernal din, "I believe that I've seen pictures of him in the newspapers. He was featured in the *Boston Times*. If I'm right, he was an officer in the German Army, Baron von Bruswitz. The story goes that a civilian brushed against him in a Berlin café, and that he accused him of insulting the uniform of a German officer. He then ran the man through with his sword – killed him."

Jan was intrigued by this story. He looked searchingly at the man who was now sat with his back against a rock, smoking nonchalantly, seemingly oblivious to the storm around him. He exuded an air of remoteness and superiority, if not arrogance.

Henry continued, “After a public outcry he was tried by a military court, cashiered and given a nominal prison sentence of a couple of years. Apparently he was soon released after the Kaiser intervened personally; then he disappeared. Fancy him turning up here.”

As they watched, the German finished his cigarette and flicked the butt into the grass. He took up his rifle and stood in full view of the enemy, took aim and fired. Smiling, he casually sat down again and lit another cigarette. Minutes passed before he repeated his performance; bullets whipped around him. He was displaying a foolish recklessness, almost as if he had a death wish - perhaps he had. Several more times he unhurriedly stood to aim and shoot, careless of the danger. Eventually he rose without his weapon, and in brazen defiance calmly lit a cigarette. He made no attempt at concealment. He just stood there smoking provocatively. The bullet hit him full in the face knocking him backwards. He lay still.

The artillery fire was subduing the Khakis, and it was safer now to adopt a fire position in order to shoot at the enemy on the plateau. In concert with the others, Jan began to snipe at the least movement.

“Observe where the enemy fires from and then lay your rifle on the spot,” Hendrick sprawled beside him. “When he next rises to shoot, you have him.”

Jan waited until a hurried shot was fired from the long sangar to his front. He noted the location and trained his rifle on it. He looked through the sights and waited; patiently he waited, ignoring the tumult around him. Many times he had stalked his prey on the open veldt; had crawled downwind into a fire position at a thousand yards from the grazing impala or kudu. The animals would chew avidly, but always alert, stopping frequently to sniff the breeze and to cock an ear to detect warning sounds. But he was an excellent shot and invariably rode home triumphantly with his white-bellied trophy slung across his saddle. Today the quarry was a man, a human being just like him, with a family, a home, dreams and hopes; he was to extinguish that life with its loves and fears and aspirations. He forced himself not to dwell on the intimacies; these were invaders who would take his country and destroy the freedoms bought with the blood and sacrifice of his parents and grandparents. There was no choice.

He noticed movement. He banished the wanderings of his mind; expelled the disturbing thoughts, the unsettling inner turbulence. A shell landed to his front, the debris and dust obscured his view; he remained focussed waiting for the air to clear. Through the dispersing dust he could now make out a helmet, a shoulder, a head. He fired. The head jerked back awkwardly and disappeared. He withdrew behind his cover.

"Well done boy!" affirmed Hendrick before moving on.

****

The fighting to the front had momentarily detracted from the threat from the right, but that had not subsided. The incoming rifle fire was intensifying. Jack could see that the number of dead was rising, particularly from head wounds; the injured lay among them twitching, thrashing, or lying stoically on the trench floor resigned to approaching death. Some were calling for their mothers or shouted the names of wife or girlfriend.

With a "whoosh" the first shell flew harmlessly over the summit. The next one crashed amongst two men lying behind a few isolated rocks in rear of the main trench. As the dust cleared Jack glanced to his rear to see only the trunk of one and a leg ripped from the other.

More guns began to fire from the two hills on the right and from another hill to the front. Soon they had the range of the sloping plateau to the yard. Every shell struck home. This chorus of Hades was joined by maxim guns of British manufacture which fired ten-round clips of one-pound shells in rapid succession: "pom-pom, pom-pom, pom-pom". The exploding shells drew an inexorable line across the dusty ground stalking their prey. Casualties grew: men were wounded several times; corpses further mangled. The trench and plateau became a hellish inferno to which there was no response. Men screamed in their helplessness.

Bill sat in the bottom of the trench, his back against the wall. He was distraught, angry, restless. Jack turned from him to see Colonel Blomfield approaching along the line from the direction of the colonials, apparently oblivious to the Mauser bullets whipping about him. He stopped by a huddle of wounded and bent over them. Jack couldn't hear, but from the emerging shouts of: "Wer with yer, sir!" he could see that the Colonel was trying to stiffen moral. He stopped by Jack, and using his telescope searched the hills to the unprotected flank. "Boers!" he shouted, apparently to anyone who could hear, but no-one in particular. "Boers! Hundreds of them moving up the slopes … about a mile or so away … towards the Twin Peaks." The Colonel noticed General Woodgate picking his way towards him along the trench, crouching to minimise his exposure; he moved off to warn him of the enemy movement. Jack saw events unfold.

The two met. "Over there, General!" Blomfield was shouting and pointing. "Coming up the slopes; hundreds!"

Woodgate looked intently in the direction indicated, squinting into the sun. But before he was heard to comment a bullet struck him through the head above the right eye. He collapsed.

Blomfield dropped to cover amongst his men. "Volunteers to carry the General to the aid post!" he cried above the racket. Dutifully, five men closed around the casualty, among them two sergeants. A fusilier removed his tunic and buttoned up the front; an improvised stretcher was constructed. The party hurriedly lifted the General onto the stretcher and scurried up the slope. A percussion shrapnel shell landed close by flinging out its ragged, hot, metal shards. Fusilier Quirk reeled and fell. Jack knew him well; he came from Wigan. He saw him struggle to his knees clutching his shoulder – bloody shredded muscle and skin where once his arm had been. He staggered towards the crest. "Thud!" Again he fell, a bullet ripping into his left lung. To the amazement of spectators, he rose once more and pitched over the summit. Sergeant Openshaw fell next; hit twice almost simultaneously, he crumpled to the ground, dead; the stretcher was dropped and the General spilled into the dust. The three remaining bearers frantically scooped up the wounded officer and staggered over the hill pursued by cracking, hissing bullets.

Blomfield shouted back to Jack's Company Commander, "Major Walter, clear those damned Boer to your front.!" He apparently assessed that it was from there that the fatal shot had come. He then set off to inform Colonel Crofton of the Royal Lancaster Regiment that, as the more senior officer, he was now in charge.

Jack waited in dread anticipation for the order to be given. Resignedly, he kicked Bill, "Get ready!" Bill starred at him; his face hardened; his eyes moist. Without a word he grasped his rifle tightly and shifted his position; his vengeance ready to unfurl like a coiled spring.

"C Company, prepare to Advance!" A pause.

"Cum on, for God's sake cum on!" muttered Jack.

"Advance! Advance!"

Jack rose from the ditch and launched himself forward with a demented scream: "Chaaaarge!" Bullets zinged past him from front and right. He had barely gone ten yards when suddenly he was overwhelmed by a terrific noise and thrown by a hot gushing wind. He could only have lost consciousness for seconds, for as the dust cleared and he rose unsteadily to his hands and knees, he saw Major Walter topple forward.

"Retire! Retire!"

Jack crawled back the few yards to the trench. He dropped to the bottom; he was shaking involuntarily. He rolled onto his back and starred upwards at the cloudless sky: Bill spilled in. "Bit of a cock-up!" he wheezed trying to recover his breath. Jack thought he detected just the suspicion of a grin.

Major Walter dragged himself along the ground; he inched his body towards the trench with the aid of stones and tufts of grass; slowly, very slowly. His movement attracted fire: "Thud! Thud!" Bullets threw up dirt around him. Still he edged towards his goal - only yards away, but for him it was a deadly marathon.

Suddenly a group of ill-clad, poorly shod, coolie stretcher-bearers from the Natal Ambulance Corps sprang forward, despising the cruel metal ripping through the air. They lifted the wounded officer onto a stretcher and hurried off up the hill at a gentle trot amid the encouraging shouts of the soldiers: "Gud on yer, body snatchers!" Miraculously they disappeared unscathed.

Blomfield nudged his way down the trench towards the devastated right flank. The men there needed encouragement and support. The trench was choked with the dead, the dying and the cowering; it was impossible to negotiate a path through the cringing mass. He climbed out onto the slope; the bullet hit him in the shoulder and spun him to the ground. Anxious hands hauled him into cover.

....

"Thank you … put it over there." Warren pointed to the "A" frame on which the orderly placed the tin bowl of hot water. He always liked to maintain appearances regardless of the trying circumstances; personal discipline was imperative. He slipped off his tunic, applied soap from the shaving stick and scraped his cheeks and chin with his cut-throat razor.

"When would you like your breakfast, sir," enquired the orderly.

"In ten minutes."

"The Quartermaster said to tell yer that he 'ad ox tongues – a special treat like," added the orderly expecting appreciation.

Warren stopped, his body stiffened, "Tell the Quartermaster that I'm of a mind to court-martial him! What right have I to be favoured above any common soldier? What's for your breakfast?"

"Bully-beef and 'ard tack, sir."

"And that's what I have."

The orderly hurried away. Warren rinsed his razor while staring at the mist which still lingered on the western summit of the hill; it was preventing direct communication with the garrison on the top. Earlier that morning he had been reassured by the cheers of success which had floated down to the valley; it appeared as if a cheap victory had been achieved. Buller's liaison officer, Colonel a Court, who had accompanied the assaulting force, had been the first to bring news of the fighting: "We can hold out until Doomsday," he had reported.

Fortunately, Warren mused, it was his own personal intervention which had forestalled a disaster when he had stopped the naval guns at Potgieter's Drift from inadvertently firing on our own forces on the summit.

Warren ate his unappetising breakfast perfunctorily and without enjoyment: the hot tea was some consolation. He sat by his waggon and turned the pages of his Bible until he found his favourite Psalm; number 91. It was a beautiful morning; he absorbed the growing warmth, delighted in God's creation as he looked across the Tugela to the Drakensberg, and felt gratefully reassured that the battle was progressing so well. He read:

> *I will say of the Lord, He is my refuge and my fortress: my God: in Him I will trust.... Thou shalt not be afraid for the terror by night: nor for the arrow that flieth by day; ... A thousand shall fall at thy side, and ten thousand at thy right hand; but it shall not come nigh thee ... For He shall give His angels charge over thee, to keep thee in all thy ways ...*

His uplifting meditation was shattered by the arrival of an agitated staff officer; "Sir, enemy fire and casualties have driven the signalling post from the west of the hill to a more sheltered position on the eastern shoulder. We don't have direct line of sight from here, and so all heliograph messages are being relayed via General Buller's headquarters. This has just arrived from Colonel Crofton." Warren took the message sheet and read: "Reinforce at once or all lost. General dead." He was surprised and alarmed at this sudden turn of events. How could this be? All was going as planned.

"Get me General Talbot-Coke!"

"Sir!"

Talbot-Coke found Warren in his tent. He brushed back the flaps and entered tentatively. "Come in! Read this!" Warren brusquely passed across the message and paused while it was read. "It seems that Crofton is now in command on the summit and is in a blue funk! It needs you there. I'd go myself if I could, but General Buller has directed me to stay here. We must send reinforcements to the summit."

"I'll despatch the Middlesex, Dorsets and Imperial Light Infantry straight away," offered Coke. "And, of course, I will leave to personally to take command."

As Talbot-Coke limped away, Warren summoned the staff officer; he needed to stiffen Crofton's backbone. "Send a message to Colonel Crofton:

> *Reinforcements despatched with immediate effect. General Talbot-Coke coming to assume command. No surrender!"*

What else could he do? He knew that Lyttleton was sitting inactive at Potgieter's Drift with a full brigade. He added, "Also telegraph to General Lyttleton and request all available assistance."

....

The heavy clouds of sulphurous smoke lay like a pall over the mountain top. They silhouetted the pigmy-like figures of the men who were holding it under an inferno of fire. Now and then he could see a small party rushing forward, only to surge back in much reduced numbers. At times the thunder of Boer guns merged to become a single dull roar, before breaking down once again into individual bursts.

Buller stood with his staff on the vantage point at Mount Alice observing the battle through telescopes. The early news had been good, but since the mist had lifted and the fight had started in earnest the signs had become worrying. Boer rifle fire had been reinforced by their artillery and it was proving impossible to locate the Boer gun positions and to destroy them. Not all could be seen, but rearward movement was hardly encouraging. Then had arrived the panicky message from Crofton stating that Woodgate was dead and the situation desperate. He had discussed developments with his staff. No-one, it seemed, had a high opinion of Crofton's capabilities; he was viewed as non-descript, uninspiring, lacking composure and grit. Then he intercepted Warren's message alerting Crofton of reinforcements and Talbot-Coke's imminent arrival. He still remained unconvinced that Talbot-Coke was the right man for the job.

"Can I make a suggestion General?" It was Court newly off the hill. "I was very impressed with Lieutenant Colonel Thorneycroft. He led the night approach and subsequent assault with great aplomb. He's very confident in command, cool-headed, unflappable. He's shown great initiative and dedication in raising his own irregular unit. I believe that he's got the back-bone to steady the defence."

Buller was unsure. Thorneycroft was not a regular officer, but a colonial. Yes, he had experience; he had fought in the Zulu campaign and in the earlier war against the Boers, but, importantly, would his authority be accepted by more senior regular officers? After all, Thorneycroft was only a temporary lieutenant colonel. He pondered; who else of that standing was in a position to grip the dubious situation on the hill? It was no time for niceties. His mind was made up, "Telegraph to Warren:

> *Unless you put some really good, hard, fighting man in command you will lose the hill. I suggest Thorneycroft."*

....

Warren studied the message from Buller. Talbot-Coke was already clambering up the hill and was to take command, but military custom dictated that a suggestion from your superior be treated with the equivalent weight of a direct order. He deliberated unhappily before reluctantly issuing instructions to his orderly officer, "Send the following:

> *With the approval of the Commander-in-Chief, I place Lieutenant Colonel Thorneycroft in command of the summit, with the local rank of Brigadier General."*

"How do we inform General Coke of the changes, sir?" enquired the officer.

"Thorneycroft will tell him on his arrival."

"And Colonel Crofton?"

"Thorneycroft will tell him!"

"It's just that if we are not careful, sir, we will have Colonel Crofton, General Talbot- Coke, and Colonel Thorneycroft each believing that they're in command of the hill."

"Damn it man! Don't you think they're capable of talking to each other?" Warren vented his irritation at Buller's meddling, "Send the message!"

....

The two signallers huddled in the hollow with spent bullets frequently whizzing over head. Earlier a near hit from a shell had wounded one of their comrades and forced them to the eastern side of the hill below the crest. The heliograph below flickered its reflected sunlight in flashes indicating letters and words. Together they strained to read the letters mouthing them in unison: F R O M – W A R R E N – T O - T H O R N E Y C R O F T - W I T H – T H E – A P P R O V A L .... Private Barrett wrote down the emerging message in his soiled notebook using a stumpy pencil. When completed an acknowledgement was sent.

That was the easy part, thought Barrett; now to deliver it. He knew that Lieutenant Colonel Thorneycroft was the Commanding Officer of the colonial troops here on the hill. They were over the summit, in the thick of the fight. He didn't fancy exposing himself to shot and shell, but there was no way out of it. He picked up his rifle and slung it over his back, adjusted his helmet and tightened the strap. Looking across at his mate he grinned, "Suppose it's my turn; am off. Wish me luck." Just then an irregular officer was hurrying by.

"Sir", shouted Barrett. "Wer do I find Colonel Thorneycroft? I've a message for 'im."

The officer slid down beside him. "What's your message soldier?" Barrett read from his notebook.

"You'll find him in that direction," advised Lieutenant Rose pointing with outstretched arm. Then he left.

Barrett moved at a crouch to the summit, the odd "over" cracking above his head. At the top he stopped and lay down. Was he to run and cover the ground quickly or crawl and keep low? With a fateful resignation he dashed forward and onto the exposed slope. He jumped over a corpse about ten yards to his front and then bounded on. Bullets thudded into the ground or ricocheted with a whine like the scream of a frightened banshee. A shell fell fifty yards to his left; instinctively he dived to the ground and sought cover. He crawled behind a shattered corpse; the legs had been ripped from the trunk. Another shell landed close by; he pushed his face into the rocky ground to hide from the shower of metal, stone and dirt.

In an interlude between shells Jack became aware of a shout behind him, "Colonel Thorneycroft, am lookin' for Colonel Thorneycroft. Wer might 'e be?" Jack raised his head just sufficient to identify someone lying close to a body, about ten yards to the rear. "'Ave a message for Colonel Thorneycroft," repeated the soldier.

He's the officer for the colonials, thought Jack; "Over to yer left, wi' colonials," he shouted as another shell landed, fortunately forward and short of the position.

Barrett could see that the shallow trench ahead was bulging with men competing for scarce cover; he would never be able to pass along it so he decided to make a final dash. He ran shouting, "Colonel Thorneycroft! Message for Colonel Thorneycroft!"

"Here lad!"

Barrett saw an arm raised; his destination; almost there now; thank God.

"Message from General Warren! ..." The bullet entered his brain killing him instantly. The lifeless body crumbled into the trench.

Thorneycroft looked sadly at the young soldier dead at his feet, "I wonder what the hell he was going to tell me?"

At that point Lieutenant Rose crashed headlong into the trench. He recovered his breath and spurted out, "You're promoted temporary Brigadier General and are to take command of all troops on the summit."

Thorneycroft was amazed. "Is there no one senior to me?" He was aware that General Woodgate and Colonel Blomfield were casualties, but what of Colonel Crofton of the Lancaster's, or others who could be despatched such as General Coke?

"That was the message," confirmed the officer. "I witnessed its receipt by heliograph from General Warren. What are we going to do? Fight or surrender?"

Lieutenant Colonel Alex Thorneycroft was an imposing figure at six feet two inches tall and weighing twenty stone. He confidently led his motley collection of colonials and disgruntled uitlanders with a firm and fatherly hand, but to assume responsibility for a regular Brigade was another unknown dimension. He was conscious of his lack of experience. He surveyed his would-be inheritance: the shell blasted plateau; the unceasing rifle fire; the mutilated corpses; the wounded and dying devoid of comfort and medical treatment; men cowering behind skimpy cover awaiting a painful and messy end.

He stood up defying the bullets and in his thunderous voice called out, "Boys, what shall we do? Surrender or fight to the last man?"

There was a pause; then in a moment of seeming silence an anonymous voice responded: "We'll make a fight of it!"

"Fight to last man!" shouted another.

Thorneycroft examined the men stretched before him: filthy with dust, red-eyed with fatigue, splattered with their own blood or that of comrades, but resolute and brave. They were looking to him for leadership. He grinned, reconciled to the inevitable, "That's what we do then. We fight to the last man!"

It was obvious to him that the situation was deteriorating rapidly. The Royal Artillery was proving incapable of silencing the Boers guns; they didn't have the range, and besides, the Boer guns were cleverly sited in the lee of the hills out of direct sight and so protected from retaliatory fire. They were firing onto the crowded hilltop with impunity. Only once had the naval guns located at Potgieter's fired on Aloe Knoll bringing momentary relief, but mysteriously this had ceased abruptly. He noticed particularly, that the Fusiliers were suffering terribly from the incessant and accurate sniping. But his immediate concern was the rocks about one hundred yards or so to his front. They provided a jump-off point for any Boer assault, and the fire coming from them was constant and accurate. To secure the main position and to relieve the right flank, he needed to clear the rocks of enemy.

He shouted above the tumult, slowly and deliberately, "We must clear the Boers from the rocks to our front. If we don't, then we shall lose this position. When I give the word we charge forward and clear the enemy. Are you with me?" This was met with a hesitant but affirmative response. "Fix bayonets!"

"Off agin!" grimaced Bill. "We're up and down this bloody slope like a fiddler's elbow!"

But Jack was ready to get to grips with the enemy. He was becoming increasingly incensed at the carnage around them, and at their own impotence. Now no more waiting for the Angel of Death to wield his scythe indiscriminately; no more cowering helplessly waiting to be picked-off; no more holding of breath anticipating the next maiming shell. It felt good: to close with the Boer, to stick him with the bayonet, to fight on their own terms. He drew his bayonet from its scabbard and clipped it onto his rifle muzzle. In so doing the tip was exposed above the parapet; it glinted in the sun inviting a response. "Ching!" a bullet struck the bayonet almost tearing the rifle from his hands. The soldier next to him reeled backwards letting out a hideous scream; his bloody face mashed by the ricochet.

"Charge! Charge!"

For a moment Jack hesitated, transfixed by the wounded man. Should he stay and care for him? He hardened his heart, turned and groped over the rock and turf of the meagre parapet: "Up the Twentieth! Avenge Majuba!"

Fusiliers and irregulars stumbled from the trench and over the parapet. The firing from the flank increased; soldiers fell, but their momentum was unstoppable. They lurched forward through the converging bullets and in seconds were amongst those Boers crouching behind the rocks. The released anger and frustration of the attackers made for an unforgiving fight. They thrust viciously and frenetically with bayonet giving little quarter. Jack, half tripping, fell involuntarily on a startled Boer. Together they rolled, clinging to each other before thrashing out wildly. They separated and started to scramble to their feet. Jack found his balance first. He snatched a nearby rifle from the ground, grabbed it by the muzzle, and with uncontrolled rage lashed out at his stout, unsteady opponent, hitting him with the butt square in the face - he collapsed. Jack kicked the prostrate body. He searched for his own rifle; picked it up, and with cold deliberation drove home his bayonet: once … twice. The Boers fell back under such fury. Jack watched with satisfaction as they retreated frantically down the slope.

At his feet was his dead enemy lying in the foetus position. He turned him over callously with his boot to reveal a middle-aged man with a long dishevelled beard. His face was contorted in pain and his craggy features exaggerated by a deep scar running from left ear to nose. He was clasping his stomach at the place where the bayonet had torn it open. Jack looked at his enemy quizzically. It was his first physical contact with the Boer - these scruffy farmers were killing so many of his friends and comrades.

Success among the rocky outcrop was short lived.

A shell landed with a deafening crash tossing a shower of dirt, stones and buzzing hot metal as from an erupting volcano. The air pressure almost knocked Jack off his feet. It had fallen short; no-one seemed to have been seriously hurt. Men took cover among the rocks as best they could, but the second shell found its target. A soldier dropped to his knees, his back torn open by a sliver of shrapnel devoid of conscience, his lung visible and pulsating with each desperate breath. Slowly he toppled forward onto his face. Another was starring helplessly at where once his legs had been. The merciless overture of death reached a new crescendo as rifles and "pom-poms" complemented the Creusots and Krupps. The attackers were tossed about in a deadly gale. Thorneycroft watched despondently as half his force was destroyed in minutes. The position was untenable. "Withdraw! Withdraw!" Yet again the girdle of rocks was to be abandoned to the Boer.

"Cum on Bill, let's go!" yelled Jack above the hellish din.

Bill had found his brother. John was dead.

Jack screamed, "Cum on Bill, let's go! Let's go!" He seized Bill's shoulder and yanked him brusquely, "There's nowt we can do!" He pulled and pushed his friend forcefully, yelling at him to move. They ran gasping, aware of others moving alongside them. The trench was just ahead; a few more steps; the bullets cracked past; Jack threw himself into the shallow depression; safe.

The shell hit the parapet and lifted him bodily into the air. The pressure wave swept over him sucking him into a consuming darkness as if dragging him helplessly into the centre of a bottomless, roaring vortex.

In the scramble for safety, Thorneycroft had fallen and badly twisted his ankle. He hobbled back to the trench trying to ignore the pain. He was furious at the vulnerability and helplessness of their situation. If only the Boer guns could be silenced! What the hell was Clery doing with a whole Division in the valley? He was a mere spectator! What was needed was a supporting attack mounted on the adjacent hills to bring relief. As he fumed he heard shouting to his front and left; cautiously he peeked over the parapet. Three of his officers were stranded amongst the rocks unable to return across the fire-swept plateau. A young lieutenant sat propped up against a rock, clearly badly wounded. He was calmly smoking a cigarette with a stoical indifference to impending death. With agonising difficulty he continued to fire his rifle in the direction of the Boer, until bullets smacked into his chest. His head slumped forward. The two remaining officers were surrounded by the bodies of their men; they continued to engage the enemy in a futile attempt to suppress the enfilading fire. It was a hopeless duel. After a short time they too lay still. Thorneycroft sank back, his head in his hands; burdened with the loss of such good young men.

....

Jack was being shaken vigorously. Grindrod was mouthing words, but Jack heard nothing. His head was throbbing; blood sang in his ears; his lungs strained to catch sufficient breath; his mouth was full of dust and cordite - he was suffocating. He gasped, urgently sucking air into his wrenching body. Gradually the voice penetrated his senses. Grindrod held him by the shoulders, “Alright Clegg? Alright lad? I’ll soon ‘ave yer sorted!”

He took Jack's field dressing from his tunic pocket and ripped off the covering. He began to apply the gauze to Jack's left upper thigh. Jack looked on somewhat detached, slowly recovering his senses. He saw the ripped flesh, red pulp, white shattered bone and spurting blood. I wonder if I'll lose the leg, he thought calmly, aloof from the reality that it was his torn limb. There was no pain. "'Ave yer any water Sergeant?" he enquired. "God am so thirsty. Feels like I've been lickin' bottom of a whore's 'andbag."

"Sorry lad, we're all out; waitin' for resupply." He unfastened Jack's putty from the injured leg and then bound it tightly as a tourniquet above the wound. The blood stopped pumping. Grindrod took another dressing from a nearby corpse and layered it over the first to cover the gaping wound; he tied the bandage tightly. "I'll get to body snatchers for yer as soon as I can, but there's plenty waitin' … need to be patient." He patted him on the shoulder encouragingly and turned to leave. He stopped suddenly. He couldn't believe what he was seeing, "What the 'ell are yer doin'!" he yelled. But it was obvious. "Yer can't! Yer bloody cowards! Yer can't surrender!"

There was an enormous explosion. The ground shook. Jack felt entombed in hot air. He was wrapped in a cloud of dust; a vicious pain poked his ears like probing red-hot needles; instinctively he covered his ears with his hands and screamed.

Slowly the air cleared and once again Jack emerged into the awful reality of that inferno: the insane whistle of incoming shells before they crashed among mangled bodies, re-ordering the dead; an unending "crack" and "thump" of rifle fire; the moans and screams of the dying squeezed into the momentary silences; the cries of the demented; the weeping of the broken. His skull was pounding as if ready to explode. It was all consuming. Only gradually did he become aware of the weight on his legs. He tried to move free, but this only served to accentuate the pain in his thigh. He clenched his fists and ground his teeth trying to hold back his cries. It was Sergeant Grindrod pinning him down; his face was frozen in shock, his eyes stared, his mouth was wide open. There was no sign of physical injury, only blood seeping from his mouth and ears. Jack couldn't budge him. Exhausted he flopped back against the trench wall.

At first he wasn't sure; there were many bodies about, but as he lay immobilised he found himself transfixed, staring at a shattered corpse. He began to mentally re-assemble the mutilated trunk lying about five yards up the slope towards the summit. There was a bloody mess where one leg should have been, whilst the other was contorted and stuck out at a ridiculous angle. The left arm was torn off at the elbow. Most of the clothing had been blown away and the naked trunk was peppered with holes from shrapnel and flying debris. At first it was instinct: a sense of shape; the sloping shoulders; the slightly arched back; then the black curly hair. But it was the tattoo which clinched it. The recognition pierced him.

He remembered goading Bill outside the tattoo parlour in Blackpool. The four friends had been drinking and Bill had boasted about having a curvaceous young lady imprinted on his upper arm – of course, carefully hidden from the critical eyes of his parents.

John had taunted his brother, "Yer not brave enough; 'aven't got the bottle."

"'Ave," defended Bill, "I'll 'ave this beautiful lass wi' me forever." He counted his money and was pennies short. Everyone coppered up and pushed Bill unsteadily through the doors. By the time the train pulled into Rochdale station that night, they had all sobered up. Bill was dreading his father finding out, and John knew that he would be in serious trouble for not properly caring for his younger brother.

Yes; the buxom lass with the hour-glass waist would be with him forever. A dribble of tears ran down Jack's dirty cheek. He couldn't stand seeing the remains of his friend, filthy and bloody like a piece of meat drawn by a mangy dog through the gutters. He slipped off his tunic, leaned forward and threw it as best he could to cover the body, but was only partially successful. The disfigured leg still protruded from beneath the garment. He stared at it; held; entranced.

He felt so very thirsty; the burning sun was relentless; cover from the searching rays was non-existent. He felt tired and weak.

The veins in his head were exploding; the darkness was thickening. He closed his eyes and thankfully sank into oblivion.

****

Jan became hot as the sun rose vertical in the sky; it seemed to pursue him, search for him among the rocks; there was little shade. Water was scarce. He chewed on a stick of biltong, his only nourishment, and tried to avert his eyes from the dead and the dying who lay among them, some horribly disfigured. As the heat intensified, flies were attracted by the smell of blood; they began to swarm over the wounds covering them like a black pall. Comfort came from the shells which sang overhead and burst frequently among the Khakis. Almost miraculously the gunners had the range to the yard and none fell among the Boers. The thump of rifle fire and the monotone "pom-pom" of the maxims from Aloe Knoll remained constant. Thankfully their casualty rate had now reduced considerably, but after the initial exhilaration of the assault a pervading atmosphere of gloom began to descend. Perhaps, thought Jan, the Khakis were content to stay behind their sangar and had no stomach to recover the rocky outcrop. He sat leaning against a rock. Latent fatigue swept over him as the soporific sun lulled him to sleep. Gradually, the din of battle faded, unable to intrude upon his unconsciousness.

"They're coming! They're coming!" shrieked Hans. "The Khakis are here!"

Thundering towards them came the English, their ranks thinned by the flanking fire, but seemingly unstoppable. Jan stood and fired into the mass, one fell, others tumbled over their comrade, sprawling in the dust. He operated his bolt, "click". The predatory bayonets glinted menacingly in the sun.

"Back Jan! Back!" Jan felt Henry grab his jacket and pull him forcefully backwards; they slid down the hillside grabbing bushes and tufts of grass to slow their descent. Pieter and Hans were with them. Bullets whizzed by, scouring the undergrowth and searching out their victims.

After an unmeasured distance they finally stopped. They grouped together, hanging on to each other, breathing heavily and exchanging fearful grins. "Steady now, Steady." They swivelled around to see a figure dressed in a brownish suit with smart top boots and spurs; he was good looking with a closely clipped beard and moustache. To one side, and slightly to his rear, stood a muscular Zulu carrying his rifle. "The Khakis won't follow. Our guns will make it too hot for them. You must return to support your friends." The voice was warm, firm and encouraging; his gaze frank and fearless. Wordlessly, and in unison, they once again began the ascent.

Above could be heard the crackle of rifle fire and innumerable shells raking the plateau. The hillside vibrated dislodging small stones and dirt which flowed in streamlets. A little shamefaced they emerged to be met by those already in place. Knowing looks and consenting grins were exchanged.

There were fresh dead and injured from both sides littering the rocks and environs; evidence of a short but brutal fight. The walking wounded picked their way tentatively and painfully down the slope; the more seriously injured were laid in blankets and carried away by friends and neighbours. It was then that Jan saw him; Hendrick lay on his back starring with sightless eyes at the searing sun, the gaping hole of a bayonet wound having torn his stomach; his intestines spilled onto the ground, the blood already beginning to congeal in the heat. His two cousins rushed to the body of their father; they crouched by him; they hesitantly touched him, ran their hands across his forehead and cheeks. They were shocked into a desolate silence; tears coursed down their cheeks; they began to sob inconsolably.

....

"They're surrendering! The Khakis are giving up!"

Jan stirred from an intermittent doze. Those around him were laughing, standing, shouting in variable English: "This way Tommy! Come! Come! Here Tommy!" The guns had stopped.

Hesitantly he stood up as if testing that the air was really free from deadly metal; it seemed reckless to be so exposed. At the trench he could see grim-faced soldiers, drawn and frightened, clasping white handkerchiefs and assorted rags. Some raised their hands; all hesitated to move forward. A nearby officer, De

Koch, leapt towards them and raced for the parapet, others followed him. "Come on, lets go!" called Jan to Henry and his cousins.

"Who's your officer?" demanded De Koch of the soldiers.

There were no officers left to reply, only exhausted, fearful fusiliers who lacked leaders and who had reached both physical and mental breaking points. As the burghers arrived, they were aghast on seeing the shallow trench containing many dead and wounded, as well as those who appeared to be groggy and disorientated. Almost sympathetically they ordered the soldiers into captivity. As if glad to find authority, the fusiliers began to numbly obey; some had obvious wounds; some were supported by friends. All were wary of their enemy wondering how they would be treated

"What's going on here? What's going on!" A large angry English officer limped towards the Boers and their prisoners, waving his pistol and shouting loudly. De Koch held his ground and confronted him, "These men are my prisoners."

The irate officer was flushed with rage, "I'm in command on this hill!" he thundered. "Take your men to hell! I allow no surrender!"

"I repeat," emphasised De Koch, "these men have surrendered and under the rules of war they are now my prisoners."

The English officer hesitated; he quickly absorbed the hopeless situation. "Then take your prisoners and no more. Go back to your positions!" he shouted brusquely.

"This is now my position. I've captured it and your men have surrendered. We're staying."

Thorneycroft reluctantly accepted the inevitability of the situation. He searched the terrified faces of the beaten soldiers; unnerved and demoralised after almost five hours of constant bombardment and sniping. "With me men, with me!" he urged, gathering as many soldiers about him as he could encourage. Like the Pied Piper, he disappeared over the summit crest, a scattered group of demoralised soldiers in tow. The dispirited prisoners stumbled into captivity.

Jan looked down from his position on the parapet into the trench. Like others he was stunned. They had been unsettled and saddened at the extent of their own casualties, but had been totally unaware of how badly the Khakis had been mauled. The dead and wounded lay intermingled, piled two and sometimes three deep.

Below him a soldier stirred. He tried to muffle a cry as he adjusted his position in an attempt to rid himself of a corpse which lay heavily on his legs. The soldier was layered with dirt, his red eyes sunken into a pallid face, his uniform in tatters. Jan noticed untidy bandages around his left thigh. The soldier shoved the body in vain; the effort drained his failing strength; he flopped back against the trench wall, his face distorted in pain. In his dazed, disorientated state the soldier seemed unaware of a spectator. Now he looked up; their eyes met. Jan noted the parched, cracked lips of his enemy. He was weak from the loss of blood and was dehydrating - even dying.

He moved towards the wounded soldier stepping over fragments of flesh which littered the ground. He grabbed the shoulders of the corpse and dragged it off the soldier's legs; from the stripes he could see that it was a sergeant. He removed his water-bottle from his belt and held it up; the soldier nodded. Greedily he drank. After a few moments Jan pulled the bottle away, conscious that he too was short of water. "Ta mate." The words were barely audible.

"Come on," said Henry. "We're to return to the rocks to cover this position. There are too many of us here."

Reluctantly Jan wandered back to his original location leaving his cousins behind. He took up a firing position, and from there keenly watched what was happening to his front.

There was shouting - a roar. The same English officer appeared over the summit still waving his revolver, but this time pointing and shooting as he lurched forwards. He was followed by a ragged mass of soldiers, screaming and hurtling down the slope. Some paused to fire; others were struggling to fix bayonets on the move. This terrifying horde swept towards them. Everyone was startled at this rapid and violent response to their occupation of the trench; they were momentarily stunned into inaction, almost mesmerized. Then a Boer fired at the attackers and the spell was broken. A soldier toppled and rolled. Others began to shoot, but within seconds they were smothered by this ferocious assault. The English threw themselves onto the farmers; they thrust savagely with their bayonets. Weapons were fired at point blank range, butts swung. It was pandemonium; a sudden hellish maelstrom which destroyed a fleeting peace.

The Boers began to fall back. Jan fired in order to cover their retreat. He aimed swiftly and carefully noting figures fall after each squeeze of the trigger: one, two, three; it was impossible to miss; it hardly seemed real. Farmers slumped behind the rocks gasping with the exertion and relief. The Khakis followed.

Hans raced for safety, but just yards from the rocks he leapt into the air with his arms outstretched, his mouth wide open in a hideous scream. He crashed to the ground. A soldier tried feverishly to withdraw his bayonet from Hans' back. Jan shot him. He fell backwards; the bayonet snapped and stood rigid.

With their casualties mounting the soldiers were happy to consolidate the trench. The attack petered out. The artillery from the Twin Peaks once more raked the plateau and the "pom-poms" sang in accompaniment.

Pieter gathered his breath and began desperately looking for his brother. He sidled up to Jan who was still firing opportunistically from among the rocks. "Have you seen him? Hans isn't with us! Did you see him?"

Jan stopped shooting and remained motionless. How did he tell Pieter that his brother was dead ten yards to the front? that the corpse with the bayonet protruding from its back was his brother.

"He's there!" shouted Hans. "He's there!" Before anyone could stop him he launched back onto the open plateau. He grabbed Hans' feet and crouching, tugged frantically at the body, dragging it the short distance towards the safety of the rocks. Jan and Henry fired rapidly to neutralize any Khakis. Helping hands reached out and pulled Pieter to safety. As Hans' remains were manhandled into cover, two bullets struck the dead boy: "Thud! Thud!"

Hans was laid at the side of his father under a thorn bush. Pieter sat by them, tense and silent. His face grew pale; he pressed his lips tightly; he vomited. His shoulders shook as the tears streamed down his face; he cried inconsolably. After a little while he grew quiet; he sat clenching and unclenching his fists, his eyes sinking. He was imploding.

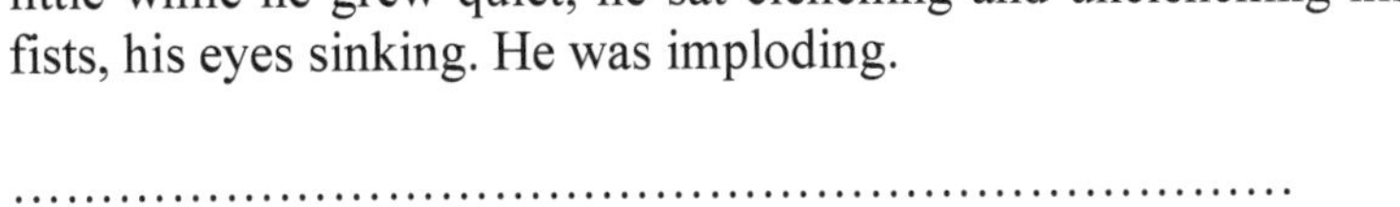

Henry edged up to Jan. He spoke loudly to be heard above the noise, "I'm going off to the left. The Field Cornet is asking for volunteers."

"Gerrit?" confirmed Jan.

"Yes, Gerrit. Those on the Knoll have identified an exposed and undefended area on the enemy's right , behind their trench and before the sheer side of the hill. If we can penetrate the position at that point, we'll get behind the trench and unhinge the whole defences."

"I'm coming with you."

"No. This position still has to be held – and your cousin needs you."

Involuntarily they both looked across at Pieter. He was sitting motionless by the two bodies, frozen in grief. There was no further discussion.

Henry pursued the disappearing backs of the Witbergers as they skirted around the hillside. Eventually he caught them as they assembled, with others, in a slight depression which was in dead ground to the English. He recognised men from the Carolina and Pretoria Commandos; there were others whom he had never seen before. Altogether, there were about sixty of them. An unfamiliar officer in customary black frock-coat was busy giving instructions; he spoke fast and in Afrikaner. Henry couldn't understand a word.

"Just follow me," a familiar Witberger smiled in encouragement.

Henry took his place in a straggly line. He checked that his magazine was full and that he had a round in the chamber. He released the safety catch. With a wave of the hand the officer initiated the advance. Quietly they inched forward, expertly using the sparse cover and undulations of the ground. The officer raised his hand above his head, and then dropped it swiftly to signal the rush. Henry clawed his way up the slope, grabbing tufts of grass to propel himself forward. He could see the crest against the sky-line. All around him the bearded farmers advanced, sure-footed, rifles in hand, success assured.

The volley sent the leading Boers reeling. Henry noticed one of them roll uncontrollably until he disappeared over the precipitous edge, his harrowing cry fading as he dropped. Others fell around him sinking into the long grass; he stumbled over them. The uniformity of the volley yielded to an irregular rattle as soldiers fired independently. He knew that they had lost surprise and the advantage it gives. They were exposed in the assault while the defenders offered lesser targets as they lay or knelt in the grass on the higher ground. Henry sensed the assault wavering; momentum was sapping away. Those around him now dropped behind cover or sought the protection of the hollows and scattered rocks.

Suddenly he was hit by a terrific force as if he had crashed into an invisible wall; he dropped like a brick. He felt a tearing pain in his left shoulder. The grass hid him from sight, but lethal, hissing metal cut through the air occasionally boring into the ground nearby. Instinctively he covered the wound with his good hand. The blood rushed out like a river bursting its banks. It gushed through his fingers quickly soaking his clothing and turning his shirt and jacket into an oozing mess. He realised that his left arm was useless; it was limp - perhaps broken. With his right hand he fumbled in an attempt to remove his necktie. He would use it as a pad to stem the flow of blood, but he couldn't release it. He pulled desperately trying to undo the knot, but it seemed only to tighten. It was useless; he was growing faint. He took off his hat and folded it as best he could, then pressed it hard against the wound. The pain was excruciating. The flow lessened, but didn't stop; blood was running down his forearm and dripping onto the ground where it was congealing in the sun …. that was the answer! He positioned himself so that his wound was exposed to the full heat of the sun's rays. Gradually the coagulating blood ceased to flow. Thank God, he thought, now I must get away from here. He edged backwards, dragging himself down the slope the way he had come, keeping low until he felt secure enough to stand. But then he felt groggy. I've lost too much blood, he thought. He sat down, shaking and dizzy. He fought to maintain consciousness.

When he came around the battle was still raging above him – he could only have been unconscious for minutes. He became aware of walking wounded staggering by. They avoided his prostrate body – probably thought he was dead. From the area of the objective he could hear yells and shouts filling the air; not those of success, but frantic and heavy with despair. Then came the retreating flow. It washed around him like the waters of a rushing stream circumventing a rock; passing him by. He tried to stand, but only managed to rise on all fours before collapsing in his weakness. All was a dizzy uncontrollable swirl. He felt nauseous.

"Come on Mr Barnham, it's time to go." Strong hands pulled him up and threw his good arm around a neck. The guttural, gravely voice continued, "The Khakis have just received reinforcements and block our way. They're too strong for us now. We need another plan."

It was Gerrit Pretorius.

CHAPTER 10

The Twin Peaks

(24 January 1900)

Ever since arriving on the banks of the Tugela ten days earlier, Major-General Neville Lyttleton had been fuming at the waste of time and ponderous progress. While Warren had moved off upstream, he had been left with his brigade to secure Potgieter's Drift and to convince the enemy that this was the direction from which the main attack would come. To that end he had crossed the Tugela and seized the group of small kopjes on the far bank, and each day made a noisy and visible demonstration. In that way he hoped to detain a sizeable number of Boers on his front.

On the morning of the assault on Spion Kop, he had cooperated by making a further feint attack against the hills to his front - towards Brakfontein. He had believed that to be part of Buller's design for battle; an integral part of the overall plan. However, he had been surprised, confused and not a little irritated when Buller signalled him, in blunt terms, to halt the offensive action. It seemed that Buller had a bloated opinion of the Boer strength facing Potgieter's, and was intent on conserving his forces by remaining on the defensive.

Lyttleton's trusted Brigade Major, Henry Wilson, brushed aside the flap of his tent and waved a telegram. He sat uninvited, but with a respectful familiarity, on a canvas chair at the table opposite his commander. "Sir, General Warren is requesting our assistance. Apparently things are not progressing too well on Spion Kop and reinforcements are needed."

The sound of battle had been reverberating around the hills all morning, and the lack of forward movement was plain to see. Lyttleton was still smarting and remained cautious after his recent brush with Buller. "Still no sign of enemy activity on our front?" he probed.

"Nothing," reassured Wilson.

"Then we could send the Scottish Rifles and Bethune's Horse?" suggested Lyttleton.

"Yes, I'm sure that would be helpful," agreed Wilson. "But perhaps we should do something more than just reinforce a crowded hill."

"You have a suggestion?" enquired Lyttleton.

"I've studied the ground and believe that the Twin Peaks to the east of Spion Kop are the key to this battle. If we could take them, then we could halt flanking fire from that direction onto Spion Kop. We could sweep along the ridges, clear the Boer from Aloe Knoll, and join forces with the garrison on the hill. We would burst open the whole Boer defences."

Lyttleton thought hard before responding; "If we reinforce Spion Kop, which I believe to be our immediate priority, we would be left with only two battalions, the Durham Light Infantry and the King's Royal Rifles. We would be vulnerable to any Boer attack here, on the Drift."

"I believe that the Boers are consumed with the battle further west. I know that the Commander-in-Chief believes that there are thousands of Boer to our front, but I see no evidence of that. The Boers are too busy blocking Spion Kop to be able to launch an offensive in this area."

"So your recommendation Major?" asked Lyttleton.

Wilson was convinced of the soundness of his appreciation, "The Durham's to protect the Drift, the Rifles to take the Twin Peaks."

"And you think General Buller would condone this plan after cancelling our operation this morning?"

"Does he need to know in advance?"

The two men sat silently for a moment. Then Lyttleton broke into a wry smile, "Make the arrangements Brigade Major."

....

From his vantage point on Mount Alice, Buller could clearly observe the men of the King's Royal Rifles clawing and fighting their way up the Twin Peaks. It was possible to make out men climbing on each others backs and shoulders to negotiate large boulders and steep slopes. Inexorably they moved upwards despite the plunging fire from the defenders and mounting casualties. "Who authorised this reckless attack?" he demanded of his staff.

"We presume Major General Lyttleton, sir", came the reply.

"Was this headquarters notified of this operation before it began?" queried Buller.

"No sir."

"Then cancel it!" he shouted furiously. "Up to seven thousand Boer may be in the hills opposite us, and yet we squander our troops on a fruitless attack. Send a rider immediately to end this unauthorised operation."

Lyttleton accepted the order with a resigned inevitability. He handed the message to Wilson with a shrug, "Signal the Rifles to withdraw." The shutters of the heliograph chattered furiously, but the advance continued as if the communication was unseen.

Buller became incensed at the lack of response to his order; he grew red with rage, "Send another rider and make sure that Lyttleton understands the seriousness of my intent … I will be obeyed!"

The flickering heliograph elicited no response from Lieutenant Colonel Buchanan-Riddell, Commanding Officer of the Rifles. The advance seemed irreversible. Reluctantly, Lyttleton addressed Wilson, "Send a rider and halt that attack. Bring back Riddell and his men."

For Buchanan-Riddell success was to hand. He had split his Battalion into two halves, each to assault one of the Peaks. Despite the almost vertical slopes and the enemy's tactical advantage, the defence had been sporadic and uncoordinated. He had seen the winking heliograph, but chose to employ a Nelsonian eye. He was not going to be deprived of victory; besides, those clinging onto Spion Kop needed relief. Finally he stood on the summit and watched with satisfaction the cloud of dust below. The defenders were scurrying off across the plains frantically galloping their guns to safety. Now he would respond to the increasingly panicky messages which had pursued him. He had no doubt that with victory his disregard of orders would be forgiven. He summoned his signaller, "Send to Brigade:

> *Objectives secured. Unless I get orders to retire I shall stay here."*

He turned to his Adjutant, and in anticipation of an affirmative reply to his communication directed, "Tell the men to entrench."

In the failing light, Buchanan-Riddell looked across to Spion Kop crowned with swirling dust and smoke. He raised his binoculars. He couldn't detect any movement, but the forward slope was littered with still forms. Importantly, however, the way to the hill was open. He turned to the north, towards Ladysmith. He could see the Boer laagers on the plain and the road twisting towards the town. Momentarily, he left the battle behind and paused to enjoy the beauty and vastness of the vista laid before him; it was breath-taking.

The sniper's bullet hit him in the head. He slumped to the ground and died silently.

"My orders will be obeyed! I'll court-martial Buchanan-Riddell if he doesn't respond!" insisted Buller. "Withdraw the Rifles!"

Lyttleton and Wilson stood together in the descending dusk, congratulating the despondent soldiers as they emerged out of the gloom and tramped towards their bivouac area. Walking wounded were supported by their comrades as they sought out the aid-post. "You did all that was asked of you. Magnificent! Well done!" consoled Lyttleton.

"Why'd yer call us back, sir. When the battle was won?"

Lyttleton had no explanation for his disillusioned, sullen and angry soldiers. "And the butcher's bill?" he enquired of Wilson tautly.

"This squandered victory has cost us seven officers and eighty two men killed or wounded."

CHAPTER 11

The Battle for Spion Kop II

(Afternoon - 24 January 1900)

Talbot-Coke winced as the stabbing pain shot up his recuperating leg after having carelessly stubbed it against a half-concealed rock on the uneven track. He struggled up the slope in the blazing sun, confirming what he knew in his heart, that he was physically unfit and lacked the stamina for this strenuous climb. His Brigade Major, Phillips, accompanied him dutifully. He found a small plateau about two hundred yards below the summit and decided that this would be suitable for his headquarters. A slight undulation gave protection from enemy rifle fire, and it was conveniently close to the heliograph station. With relief he sat on a rock, removed his helmet, and with a large handkerchief wiped the grimy sweat from his brow and face. En route he had extracted information from a number of officers and soldiers and he felt that he had a good understanding of the situation. He had sent orders to the Commanding Officer of the Dorsets to remain this side of the crest in reserve and not to get embroiled in the fighting. He assessed that there were enough units in the forward positions to hold the Boers at bay. With a wave of his hand he summoned Philips to his side and addressed him in stuttering breaths:

"Best let General Warren know we've arrived, and that all is in hand."

Philips took pencil and message pad from his tunic pocket and made ready to write. He recorded the time as 12:50 p.m.

"Send the following signal:

> *I am now on the plateau of Spion Kop slopes. The top of the hill is reported crowded with men and as these are exposed to shell fire they are suffering, but holding out well. I have stopped further reinforcements beyond this point, but troops engaged know that help is near to hand. Ammunition is being pushed up."*

He felt a rising weakness; a strenuous climb and not enough to eat, he told himself. He spotted a slight fold in the ground about fifteen yards away and indicated it to Philips, "There's nothing more I can do at the moment. I'm seizing the opportunity to get a little rest. Wake me if there are any developments."

Philips walked over to the signallers and handed them the message. He watched as the shutters of the heliograph clattered methodically. A moment later the receiving station winked in acknowledgement. He returned and sat by the track, there to observe the ant-like activities of soldiers on this vital artery. They carried water, ammunition, sandbags and empty stretchers; this was the life-blood of war; the umbilical cord sustaining those fighting for possession of the hilltop. And all the time the hillside vibrated as the Boer shells impacted; the hills echoed to the sound of the gunfire. He sat inert, sucking in the racket, but feeling strangely remote.

A colonial soldier descended, teetering with fatigue. He flopped on a boulder to gather his breath and strength.

"Are you wounded man? Do you need help?" enquired Philips.

The soldier looked up, "No thanks sir. I'll be off in a minute."

"Off where? Shouldn't you be with your unit?" Philips suspected that the man was deserting the fight.

"I've a message for General Warren from Colonel Thorneycroft."

Philips stepped forward, interested, "Let me have it."

"It's for General Warren," asserted the soldier protectively.

Philips pointed, "Over there you see General Talbot-Coke; he's in command of the battle. He must see the message."

Reluctantly, the soldier handed the paper to Philips.

"Wait here." With that Philips moved across to Talbot-Coke and shook him gently, "A message from Colonel Thorneycroft. I intercepted a runner." He passed the message- sheet to his drowsy commander and waited patiently for the response.

Talbot-Coke sat upright and begrudgingly began to read. He noticed that it was addressed to General Warren and not to himself as the officer in command of the hill. He read:

Hung on till last extremity with old force. Some of Middlesex here now, and I hear Dorset's coming up, but force really inadequate to hold such a large perimeter. The enemy's guns are north-west, sweep the whole of the top of the hill. They also have guns east; cannot you bring artillery fire to bear on north-west guns? What reinforcements can you send to hold the hill tonight? We are badly in need of water. There are many killed and wounded – Alec Thorneycroft.

P.S. If you wish to really make a certainty of hill for night you must send more infantry to attack enemy guns.

Why is this colonial officer communicating directly with General Warren? he wondered. The officer in command until I arrived was Colonel Crofton. Why is Thorneycroft bypassing the correct chain of command? He's a temporary Lieutenant-Colonel of a small unit, yet he writes as if in command of the whole hill. What impertinence from an irregular officer. Besides, the situation will have improved with the arrival of reinforcements, and mules are fetching water constantly; they passed me on the track. In a state of exhausted irritation he annotated the message:

Major General Coke to Sir C Warren; 3 p.m. I have seen the above and have ordered the Scottish Rifles and the King's Royal Rifles to reinforce. The Middlesex Regiment, Dorsetshire Regiment and Imperial Light Infantry have also gone up, Bethune's Infantry (120 strong) also reinforce. We appear to be holding our own at present.

Dismissively he handed the amended paper back to Phillips, "Tell the runner to deliver this to General Warren immediately." With that, he again sought his well earned sleep.

....

Cautiously he edged to one side struggling to keep his footing on the narrow, stony track in order to allow the mule to pass. It was laden with square, open-topped biscuit-tins which spilled their contents generously as the water sloshed from side to side under the awkward, jerky motion of the animal. The track was full of men and mules competing for space as they wearily negotiated the hill under a searing sun. He stopped momentarily to examine a discarded corpse with its ashen skin and blank starring eyes. Nearby a soldier was crawling on his hands and knees moaning incomprehensively; he stepped around him and continued the climb. He gave way to a scruffy, coolie stretcher-party straining to keep their footing as they descended under the weight of their moaning load. A little further on he was barged by a soldier hurrying to escape the hell above; he looked stunned, stupefied; was careering as if drunk. The occasional bullet zizzed overhead or burrowed angrily into the ground; people were too consumed in their tasks to take notice or too tired to care. There was an oppressive air of confusion and numbing fear; and all this to the backdrop of the deep, staccato rumble of guns whose erupting shells set the hillside quaking.

The South African Light Horse had not been committed to this battle, and for several hours Lieutenant Winston Churchill watched with concern from his vantage point as events unfolded on the hill. He had been woken in the early hours by the muffled cheers from the hilltop and the noisy, dazzling reply of the star-shells. With his fellow officers he had celebrated the victory by drinking warm champagne, courtesy of Fortnum & Mason in London, but now that rejoicing seemed premature. As the battle dragged on he watched from his vantage point and counted the "crunches" as Boer shells exploded on the smoke-hazed summit: one, two – six, seven. And all within a minute! Eventually he could contain himself no longer and decided to assume his other role, that of war correspondent for the *Morning Post.* He galloped off to the foot of Spion Kop and wended his way through the disorderly village of echelon wagons and ambulances. He left his horse in the care of an obliging quartermaster before starting the climb. A couple of hundred yards short of the summit he came across a familiar face,

"George, how good to see you! I heard that you'd joined Coke's staff. Where is he?"

Somewhat sheepishly Philips pointed to a prostrate figure a little distance away.

"I need to speak to him."

"You can't disturb the General, he needs his rest."

"But I need to know how the battle's faring; I must write about it, and perhaps I can help by taking a report to General Warren."

"I'm to disturb him only if the battle requires," stated Philips.

Churchill felt disturbed; how could Coke sleep at this critical time? He shrugged, "I'll go up and see for myself." He didn't wait for a reply.

He clambered upwards, taking care to crawl the final few yards as he found a place from which to cautiously peer over the summit onto the forward slope. It was like drawing a curtain and peering into Hades. His worst fears were confirmed. Dead and wounded littered the slope; it was a bloody shambles. Through the drifting dust he identified the large frame of Thorneycroft flitting along a primitive trench. But men were lying pressed to the ground, hands covering heads, fearful to move and invite death. Wasn't Colonel Crofton in charge of the fighting? No sign of him. He sensed there was no real grip, no-one properly in overall command - except the sleeping General. All this served only to confirm the impression gained from his experience on the track, and to reinforce the sense that morale was fragile. He must alert General Warren and plead for remedial action.

……………………………………………………………

Huddled in the shallow depression and compressed by the din of battle, Talbot-Coke was finding it impossible to sleep. What with all the shouting and clatter on the nearby track and the infernal noise of the guns; besides, he felt perturbed by the near panic of Thorneycroft's message. There was nothing for it, he would have to go and see for himself. "George!" He summoned Philips. "I'll take an escort and reconnoitre the battle. You remain here and respond to any instructions from General Warren." With that he gathered two soldiers and reluctantly ascended the hill. Stray bullets whizzed by him, some seemingly cracking just above his head; he nudged over to the safer right flank. He crawled the last ten yards and tried to peer over the crest. As he lay on the trembling hillside, he could see little through the swirling dust and smoke.

"Good to see you, General." Colonel Hill - commanding officer of the Middlesex - dropped beside him. "I heard that you were about and I was on my way to see you; just wanted to confirm the plan."

Inwardly Talbot-Coke sighed with relief; thank goodness he had found a commanding officer; he needn't go further forward. "The plan …" he shouted above the noise of an explosion, "the plan remains unchanged. You are to hold on, improve your defences during the night and we will bring up the guns and reinforcements under cover of darkness. Can you hang on?"

Hill hesitated; he too shouted, "The Fusiliers are all but done; we've filled the gaps but are taking heavy casualties. Can we silence the Boer guns?"

"Not until we get our own guns up here." Again he pressed for reassurance, "Can you hang on?"

"We'll hang on today; but tomorrow …" his voice trailed away.

"Good … good. Have you seen Crofton? He's supposed to be in charge of the forward positions."

"Haven't seen him since I arrived; not heard from him, but I was told that he was badly wounded. Because of the intensity of the shelling and accuracy of the rifle fire, I haven't been able to move about to confirm or otherwise," offered Hill.

"Then you are to assume command."

"Of course, sir ... thank you, sir." Hill felt uneasy at this dubious honour.

Gratefully, Talbot-Coke returned to his chosen sanctuary. He removed his helmet, wiped the sweat from his eyes and enjoyed the sweet taste of water; albeit warm – equates to champagne in these circumstances, he mused, and it tastes just as good. His pleasant interlude was shattered by the abrupt arrival of Colonel Cooke - commanding officer of the Scottish Rifles. He spilled into the hollow pursued by flying metal. His Battalion had arrived just in time to push back a Boer counter-attack at the point of the bayonet. But now he was pursuing a different kind of confrontation. In the safety of the dead ground he gathered his breath and dignity before addressing Talbot-Coke; he raised his voice to be heard above the incessant noise of battle and mouthed his words deliberately, "I met Thorneycroft who says that he is in command; apparently General Warren appointed him this morning. I am by far senior to him, and I have no intention of being subordinated to a junior and irregular officer."

Talbot-Coke was taken aback; then he remembered the presumption of Thorneycroft's earlier message. He affirmed, "I was given command this morning on the death of General Woodgate. No one has told me any different, and as far as I'm concerned, nothing has changed. I have liaised with Colonel Hill as the senior unwounded officer on the summit, and have confirmed him as officer-in-charge of the front line." He was screaming to be heard.

"But General, I'm senior to Hill and should be given command!"

Coke was becoming annoyed, in fact infuriated, "We cannot constantly change command every time a reinforcing unit arrives; we must have continuity, anything else is a recipe for disaster. Colonel Hill remains in command of the immediate battle." He looked Cooke in the eyes, "Colonel, you have left your Battalion at the height of the fighting to argue seniority. I suggest your place is with your men."

Stung by this blunt criticism and pained at the decision, Cooke tightened the chinstrap of his helmet, picked up his rifle and left with a curt, "Yes, sir."

"Bloody arrogant, egomaniac!" declared Coke to the unlistening world, "as if I didn't have enough problems without having to deal with self-seeking upstarts!" He cast about, "Philips; I need to send a message to General Warren."

"Sorry, sir, we can't use the heliograph, the thickening clouds are obscuring the sun. Your message will have to go by runner."

"Then send it by runner!" replied Talbot-Coke hotly. He dictated:

> *"The situation is as follows – the original troops are still in position, have suffered severely, and the dead and*

wounded are still in the trenches. The shell fire is, and has been, very severe. If I hold on to the position all night, is there any guarantee that our artillery can silence the enemy guns? Otherwise today's experience will be repeated, and the men will not stand another day's shelling……

The situation is extremely critical ….

Please give orders, and should you wish me to retire, cover retirement from Connaught's Hill."

………………………………………………………………

It had been with a sense of renewed reassurance and relief that Warren had read his first signal from Talbot-Coke; so much for Crofton's panicking. The subsequent message amplifying Thorneycroft's rather pessimistic appreciation demonstrated that Talbot-Coke had brought a steadying hand to the situation. This was corroborated by a verbal report received just a short time before by another of Buller's staff officers sent to observe the battle. But the day was passing, and for several hours his signals had gone unacknowledged; the situation on the hill had become unclear. He could only assume that the heliograph was out of action. He was content that all was being done to secure the hill. The next phase would come with darkness; guns would be hauled up to the summit, and reinforcements would improve the entrenchments and consolidate the position. He needed to confirm that all was properly in hand. He summoned a staff officer, "Call a council of war for 8 p.m. I want to review our current plans."

The shell landed amongst the headquarters' wagons with an ear-splitting explosion. The hot pressure wave sent him tottering, but he kept his feet. Horses screamed fearfully, men shouted in momentary panic; there was confusion amid the acrid smoke, dust and disorientating clamour. Composed, Warren strode over to where the shell had struck; two wagons lay on their sides, their shattered contents littering the hillside. One man was wounded, but already comrades were attending to him. Warren drew his pistol and placed the muzzle behind the ear of an injured horse lying helplessly on its side. Its rump was ragged with bloody flesh, a hind leg misshapen grotesquely. It was whining pathetically. He pulled the trigger. In similar manner he dispatched two other injured animals.

"Move the headquarters!" he commanded. "Looks like the enemy have our location." He pointed, "Over there!" The terrain didn't offer many options for redeployment, but about two hundred yards away was a slight depression – an acceptable alternative.

……………………………………………………………………

By the time he had hurried down the hill and galloped to the group of wagons which constituted Warren's headquarters, he was hot, sweaty, tired, agitated and full of foreboding. In the approaching gloom of dusk he identified the General; he was alone, pacing up and down slightly apart from officers who were assembling in a nearby tent.

"General, you must silence those guns!" he shouted as he strode towards the Commander. "Your troops are suffering unsustainable casualties; it's a slaughterhouse up there!" He drew level. "If you don't do something then this will be a second Majuba. The great British public will not stand for this!"

Warren, taken aback at this sudden intrusion and vehement, verbal attack, looked from his agitated informant to his staff officers, "Who is this man? Take him away! Put him under arrest!"

An officer stepped forward, "Sir, this is Mr Winston Churchill, war correspondent".

Warren knew of Churchill; who didn't? This was the young reporter who had taken command of troops when ambushed in an armoured train near Estcourt; who had led them gallantly before final surrender. The Boers had incarcerated him in a prison camp in Pretoria from where he had escaped and jumped a train to Portuguese East Africa. Now he was back as both subaltern in the cavalry and war correspondent. He was famous for his recent exploits, a lone hero in this war of villains and disasters, the current favourite of the "great British public" that he harped on about so much. But Warren was not to be browbeaten.

"I don't need a war correspondent masquerading as a junior officer to tell me how to conduct my battle!"

"Sir," Churchill hung in like a terrier, "one thing is certain, unless good and effective cover can be made during the night, and unless guns can be dragged to the summit to match the Boer artillery, the infantry cannot endure another day!"

Warren restrained his anger and summoned reserves of patience, "Thank you Mr Churchill! I'm about to attend to these matters; my officers are assembling for a council of war. You may sit at the back of our meeting, but without comment."

Warren was gripped by a feeling of disquiet and unease. He had been eagerly awaiting news of the battle, and just prior to Churchill's intervention he had been handed a note from Talbot-Coke. It was this that he had been considering with mounting alarm. Until now all reports received had been positive; previously Talbot-Coke had been reassuring saying that we could hold our own; Colonel Sandbach, one of Buller's staff officers who had visited the summit, had given a good account of affairs. Now, inexplicably, the situation had turned around one hundred and eighty degrees - there was even mention of withdrawing! He was confused. But Churchill was right; there could be no deviation from the original plan. He must use the night to reinforce the infantry and to improve the defensive position, and he must get guns up there to neutralise and, even better, to destroy the Boer artillery.

It was crowded in the tent and the flickering half-light from the six or more storm lamps cast ghostly shadows on the subdued proceedings. Warren scoured the expectant faces of the assembled officers, "Where's General Clery?" he snapped.

"He's ill and confined to his wagon, sir," reported a staff officer.

Warren felt no surprise. He would fight the battle without him. He addressed his officers, "The key to our plan is to hold the summit with guns; whoever does that commands the heights from the Rangeworthy Hills in the west to Brakfontein in the east." He questioned his artillery representative aggressively, "What of the arrangements to get field guns on the hill during the night?"

"I've had an officer on the hill all day and he reports that it's not possible to get the field guns up the slopes. However, we should be able to get the mountain guns on the top, they're carried on mules. The 4th Mountain Battery detrained at Frere and has been marching for two days. It arrived at Trichardt's Drift this afternoon. Men and mules are exhausted. I received orders that they were to be rested before ascending the Kop. This they're doing and will move forward shortly."

Indeed, reflected Warren, it was Buller who had ordered the Mountain Battery to rest - once again interfering in his operation. But regardless, in his heart he knew that the light calibre and limited range of the mountain guns would be no match against the Creusots and Krupps; they would quickly be annihilated. In despair he turned to the naval representative, "And the 12 pounders?"

Lieutenant James RN was inwardly scathing of the gunners and their defeatist attitude, "Yes, general, we can get our two guns to the top. They should be at the bottom of the hill in a couple of hours ready to be hauled up the slopes."

"What of the arrangements for engineering tasks?" Warren quizzed the senior Royal Engineer officer.

"Sir, gun-slides have been completed on the slopes for the movement of the naval guns, and three inch ropes have been pre-positioned. Every available pick, shovel and sandbag has been despatched to the summit. We completed a dam for water at the foot of the hill for containers to be filled and transported by mule. I have arranged for the exhausted engineers on the hill to be replaced by a fresh company.

A staff officer interjected to add further details, "Sir, it's arranged for a fatigue party of six hundred men from reserve units to precede the guns and to dig emplacements. Also, in total General Talbot-Coke presently has seven battalions at his disposal."

"Thank you." Warren felt heartened, confident; preparations were going very much as planned despite the miserable performance of our artillery. "There's much to be done gentlemen." With that the meeting began to disperse. Warren called to Churchill, "A moment!" The tent cleared. "I want to know the true position on the hill. I want you to return and to brief Thorneycroft on all that you've just heard. He must understand that fresh troops, supplies and guns are on their way up. I want to know his views."

As Churchill left, Warren beckoned a staff officer. He was worried by Talbot-Coke's apparently weakening resolve – retirement; never! "Signal to General Talbot-Coke," he announced tetchily, "I want him here to personally update me on the situation on Spion Kop."

....

Thorneycroft lay back behind his meagre cover, exhausted and angry as he endured the relentless bombardment of the enemy guns and the unceasing sniper fire. He could not understand why nothing had been done to silence the Boer artillery. Why, he reasoned, had the ten thousand troops under Clery at the foot of the Rangeworthy Hills remained passive? Why had he not attacked? Why had the hills to the east - Aloe Knoll and the Twin Peaks - not been neutralized, at least with artillery fire? While he and his men had been locked in a bitter, bloody battle, the bulk of the Field Force had remained in a state of aimless inertia; they were mere spectators. How, he wondered, could the shattered remnants which constituted his command possibly endure another such day? His earlier message to Warren had failed to elicit a reply; he must make one more appeal before it was too dark to write. He took out a pencil and scribbled on the message pad;

> *To Sir C Warren - The troops which marched up here last night are quite done up – Lancashire Fusiliers, Royal Lancaster Regiment and Thorneycroft's Mounted Infantry. They have no water and ammunition is running short. I consider that even with reinforcements which have arrived, that it is impossible to permanently hold this place so long as the enemy's guns can play on this hill. They have the long range gun, three of shorter*

> *range and one Maxim-Nordenfelt which have swept the whole of the plateau since 8 am. I have not been able to ascertain the casualties, but they have been very heavy, especially in the regiments which came up last night.*
> *I request instructions as to what course I am to adopt. The enemy at 6:30 pm were firing heavily from both flanks with rifles, shell and Nordenfelt. If casualties go on occurring at present rate I shall barely hold out the night. A large number of stretcher bearers should be sent up, and also all water possible. The situation is critical – Alec Thorneycroft*

He turned to his Adjutant and spoke wearily, "Please send by reliable runner …it's very important."

……………………………………………………………………

The flickering signal lamp penetrated the night. Corporal Sexton wrote down the message on the pad and passed it to Major Phillips. Philips shook the sleeping General, "Sir, General Warren is summoning you to his headquarters. He wants your personal report on the situation here."

Talbot-Coke was incredulous, "Point out to Sir Charles that the night is so dark and the country so rough, that the whole night would be taken up in the journey. Is it not possible to give orders without my presence?"

Phillips returned to the signal station, "Corporal Sexton, I want you to send this." He passed the message pad. His request was met with a nervous silence.

"What's the matter Corporal?"

"It's th'oil, sir."

"Oil! What about the oil?" enquired Phillips suspiciously.

"We don't 'ave none," stuttered the corporal. Hesitantly he explained, "We forgot to bring it."

"Forgot! Forgot! It's your bloody job to remember!" But what could be done?

Talbot-Coke was furious, "You know what this means? I have to clamber down that damned hill at night with a gammy leg. God knows how long it'll take; and then I'll have to come all the way back up again in the dark." In temper he flung on his harness and picked up his helmet.

"I have an escort of two men for you, sir," consoled Phillips.

"I'll be back in the morning, until then you may act with my full authority. Colonel Hill remains in charge of the summit." And with that Talbot-Coke shuffled off into the night.

CHAPTER 12

The Battle for Spion Kop III

(Night 24/25 January 1900)

The sun was merciless. There was no food and water. Fatigue was overwhelming, dulling mind and body. The injured lay groaning on the slopes. The dead with blackening wounds were infested with buzzing flies. A feeling of discouragement set in amongst the farmers. Where were the reinforcements? Where were the supplies? Where were the bearers to care for the wounded? The only comfort came with the constant explosions and shaking earth, and the knowledge that the enemy was being pounded into a pulp.

Jan was no longer surrounded by familiar faces from his own Corporalship or even Commando. In the general tumult and chaos, everyone had become inextricably mixed. Reinforcements had arrived from a number of Commandos: Krugersdorp, Ermelo, Standerton and Johannesburg, but never in large enough numbers, and now the flow had ceased completely. Jan looked across at Opperman who was commanding this sector. Earlier he had been reassuring: "Reinforcements will come soon." However, from their position they could clearly see the plain below and behind. Numerous burghers and wagons were moving about, but they were heading away, northwards towards Ladysmith. Jan, like the others, felt increasingly isolated. Opperman was becoming visibly uneasy as men unashamedly sought excuses to slip away down the slope. At first Opperman had cajoled the disheartened: "You have a duty to your country and to your God!" And for a time they had been cowed into compliance; the haemorrhage stemmed. But now, with the lengthening shadows, the faltering burghers were slipping away: "Are you to desert your comrades? How do you tell your children that you are a coward?" He lambasted those who would flee the battle. But even the strength of his personality and the sharpness of his tongue could not stop a trickle becoming a wholesale defection.

With darkness the firing stopped. Jan could hear the voices of the Khakis and the noise as they stumbled about. Then out of the gloom, from behind him, appeared shadowy figures. They struggled with the weight and ungainly bulk of a laden blanket. Immediately Jan guessed that this was yet another body being recovered by family and friends – a too familiar sight on this bloody day. As they drew level he recognised the bulk of Hendrik Prinsloo; he recalled his prophetic words of a few hours ago, "….all of us will not return." He was to learn that the body was that of Prinsloo's brother, Willie, and that of his small band more than fifty had been killed or wounded. The macabre group passed by. Jan felt a chill rush through his body; something more than the penetrating cold of the night. He edged closer to Opperman; his immediacy brought a sense of security, of warmth, of hope – stick close to him and perhaps I'll survive, he thought. Opperman was the only certainty on this hill of random fortunes where death had become a common visitor. Jan lolled against a rock, exhausted. The moans and cries of the English wounded lulled him to sleep.

"It's time to go boy," Opperman shook him gently. "I have no new orders and we few can do no more here."

During his short sleep the numbers had thinned even more. Jan counted; only about a dozen men were left to assemble among the rocks – he could not identify anyone that he knew. The frontal assault had failed; the citizen army was dissolving; there was no food and water; everyone was spent; yes, it was time to go. Thankfully, he followed the Commandant cautiously down the slope. He trod carefully, but on several occasions he sickeningly struck his foot against the dead bodies on the path. He was relieved to reach the bottom where he found his faithful pony still tethered to the tree where he had left her more than twelve hours ago. Many mounts had gone, but those of the dead and wounded still waited placidly, expectant of their owner's return.

"What's your name boy?" asked Opperman kindly.

"Jan … Jan van den Berg."

"You've done well today Jan; now one last task. You see the light in the farmhouse over there?" He pointed to the farm on a small rise about a mile away – the one that Hendrick had visited earlier that morning. "There you'll find our General, Louis Botha. Go and tell him from me that the burghers have played their part. That we have suffered greatly, and that we have retired. The hill belongs to the Khakis."

Jan looked at this huge, brave man, now overcome by sorrow at the loss of so many of his friends and neighbours. He saw a man tired and despondent, dispirited and beaten. Opperman continued, "I must hasten to my laager and take charge of my Commando before this withdrawal becomes a rout." He placed a hand on Jan's shoulder, "You are a brave young man; may God go with you."

Jan was ravenous and dehydrated; near collapse. Guiltily, he scavenged for food in the saddle-bags of unclaimed horses, before leading his pony to a nearby spruit where both drank greedily. En route he passed an old Boer who was caring for a group of men too badly wounded to be moved. The ancient attendant had little to offer other than compassion. He moved about solemnly by the light of a candle-lantern talking quietly and comforting his patients; death hung in the air.

....

With the darkness the Krupp gun adjacent to the farmhouse and nearby bell-tent ceased firing; a palpable silence descended. The coffee had gone cold in the metal cup. He shook himself awake and looked across the wooden packing case which served as a table, to his friend and secretary, Sandberg. The lamp flickered weakly; the yellowish light played hauntingly on the tent canvass – booty liberated from English stores. The eerie glare revealed Sandberg slumped over the case with his head on his hands. He moaned sporadically; his body twitched; he was utterly spent.

Botha too was drained; more than that, he was ill. He felt sapped by the tensions and anxieties of the previous weeks, and by the constant pressure of work; day and night he had been riding, organising, encouraging, persuading. For weeks he had existed under the English shell fire. He recalled how, after

Colenso, he had appealed to Kruger for leave and the reply: "I regard your presence in the difficult circumstances on your front as indispensable. God will help and sustain you in your onerous task." That was that.

The candle was all but finished. He removed the stub and set a replacement in the bed of molten tallow at the bottom of the lantern. In the renewed light he gently shook his friend, "We have work to do."

That morning he had not been unduly concerned to learn that the English had taken Spion Kop. Despite its psychological, gravitational pull, it was not vital ground. It was an unsuitable site for his artillery to fire southwards on the enemy without being exposed to their superior firepower, and should it be occupied by the English, then, with his intricate knowledge of the terrain, he was confident that he could bring converging fire from adjacent hills and make their stay untenable. He had been content to place a small piquet on the hilltop. He had, however, been anxious for the Twin Peaks; if the English captured them then his whole flank would be ripped open. He had placed its defence in the hands of the Lyndenburgers under General Shalk Burger. He had also sited a gun and pom-pom there from where they had an uninterrupted view of Spion Kop. He had thought the position practically impregnable, protected as it was by the steep, unassailable southern slopes.

He was not surprised to learn that in the failing evening light, burghers were abandoning the Kop in considerable numbers, but that didn't worry him. They needed rest, food and water; tomorrow they would return refreshed for the fight. He had, however, been worried about Shalk Burger who, on being driven from the Twin Peaks, had sent him a message saying that further resistance was futile, and that the front could no longer be held. He had replied urging Shalk Burger not to lose heart:

> *Let us fight and die together, but brother, please do not let us yield an inch to the English. I am confident and convinced that if only we stand firm our Lord will give us victory.*

"We must inform Kruger of our present position. I believe that the battle is won," urged Botha.

Sandberg fought to shake off his tiredness; was he hearing correctly?

"Even in this gloom I see in your face that you don't share my conviction." Botha went on to explain, "All day the English have sat idle opposite Rangeworthy. They out-number us ten to one, and yet refuse to renew their attacks. The English took the Twin Peaks. It gave them the opportunity to roll up our defences and yet, inexplicably, they withdrew. All day they have endured our punishment on Spion Kop and made no attempt to break through. Almost two hundred surrendered and we know of their heavy casualties; morale is low. The English procrastinate; their will is broken. I anticipate that they'll withdraw."

He stood up, pulled back the tent flap and stared into the blackness of the night. Without turning he directed, "Write that in the despatch to the President. Say, however, that I will make the necessary preparations in case the battle will have to be resumed in the morning." The firmness in his voice dissipated, more softly he added, "I'll fetch the coffee."

It was almost mid-night when Jan arrived at the farm. He was shown by a sentry to the bell-tent where two men were drinking coffee. It took a few moments for his eyes to adjust to the light; then he recognised the man on the hillside, the one who had coaxed them to return to the fight. "Sir, Commandant Opperman sent me with a message. I am to tell you that all the burghers have left the hill, and that it now belongs to the Khakis."

"There is no-one on the hill?"

"None, sir. We were the last to leave," confirmed Jan.

Outside could be heard a ruckus as a horseman arrived. There was an agitated exchange of indiscernible words, and a moment later the sentry ushered in another burgher, "Sir, he has a report for you."

The despatch rider handed Botha a message. It was his own; the one which he had earlier sent to Shalk Burger.

The rider strove to control his heavy breathing and spurted out his explanation, "Sir, General Schalk Burger's laager is empty.

He's left with his Commando for Ladysmith. Other commandos are leaving. The word is spreading that the battle is lost!"

Botha was horrified by the news. If his civilian army disintegrated now, all would be thrown away at the very moment of success. He spoke urgently to the sentry, "Have my horse saddled!"

Jan galloped behind Botha as he headed for the Carolina laager, his plucky pony struggling to keep up with the sturdy Cape Horse - the laager was also the administrative area of his own detachment from Witberg. They rode into the circle of wagons. There was panic in the camp. Everyone was hurriedly packing. Some had already left.

"Stop! Stop!" He identified himself in the darkness, "I'm your Commanding General, Louis Botha."

Gradually men ceased their preparations as Botha's voice and authority cut through the bustling activity and pandemonium. He addressed the men from his saddle, "It's been a hard fight, and we have paid a high price. Your bravery will be spoken of by generations to come. But we must continue to hold the line. If we don't, then with the daylight the English will stream through the breach and roll up our defences on the Tugela and reach Ladysmith." He paused to let the significance of his words sink in. "Shame on you, if now you desert your posts in this hour of greatest danger!"

These were men who for seven long days and nights had been digging defences, manoeuvring to parry assaults, attacking, living under heavy shellfire; they felt broken, defeated, haunted by the horrors of the recent days. They were grieving for so many friends lying on the slopes of that devouring Kop. Now they were being asked to return, without sleep, without rest, with little hope of victory. The weary, surly men absorbed the plea: discussed, argued, evaluated.

Jan felt uneasy in the charged atmosphere. Would the Burghers respond, or was this the end of the fight? Would they lose Ladysmith? Would they be forced to return defeated to their Republics? His mind was swirling with anxious thoughts when he saw Commandant Hendrick Prinsloo step from the shadows into the glare of a camp fire – hadn't he last seen him carrying his dead brother off the hillside?

"Who's with me?" He called. He looked around at his exhausted, pained, sullen men, "Today we have lost family and friends, but the work remains unfinished." Without further ado, he mounted his roan pony and trotted off towards the Kop. Burghers exchanged grim looks. For a moment no one moved; then first one and then another untethered his pony from his wagon and mounted; they followed, resigned to their fate.

Botha galloped off into the night searching out other laagers.

Jan found his wagon which had been brought forward by the Bantu servants. Henry was there sat on his saddle, leaning back against a wheel, drinking coffee and nursing a bandaged arm and shoulder. They greeted each other warmly.

"Am I glad to see you!" shouted Henry, rising awkwardly and thrusting out his uninjured hand.

Jan shook it vigorously, with relief, "And me you! I thank God you're alive. What happened to your shoulder?"

"Nothing too bad," explained Henry. "A bullet in the shoulder and arm; went straight through - sore as hell; but if it doesn't get infected I should soon be right." He sat down feeling weak and unsteady. He pointed into the body of the wagon, "Pieter," he said quietly, "he's been badly affected by the death of Hans and his father."

"I'll go to him," suggested Jan.

"No; no I wouldn't. He's grieving; he won't see anyone or talk. Give him time."

Jan eagerly took a coffee handed to him by one of the servants and sat by Henry. He slurped noisily. "I must go back," said Jan. "I don't want to, but I must. Besides, Botha told me that we'd won. He believes that the English will withdraw. But just in case, we must be ready." He paused, "When this is over I'll sleep for a week."

Jan mounted his faithful, indefatigable pony and trotted off to join the other reluctant warriors at the foot of the Kop. Heidelbergers came across from the Rangeworthy Hills to strengthen the assembling assault force. Jan wrapped himself up in a blanket and lay by his tethered pony; with anxious expectations he awaited the dawn and whatever the new day held.

****

It was dark when Churchill set off once again to climb up the hill. He found that he was moving against a flow of men who were groping down the track; worn-out, stumbling, cursing, and eager to reach the valley below. It was an ominous sign.

With the coming of night the firing had virtually stopped; just the odd speculative bullet searched the darkness. He eventually found Thorneycroft sitting on a boulder surrounded by the spent remnant of his Regiment. They huddled together for warmth against the intrusive cold of the night. They were but a handful of the two hundred who had climbed the hill that morning.

"General Warren sent me to brief you on the current plans," explained Churchill. "They can't get the field guns up, but the mountain guns will set off at midnight and the sappers are preparing to haul up two naval twelve pounders. Food, ammunition and water are on their way. A six hundred strong entrenching party is assembling; fresh reinforcements are available." He became aware that his news was not exciting the anticipated response. He continued, "Warren wants to know what else you need to hold the hill?"

Thorneycroft sat with his head lowered into his hands as if listening attentively. When Churchill had finished he slowly looked up at him. He spoke with a smouldering anger, "This morning I was placed in command of this hilltop. Only now does General Warren communicate with me and this through a war correspondent. All day I have waited for help, for news, for ammunition, for water, for orders. All day this hilltop has been swept by Boer artillery and Mausers. Despite my pleas nothing has been done to silence them. We have suffered unmercifully. In the meantime a whole damned army has sat on its arse, whilst my soldiers have fought like lions and died like heroes!" He paused. He wiped the emerging wet from his eyes with a bloody sleeve. "And what of tomorrow? You know, as I know, that it's too late for our guns to be in position by daylight. It's not possible to dig protection for them in this rock. And how long would they last against the Boer Krupps and Creusots who have our range to the yard? Better six battalions safely off the hill than a mop-up in the morning."

With compassion and admiration Churchill examined the man who had all day fought ferociously, who had personally led attacks and counter-attacks, who had cajoled, bullied and inspired soldiers of different regiments, in the absence of their own officers, to fight beyond their imagined limits. Now this man was sagging with fatigue: heavy-hearted, despondent, deflated, of broken spirit - all fought out. Unimaginably brave, but he had passed the limit of endurance. The reality of the situation was forced upon him. No guns dragged to the summit would survive in action for more than a few minutes. And the distressing work of burying the dead and removing the wounded would occupy the intervening hours before daylight leaving no time to improve defences – and digging in rock? Unless the Boers were attacked in their flanking positions and attention drawn from Spion Kop, then how could the defences withstand the fire of another day? And Churchill knew that there were no such plans.

Thorneycroft rose wearily, "Come on men; it's time to go." His voice was soft and endearing as if speaking to children. Churchill accompanied Thorneycroft as his men followed in a straggling line. They passed over the summit and drew level with the first-aid station. There they were confronted by a furious Colonel Hill, "What the hell's going on?" he asked indignantly. "I understand that you've ordered the hill to be evacuated. On whose authority? I'm in command here!"

Thorneycroft was resigned and determined. From his advantage of height he looked down on this ineffectual officer and fixed his stare; he was in no mood to argue, "General Warren placed me in command on the demise of General Woodgate and with the approval of the Commander-in-Chief. He also gave me the temporary rank of brigadier general. In that capacity I now order the evacuation of this hill." He continued scathingly, "For someone claiming to be in command, you were conspicuous by your absence in the front line, nor am I aware of a single order which you have issued. Sir, you may stay behind with your Battalion and exercise command. As for me and everyone else, we're leaving."

He brushed passed Hill uncompromisingly, leaving him by the track, speechless.

Phillips was aroused from his heavy sleep by the sound of men scurrying past his location. "What's happening?" he called out.

"We're withdrawing."

"But you can't!"

He hurried to the track, "Stop! Stop! We're to hold the hill!" Soldiers hesitated, but were propelled forward by the crush of those behind. He found an officer, "Someone without authority has given orders. Were General Talbot-Coke here he would order an instant reoccupation of the heights." But he wasn't listening; no-one was listening. Philips was cast aside by the momentum of the fleeing men.

Half way down Thorneycroft came upon Captain Braithwaite of the Somerset Light Infantry with two hundred of his men carrying entrenching tools.

"What are you doing?" asked Thorneycroft roughly.

"I'm on my way to improve the trenches. I've a note for you from General Warren." He passed it across. The light from the stars and moon was poor and Thorneycroft, in his agitated state, struggled to read the small handwriting.

"Here let me read it," Churchill took the letter. "It says that you are to hang on and that this party is to dig your trenches."

Thorneycroft felt the rage and indignation rising hotly within. He burst out, "I've done all I can and I'm not going back!" He stormed off sweeping aside Braithwaite and his men; Churchill followed in his wake.

Braithwaite, realising that there were no troops left to occupy any trenches that he might dig, ordered his men to turn about.

....

"Damn!" He banged his leg on yet another stone. For more than two hours he had been stumbling and staggering around in the blackness trying to find Warren's headquarters. It wasn't where it had been the previous morning. He wandered from wagon to wagon, lamp to lamp, camp-fire to camp-fire; no one knew its whereabouts. He recalled with anxiety his disorientation of two nights ago and his long uncomfortable vigil until dawn came to his aid; oh lord, not again! he thought as his stomach tightened with rising angst. He was tired, aching and fed up. Ahead there was yet another light in the gloom.

"'alt! Who goes there?"

"General Talbot-Coke looking for General Warren."

"Pass, sir," welcomed the sentry. "General Warren's tent is over there." He pointed to the watery light straining through the white canvas. "I'll fetch him from his wagon."

With relief Talbot-Coke fell through the tent flaps and collapsed into a chair. Soon Warren entered, his eyes red from sleep. "It's good to see you, but I rather hoped that you'd be here sooner," opened Warren. "Can I get you a cup of tea?" Without waiting for a reply he called, "Orderly! pot of tea and two cups."

"Sir Charles," panted Talbot-Coke, "I've been blundering around in the vicinity for at least two hours trying to find your wagons."

"The Boer got our range and we had to move," explained Warren, "but my new position is known by the artillery headquarters."

Talbot-Coke suppressed his anger and frustration, "And you wanted my personal report?"

"I received your message in which you considered withdrawal. I was concerned. I believe we must discuss the situation thoroughly and plan to hold the hill. Withdrawal is out of the question."

An orderly interrupted, "Sir, message from Colonel Thorneycroft." Warren took it and read:

6:30 p.m

To Sir C Warren - "The troops which marched up here last night are quite done up……………The situation is critical.

"Why has this message taken so long to reach me?" he demanded.

"Runner couldn't find us, sir."

There was a sudden, noisy commotion outside. "Thank God I've found this bloody place!" Thorneycroft burst into the tent.

Warren and Talbot-Coke jumped up from their seats and stared in amazement at the large, filthy, dishevelled, fuming officer. His hair was matted, his face grey with ingrained dust, and his tunic splattered with the blood of his men.

Thorneycroft spoke first. He looked at Warren with contempt and disgust; this was the man who had deserted and ignored him. He spit out, "I've come to inform you that Spion Kop has been evacuated!"

Talbot-Coke exploded, "Evacuated! What the hell are you talking about man? When I left everything was under control!"

"Left! Left!" erupted Thorneycroft. "I never bloody well saw you there, General, so how could you have left?!" All pretensions of rank and respect had gone.

Ignoring this obvious insubordination Talbot-Coke demanded, "Who ordered this withdrawal and by what authority?"

"I ordered the withdrawal!" shouted Thorneycroft. The tent shook with the angry voices. "I made the decision as the officer in command of the hill and in the light of prevailing circumstances … and in the absence of contrary instructions!"

"I am the officer commanding Spion Kop!" countered a confused Talbot-Coke. "And what's more I delegated the defence to Colonel Hill!"

Thorneycroft was seething at this assertion. He spoke slowly and deliberately, explaining himself yet again, "At about mid-day yesterday I received a signal from General Warren appointing me officer in command of the hill and the fight. I was awarded the temporary rank of brigadier and that with the approval of General Buller." He looked towards Warren for confirmation.

An abrupt and heavy silence descended.

………………………………………………………………

After the torrent of retreating men had swept by, the hillside became eerily quiet. Phillips was gathering his equipment together ready to descend the slope with his small party.

"Sir, sir, we found some!" It was Corporal Sexton.

"Found what?" queried Phillips sharply.

"Oil, sir; we found some in a tin, enough to send a message."

Phillips thought for a moment, then dictated:

> *"To General Warren; summit of Spion Kop evacuated by our troops. An unauthorised retirement took place."*

....

Buller had a premonition of disaster. He rose early, gathered his staff officers about him, and rode off to see Warren. The first streaks of light heralded the dawn when he was accosted by a courier with a message from Warren; he read:

> *Warren to Chief of Staff, pressing. Colonel Thorneycroft has on his own authority abandoned the position of Spion Kop, and the troops are evacuating the place; can you come at once and decide what to do?*

"Thorneycroft was your man. He ordered the withdrawal," Warren confronted Buller. "Everything was in place to reinforce the hill and to establish guns on the heights. Success was in our grasp." He was finding it difficult to contain his anger. "The Boers have gone – totally demoralised. I have native intelligence and a report from a patrol which I sent to the summit to confirm that. It's not too late to retake the hill."

Buller was strangely distant; preoccupied.

Warren continued, unwilling to admit defeat, "We still have three options: reoccupy the hill; renew the attack on our left against the Rangeworthy Hills; or withdrawal. I recommend that we attack the hill now and reinstate the original plan."

Buller took solace from the discomfort of his once cocky rival. Now he was pleading for Buller to get him out of this mess. London would soon know who was responsible for this disaster; and it wasn't him. Indeed, he had seen this coming, what with all the dilatory manoeuvres and lack of decisive action. It had been apparent to him for days that his plan had been spoiled and that a breakthrough at this point was now impossible.

"I have other plans," announced Buller. "I have the key to Ladysmith." With a self-satisfied grin he added, "Sir Charles, I am taking back command and will personally supervise our withdrawal to the south bank of the Tugela."

Later that day when back at Spearman's, Buller called for his shorthand clerk, "Send to General White in Ladysmith:

> *Warren took Spion Kop the 24th and held it all day, but suffered very heavily; General Woodgate dangerously wounded, 200 killed and 300 badly wounded, and his garrison abandoned it in great disorder at night. I am withdrawing to Potgieter's and mean to have one square try to get with you, but my force is not strong enough I fear."*

The clerk left to arrange transmission of the message; Buller surreptitiously penned a short report to the War Office.

The following day, Friday 26 January, the later editions of the London papers announced the war news:

> *The following telegram from General Buller was received at the War Office 6 a.m. today: "Spearman's Camp, January 25 12.5 p.m. Warren's garrison, I am sorry to say, I find this morning had in the night abandoned Spion Kop."*

PART II

CHAPTER 13

Dulce et decorum est …

(January 1900)

Jack was prodded into consciousness by the pain and cold; he shivered involuntarily. The night air was chilled and damp. Gradually, as his addled brain slowly cleared, he realised that the fighting had stopped; no more ear-splitting shells landed, or bullets cracked through the air. He listened; a low, agitated murmur hung over the hilltop like the deep-throated humming of an angry bumble-bee. Suddenly the darkness was rent with a piercing scream; a shrill cry: "Mam! Mam!" A ghostly silence followed. Then once again the wretched lullaby of the doomed serenaded the dead. Jack surveyed the dark mounds around him: most were still; a few twitched; one moaned. His brain swam; desperately he tried to focus. Pictures of home flitted through his mind: his mother dishing out the hot-pot; his father in the mill carefully tending his mules; the noise and smoke of the Spinners' Arms – were they talking about him as they heard the war news? And Mary - she was smiling at him; but her eyes were watering; those were tears coursing down her pale face; she beckoned to him wistfully. He smiled back at her; a peace descended as his aching, spent body dragged him back into senselessness.

****

There was a commotion. Jan peered out from beneath his dew-soaked blanket into the breaking light. How quickly the night had passed and the time to attack arrived. Men stood about stamping cold feet to revive circulation, when there arose an unexpected excited banter. People were pointing to two shadowy figures on the top of the Kop; barely distinguishable. The silhouettes were shouting and waving their felt hats. The realisation struck home; they are our neighbours, our friends on the hilltop.

"The Khakis have gone!" exclaimed someone. The cry was taken up: "The Khakis have gone! We've won! The victory is ours!"

****

The dew was heavy. A white ghostly vapour lingered as a shroud concealing the shattered, contorted bodies; it was reluctant to relinquish its hold. But the daylight crept across the hills; an unstoppable force, which gradually and inexorably banished the darkness. The first glimmers of light accentuated the glistening dew drops and the curling wisps of mist as they dissipated in the warming rays. It was a moment of freshness as the damp of the night gave way to the warmth of the day. Greyness turned to colour, silhouette to form. The ground-thrush rose into the sky twittering incongruously above the hilltop.

For several hours the guardians of the hill had been the dead and the dying - both Khaki and Boer.

Lieutenant Blake-Knox, Royal Army Medical Corps, reached the summit with some apprehension; behind him straggled the stretcher-bearers and a chaplain, the Reverend Collins. As he came over the summit he stopped suddenly as if hit by a shock wave; his stomach heaved. He gazed upon the swathes of shapeless bodies; the disembowelled corpses; the bloody jetsam of war, "Dulce et decorum est pro patria mori…"

"What was that?" panted the chaplain as he drew level.

Blake-Knox repeated it. "A cynical reflection. Do you know it?"

"Of course, doesn't everyone; from the Roman poet Horace. I was compelled to learn it by heart at school:

How sweet and fitting it is to die for one's country."

They had attended the wounded from Colenso, and all through the previous day worked ceaselessly to stem flowing blood and clean and bind shattered bodies in the dressing station at the foot of the hill. They had seen and experienced much during this short war and thought themselves hardened, but now they stood silently together, surveying the grim scene.

"Hands up! Hands up!" Their reflections were interrupted as resurgent Boers scrambled over the rocky ledge and rushed towards them. Knox scrutinised them as they approached: rugged men in tweed suits, leggings, spurs and soft hats with the Transvaal colours around the brim.

"I'm a medical officer, a non-combatant. I've come to collect our wounded," explained Knox.

"What proof have you of that?" demand the leading Boer in good English, his rifle pointed at Knox's chest. Other burghers were hurriedly assembling.

Knox glanced at his right arm and realised that his red-cross brassard had slipped off during the climb. He was flustered; what to do?

"Hands up! This way. You're my prisoner."

He was pushed unceremoniously down the slope while the gathering stretcher-bearers were herded together as they arrived, confused and afraid. He noticed a group of Boers conversing; some wore long black frockcoats, another in a smart brown suit - he was unharmed, but close by was a native carrying a handsomely carved rifle. They had an air of authority. As he passed he called out, "Gentlemen! Gentlemen! I'm a medical officer come to collect the wounded. I should not be taken prisoner. It's against the conventions of war!"

The man in the brown suit looked up, "Bring him here!" He scrutinised Knox, "Tell me, how do we know that you're a medical officer?"

Before he could answer another interjected, "Where did you train and when?"

"Edinburgh; I qualified three years ago."

"And who was your consultant?"

"Edwards … Professor Edwards."

"I'm a Doctor and I also trained at Edinburgh. I knew Professor Edwards." He turned to his companion, "General, we should allow the Doctor to do his work."

"Yes, of course." He addressed Knox, his manner sympathetic, "If there's anything we can do to help, then please ask. There will be a truce until all wounded have been collected and the dead buried."

"Thank you, sir."

Botha addressed a nearby burgher, "Return to my headquarters and fetch coffee for the doctor and the others – they have much to do."

Gratefully Knox returned to his men. He allocated areas to stretcher parties, "Search carefully; we must quickly recover the wounded if they are to survive. Be thorough. And chaplain, could you organise the burials. Do ensure that we collect the names of the dead. Brief the men to extract the calico patch with identification details which they'll find sewn into an inside pocket of the tunics." Everyone moved off to their allocated tasks.

"Cigarette?"

Knox turned; it was Botha.

"Thank you General."

"You see, we honour the Geneva Convention. Unlike the English; we are not barbarians."

"Why do you say that?" enquired Knox defensively.

"Because it's true!" Retorted Botha angrily. "Let me give you three instances: after the skirmish near the village of Acton Homes the wounded were ill treated; our ambulances seized in the Orange Free State have been sent off to Cape Town; and our prisoners are tied to wagons and dragged along the roads."

Knox inhaled the cigarette and slowly, struggling to maintain a respectful composure, blew the smoke through his nostrils. He watched it dispel quickly in the gentle breeze. "General, can you corroborate these accusations personally or produce witnesses?"

"No; but these reports are common in our lines."

"General, I treated the wounded from Acton Homes. As for the ambulances, I cannot comment. And your third accusation is too preposterous to discuss."

Botha remained silent and thoughtful at this rebuke. Together they stood smoking, quietly watching the macabre scene unfold before them. Now the sun was warming the ground, and the rising heat brought the stench of blood and putrefying flesh, heavy with a repulsive sweetness. Botha indicated the valley below; there was an army in retreat. Long columns of wagons were crossing the Tugela via the pontoon bridges. The Khakis were also withdrawing from their gains in the Rangeworthy Hills to the west. Botha finally intruded upon their silence; reflectively he commented, "Your soldiers are the best in the world, your regimental officers the bravest." He paused for a moment; he smiled self-assuredly, "We rely on your generals."

> *"He shall judge among the nations, and shall rebuke many people; and they shall beat their swords into ploughshares and their spears into pruning hooks: nation shall not lift up sword against nation, neither shall they learn war any more………"*

Knox and Botha swung around to find an old burgher with a long, white beard standing on a nearby rock. With Bible in raised hand he loudly berated his enemies and called upon them to renounce war.

"Excuse me, General, I must attend to my patients." Without waiting for an answer, Knox strode off across the plateau.

…………………………………………………………………

Jack was jolted into consciousness by an excruciating pain rushing from hip to toe like a slug of molten metal tearing through his limb. He screamed. As his senses cleared he found that he was starring at a leathery, be-whiskered face beneath a wide-brimmed hat. At first the face was bemused, but gradually broke into a guarded smile of understanding. Jack realised that his right boot had been removed, and that the owner of this face was trying to take his left one.

"Bugger off! Bugger off!" It was a pained effort to shout.

A hand appeared and touched the rim of the hat as if offering a salute. With a kindly nod and widening grin the old Boer moved on to rob the next corpse. He cut away the sergeant stripes and tunic buttons as trophies.

Jack's recollections were vague – when did they climb this hill? He remembered Grindrod applying his field dressing, and wasn't there a young Boer who gave him a drink of water; or was that the fever taking over? And Bill; he checked, yes his tunic was still lying on the corpse. He felt so tired and racked with pain; he trembled uncontrollably. His throat was dry and burning from the dust and lingering, noxious fumes of battle. He willed for sleep to once again bring him relief and peace. The discomfort was almost unbearable; the rough stony ground bit into his back. Unthinkingly, he moved to adjust his position - he screamed instinctively. He heard babbling; he couldn't make out what was being said. It wasn't a language he knew. Was it the Boers coming this time to take him prisoner or to finish him off?

"Sahib! Sahib!"

Knox wandered the plateau supervising the bearers. He offered thanks to those Boers who helped to identify the wounded and to render first aid. He was still grappling with the enormity of the slaughter. Body lay upon body; some twitched and squirmed. One seeming corpse stirred, the head turned revealing a nauseating, ragged wound to the jaw and a face of congealed blood. He stepped forward to help; the face fell back into the dust with an indecipherable groan; it was still. He stared into the waxen face and at the gapping eyeballs – there's no dignity in death, he thought. Then he heard the excited shout and looked across to a party of coolie stretcher-bearers; they had found a survivor.

"I'm a doctor … I'm going to re-bandage your wound and then tie your good leg to the injured one to act as a splint. It'll stop it moving as we carry you down the hill."

Through his hurt and semi-consciousness Jack felt the probing of his body and the movement of his injured leg. He clenched his teeth to contain a scream. Gently he was lifted onto a stretcher and a blanket was thrown over him; at last he felt some warmth. He later remembered that at one point he was given a drink of hot Bovril before being laid on blood-stained straw in an ambulance wagon. He bit his tongue in an attempt to contain his cries as he jolted and rocked across the uneven veld. The man lying next to him at first moaned and cursed, but then, mercifully, grew quiet. Jack drifted into blackness.

****

Botha turned and made his way back to his headquarters. He shared the track with parties of farmer-warriors as they stumbled down towards their laagers, burdened with the bodies of their fallen relatives and friends wrapped in blankets. He was moved by the tears of some and the grim stoicism of others. He carefully negotiated other corpses of friends and neighbours waiting to be claimed. As he looked on them he became disturbed and distressed by the distorted, anguished, pallid faces and the stiffening limbs of those with whom, such a short time before, he had argued, laughed and worshiped. Freedom is a carnivore, he mused. He felt no triumphalism in this victory, only grief.

The farm by his headquarters had been designated a collection point and aid post for captured English wounded. They lay in neat rows or sat propped against the building wall. A Russian doctor and his attendants provided care. He passed them and entered his tent; Sandberg was startled from a heavy sleep. "My friend, we both need rest, but first one final telegram to President Kruger and General Joubert." Sandberg wrote as Botha dictated:

> *"Battle over and by the grace of God a magnificent victory for us. The enemy driven out of their positions and their losses are great. At least 600 dead and a large number of wounded are still lying on the battlefield. The enemy have asked me to remove their wounded and bury their dead, to which I have agreed. The battlefield therefore is ours…………It breaks my heart to say that so many of our gallant heroes have also been killed and wounded…It is incredible that such a small handful of men, with the help of the Most High, could fight and withstand the mighty Britain for six consecutive days and drive them back with heavy losses."*

"Now I must sleep." He stood and made as if to leave, then stopped and looked back towards his Secretary, "Order the firing of one shell – one shell only, in the vicinity of the withdrawing enemy."

Sandberg was perplexed by this curious instruction. Botha read his body language and explained, "To bid farewell - a salute."

The shell splashed harmlessly in the Tugela.

....

Jan rode back to the laager and brought forward the wagon to the foot of the Kop. He took the native servants and retraced his steps up the hill. Henry, in his weakened state, remained with Pieter in the wagon. They soon located the bodies of Hendrick and Hans under the thorn bush where they had been laid. Hendrick's mouth hung open wide, his lips were blue, his nostrils waxen and caved in. Hans' waxy, yellow face peaked out from beneath his wide-brimmed hat which his brother had carefully replaced. The bodies had stiffened - rigor mortis was setting in. They rolled them into blankets. First they lifted Hendrick - he was very heavy. They staggered down the rocky slope, occasionally bumping the corpse against a rock or on the ground – Jan was becoming distraught at this disrespectful handling of his Uncle. Then survivors from the Corporalship came to help. With all possible care they hoisted the corpse into the vehicle, before returning to fetch Hans.

Ruth and Jacobus had been disturbed in the early morning by the noise of the fleeing Lyndenburgers and others from the Tugela front. The word spread rapidly: "The English have broken through!" There was confusion and disarray among the besiegers of Ladysmith.

Jacobus had recovered limited mobility, and he consoled the troubled Ruth, "Our wagon is with Hendrick and the boys; neither of us is capable of riding far. We'll pack our things together so that we can move quickly if necessary when they return."

But by mid-day the victory was being loudly announced; the gloom lifted and the predikant quickly declared a special service of thanksgiving. Ruth didn't attend; she waited for the wagon, fretting and ill at ease. In the failing light it rumbled into the laager; she ran with relief to meet it. But she stopped in her tracks; she saw Henry in bandages and the riderless mounts tied to the wagon. She bellowed and broke down, trembling in a flood of uncontrollable tears.

Jacobus sat by Jan on the front seat of the wagon. Ruth was in the back; she drew close to Henry, snuggling against him for protection, support and love. Pieter remained silent as he watched over his father and brother.

With the ponies tethered to the back of the wagon, and the two servants on foot guiding the lead oxen, the van den Berg's began the long, slow trek home.

CHAPTER 14

Number 4 Field Hospital

(25 January 1900)

He sat at the bottom of the hill on a stone at the side of the track. He was tired, but still in good spirits despite the exertions of the past six days. He bit into a hard army biscuit. Experience had taught him that the best way to tackle this food was to break away the edge and then to nibble towards the centre. He took a swig of water from his bottle. The sun was now rising to its zenith. It was hot after the cold night. He picked up his slouch hat which had been on the ground by his side and placed it casually on his head. This completed his untidy uniform of baggy, khaki trousers and jacket buttoned up to the neck.

As he rested he looked towards the river. The armada of wagons was rolling across the two pontoons, unhurriedly, but steadily; the atmosphere was one of a depressed resignation; a reluctant recognition of defeat. Out of the comparative silence a shell whistled overhead and crashed into the river about two hundred yards from the nearest pontoon. He saw oxen, mules and horses shy; there was a moment of frantic activity amongst the soldiers as they struggled to restrain and to control the animals, but soon the situation settled down to an orderly movement, as the expectation of further shells failed to materialise. He pondered at the significance of that single Boer shell.

As he reflected he was not unaware of the irony of his position and circumstances. He had come to southern Africa, a son of the Empire and a newly qualified lawyer having studied at Edinburgh. But ever since his arrival he had been confronted by the endemic racism of the whites. He still smarted at the memory of being struck across the head by a railway conductor, and thrown off the train at Pietermaritzburg for the impertinence of travelling in a carriage reserved for whites only. He had quickly become the leading activist seeking equality for Indians. This war between the two white tribes had brought with it a fine political opportunity to further his cause. Here was an occasion for Indians to demonstrate their loyalty to the Empire, and to legitimize their claim for full citizenship. Inwardly he admired the spirit of the Boers in their fight for freedom; he believed that justice was undoubtedly on their side, but publicly he proclaimed the duty of every citizen of the Empire to support the government from which they expected succour. He was a pacifist - determined to conquer hate by love in line with the teachings of the Jain sect of Hinduism - so he had mobilized the Indian community of Natal to fund and to supply recruits to his Ambulance Corps. About three hundred had volunteered with an additional eight hundred indentured labourers being despatched by their employers - willingly or otherwise. He had offered the services of his Unit to the British Army, and after due procrastination it had been accepted. Indians were not allowed to hold the Queen's Commission, and so it was as a Sergeant-Major that Mohandas Gandhi led his scruffy, undisciplined unit of stretcher bearers.

It was the afternoon of the preceding day when he had first been tasked to send his men up the hill. It had not been just a simple job of removing the wounded - although carrying heavy, human loads down a steep, uneven track was bad enough - but rather, a matter of survival. The artillery shells were indiscriminate, and the small red-cross brassard worn on the left sleeve was not visible to the distant, sniping Boers. Several of his men had been killed and wounded whilst retrieving casualties, but their pluck, fortitude and courage had drawn praise, respect and thanks.

This morning had been disturbing as they had picked among the mangled bodies searching for survivors. The wounded, dying and dead had lain intertwined; a few seemingly unwounded were uncovered in a state of collapse and exhaustion, they appeared to have been sapped of life: stupefied, disorientated, distant, unreal. But now all the wounded had been removed and brought to the aid post at the bottom of the hill. On the orders of the Army Surgeon, his men had prepared and served fresh, hot Bovril to the casualties before loading them onto the straw in the back of rigid ox wagons and ambulances. They were despatched to the Field Hospital five miles away. Those who would never survive such a painful journey were to be carried the whole distance on stretchers by a relay of bearers.

The last party of bearers had left. Sergeant-Major Gandhi wearily rose to his feet slapping the dust from the rear of his trousers. He smoothed his short, neatly clipped moustache, arranged his broad-rimmed hat which he turned up jauntily on the left, and began the long walk to Spearman's farm and the hospital.

Gandhi was familiar with Number 4 Stationary Field Hospital. Days before, his men had helped to erect more than one hundred bell-tents and four operating marquees ready to receive the casualties from the imminent battle. They had unloaded the numerous stores from the sixty wagons which made up the hospital train, including iron bedsteads and mattresses. There seemed to be an abundance of supplies.

The hospital sat in the lee of a kopje on which was sited a naval gun, and close to the farm which gave the location its name. It had been a modest farm; a single storey building with the ubiquitous corrugated-zinc roof. There were a few outbuildings, but now it was in a sorry state – looted and damaged by Boer marauders. Doors hung crazily and every window was broken.

Gandhi watched the melee of arriving ambulances, each with its load of suffering, misery and death. They were drawn by ten mules and driven by a black native. Over the dusty, white hood flew a red-cross flag. Willing hands helped the walking wounded to alight, while stretchers were removed compassionately by relays of his coolie bearers with their bare, spindly legs protruding from dirty, tatty khaki. The casualties were covered in dust and sweat, many blistered by the sun. Some were without tunics, their blue army shirts stiff with blood. Wounds were varied: shattered arms; heads wrapped in bandages their faces lined with black streaks of blood; one man was blind and clung to the tunic of a comrade; some fell to their knees vomiting and coughing blood. All were dazed, weary and disheartened. Personal equipment was jettisoned: helmets, rifles, canteens, mess-tins, boots; all littered the area. Ghandi noticed a doctor carefully, but quickly examining the new arrivals as they were unloaded, and occasionally directing a patient to an area set aside. There they received morphine by hypodermic needle, but were never moved into the operating theatre.

Soldiers sat on the ground amid the stretchers by the operating marquees, waiting fatalistically and uncomplaining for their turn at the surgeons' hands. A few were delirious writhing on their stretchers or rolling in the dust; some were ominously quiet.

Gandhi filled his water bottle from a nearby barrel and joined the other orderlies who were moving among the wounded, dispensing comfort and relief. "Here soldier ... water." The man raised himself up on his elbows and gratefully gulped the liquid.

"Ta mate." The soldier grimaced fighting obvious discomfort.

"And what's your name?" asked Gandhi

"Jack …Jack Clegg."

"And where are you from Jack?"

"Rochdale."

"Isn't that where the cotton is spun?"

"Yes. I were a piecer … would 'ave been a spinner soon wi' me dad." Momentarily Jack nostalgically visualised the mill and the clattering mules. "Aaah…" he moaned, clenching his teeth grimly, trying not to shout out as the hurt from his thigh swept upwards through his body.

When the pain had eased and the soldier relaxed, Gandhi continued, "I know of it. The cotton from my country is sent there. You see, we share a common interest. We grow the cotton and you manufacture it. We are each dependent upon the other."

"Aye." Jack acknowledged weakly.

"Bring him through!" A surgeon in riding breeches stood at the entrance to the operating marquee and was pointing out Jack to two orderlies.

"I'll help." Gandhi took hold of the front of the stretcher, and assisted by one of his own men carried Jack into the operating tent. In the centre was a table which only just fitted between the vertical tent poles. Inside it was hot, dusty, and plagued by flies attracted by the plentiful blood.

"Put him on there!"

They laid the stretcher down on the table. Gandhi noticed that along the sides were field panniers which served as tables; lying on them were instruments and dressings. Inside the operating tent were the surgeon, anaesthetist, and two unshaven orderlies; all were in shirt sleeves; sweat ran liberally down their grimy faces; blood splattered their clothes. They were tired. Immediately the orderlies removed the bandage which secured the legs together. They drew vicious-looking knives from sheaths hanging from broad leather belts, and cut away the clothing to reveal the wound. They stepped to one side. The surgeon examined the bloody flesh and visible bone and nodded to the anaesthetist.

"Yer won't feel nothin'," encouraged the orderly as he held Jack's head firmly from behind.

Jack was consumed by a strong smell of chloroform as a mask was placed over his face. He drifted into a painless oblivion.

Expertly the surgeon removed the dead tissue, cutting away chunks of skin and muscle. He cleaned the raw wound with a sterilised pad, "Lot of dirt in here … possible infection," he said concernedly without looking up. He cleaned some more. All right, we leave it open, let's pack and dress it."

Gandhi watched in admiration. The surgeon set the break and with the help of the two orderlies immobilised the leg in a special splint of canvas into which was sewn a strip of bamboo. It was all over in ten minutes.

"Take him out," ordered the surgeon. "Next!" he cried wearily.

……………………………………………………………

The corporal and his six dishevelled soldiers shamble by. They are unshaven and scruffily dressed: sleeves rolled up carelessly, helmets pushed back jauntily, shirts unbuttoned at the neck. They carry spades on their shoulders and smoke clay pipes. Light-hearted banter flies between them: "So 'ow many died durin' night? One; just one; we'll soon be out a business."

The gravediggers shuffle to the back of the farm and stop in the vicinity of a small burial ground. In it are the graves of two hardy pioneers, George and Susan Spearman. They are shaded by the only visible trees, and the whole is enclosed by a solid iron railing, more typical of an English country cemetery than of a desolate spot on the sprawling veld. With practised movements the diggers begin to shape the grave in the designated area about fifty yards away. Each shovel-full of spoil square and compact, nothing is spilled; no effort is wasted.

Some hours later the funeral party assembles. The stretcher-bearers emerge from the mortuary tent carrying a blanket-covered object. It is a soldier - officers get a coffin. The firing party forms up under a sergeant, their rifles reversed. "Slooow … march!" They step off in precise military formation leading the bearers with their sad load. Waiting at the graveside is the Chaplain wearing a college cap, white surplice, and riding breeches and puttees. The funeral party arrives, and with practised precision the brown bundle is lowered into the hole by ropes, and the firing party takes up its position by the grave. The Chaplain breaks the silence as he reads the service:

> "*We entrust into your merciful hands, Father, the soul of our brother, And we commit his body to the ground: earth to earth, ashes to ashes, dust to dust; in sure and certain hope of the resurrection to eternal life through Jesus Christ our Lord.*"

All respond, "Amen."

"Present Arms! Ready! Fire!" Three times the volley of shots ring out.

As the funeral party marches briskly back to camp, the grave diggers busy themselves once more, filling in the hole under the dazzling sun, at the foot of a kopje, on the vast expanse of South Africa.

CHAPTER 15

Spearman's Farm

(30 January 1900)

As he trotted towards his tent the cheers of the assembled troops rang loudly in his ears. Five thousand or more had been drawn up in a hollow square, rank upon rank, to be inspired by his promise that they would be in Ladysmith within the week. He had scanned the soldiers' resolute faces; how eager they were to avenge past defeats and to close with the Boer for the third and last battle to break the enemy's lines. Since the withdrawal, the troops had been rested and well fed; reinforcements meant that the Force was now stronger than ever before. He took comfort in the belief that the Boers must have lost at least five hundred men; they could never win this battle of attrition. Yes, he and his soldiers had been cruelly disappointed by the inadequacies of his subordinate generals. But his men's devotion towards him clearly remained undiminished by the recent set-back. They trusted in his judgement and his concern for their well-being. Now it was time for him to do things himself. He had a new plan; as he had announced, he had the key to victory.

As he approached his tent a young horseman drew alongside. Buller recognised the face, but struggled to put a name to it.

"Good morning, General" He didn't wait for a reply. "I see your men are in good heart despite a second failure, and remain eager for the fight – says something for the courage of the Englishman...don't you think?"

"Your name again?"

"Leo Amery."

"Yes.... *The Times*."

"General, could I interview you about the imminent battle … in Ladysmith within the week, you forecast. What is this key?"

"I though I'd made myself perfectly clear the last time we met." He spoke slowly with deliberate emphasis, "I do not speak to the press. Kindly leave my headquarters before I have you removed."

Irritated, he dismounted, handed the reins of his bay to his groom and entered his tent. His aide-de-camp followed, "Sir, I have the despatches from General Warren and Colonel Thorneycroft."

"Place them on the table and close the tent flap as you leave … and send me in a drink; the usual for this time."

Buller opened the leather wallet on the table and removed the reports. He was required to send an account of the battle to the War Office which convention demanded be released into the public domain. He considered. There was much to be said, but some things should remain confidential.

"Your drink, sir," the orderly stood outside.

"Come in … here, on the table." The orderly set down the tankard of champagne and withdrew.

Buller sat down, drank eagerly – it was getting hot. He read the reports. Things had not gone according to his plans. He had given clear orders and delegated the execution to Warren. The failure to break through was not his fault. "Johnson! Johnson!" An earnest young staff officer appeared, "Send the short-hand clerk to me. I have despatches to write." With the clerk sitting opposite him he began to dictate:

"Spearman's Hill, 30th January 1900. To the Secretary of State for War…" He recounted the machinations leading up to the attack on Spion Kop and the subsequent withdrawal. Then he added:

> *"If at sundown the defence of the summit had been taken regularly in hand, entrenchments laid out, gun emplacements prepared, the dead removed, the wounded collected, and, in fact the whole place brought under regular military command, and careful arrangements made for the supply of water and food to the scattered fighting line, the hills would have been held I am sure. But no arrangements were made. General Coke seems to have been ordered away just as he would have been useful, and no-one succeeded him. Those on top were ignorant of the fact that the guns were coming up, and generally there was a want of organization and system that acted most unfavourably on the defence.*

> *Preparations for the second day's defence should have been organised during the day, and have been commenced at nightfall. As this was not done, I think Colonel Thorneycroft exercised a wise discretion.*
>
> *Our losses, I regret to say, were very heavy, and though we were not successful in retaining the position, the losses inflicted on the enemy and the attack generally have had a marked effect on them."*

"Write that up and send by telegram immediately." The clerk left.

That was not enough. The Government and the Commander-in-Chief South Africa, Lord Roberts, needed to properly understand the extent of Warren's incompetence. He emptied the tankard; by now the champagne was warm and lifeless. He picked up his pen. He would need to write this himself; it was not for everyone's eyes:

> *To the Secretary of State for War – In forwarding this report, I am constrained to make the following remarks, not necessarily for publication.*
>
> *I had fully discussed my orders with General Warren before he started, and he appeared to entirely agree that the policy indicated of refusing the right and advancing the left was the right one. He never, though, attempted to carry it out.*
>
> *The arrival of the Force at Trichard's was a surprise to the enemy, who were not in strength. Sir Warren, instead of feeling for the enemy, elected to spend two whole days in passing his baggage. During this time the enemy received reinforcements and strengthened his position. On the 19th he attacked and gained considerable advantage. On the 20th, instead of pursuing it, he divided his force, and gave General Clery a separate command. As the days went on, I saw no attempt on the part of General Warren either to grapple with the situation or*

to command his force himself. We had really lost our chance by Sir C Warren's slowness. He seems to me a man who can do well what he can do himself, but who cannot command, as he can use neither his staff nor subordinates.

I can never employ him again on an independent command.

On the 19th I ought to have assumed command myself; I saw things were not going well. I did not because I thought that if I did I should discredit Warren in the estimation of the troops. Anyhow I felt convinced that we had a good chance on the 17th and that we lost it.

Redvers Buller, General

CHAPTER 16

War News

(February 1900)

Mary met her father as he left the mill at the end of the Saturday morning shift. Together they walked home.

The paper-boy was standing at his usual pitch on the corner of Albert Street and Manchester Road: "War news! War news! Fusiliers suffer casualties!"

Mr Kenyon bought a paper and attempted to read it, but it unravelled in the wind and was getting wet in the fine drizzle. "We'll 'ave to wait 'til we get 'ome lass," he explained to Mary.

Once in the cottage they quickly threw their coats onto the hooks behind the door and headed for the chairs around the fire. "Celia, think yer should listen to this lass," Mr Naylor summoned his wife. "I've got th' Observer." He read aloud:

WAR NEWS

SPION KOP ABANDONED

Heavy British Casualties

Lancashire Fusiliers Suffer Severely

> *On Thursday morning we learned from General Buller that General Warren had surprised Spion Kop on Tuesday night, that the small Boer garrison had fled, but that Warren's men were subsequently attacked by the Boers in a strong force, and that our losses are considerable.*
>
> *We understand that a private telegram was received on Tuesday night at the Depot of the 2nd Battalion Lancashire Fusiliers to the effect that the casualties of the Battalion in the Spion Kop engagement numbered 57. No information was sent as to the proportionate*

> *number killed or wounded and no names have been received.*
> *Up to a late hour last night no further details had arrived.*

There was silence. They were fearful for John and Bill. Mary was also anxious about Jack.

"Wen do yer think we'll know about John and Bill?" she asked her father.

"Don't know lass." There was an unfamiliar warmth in his voice, "We all 'ave to be patient and wait for the names of casualties to come through. 'Til then, no news is good news." He picked up his paper and read on. With that the women folk were summarily dismissed.

Mary's inner turmoil was compounded by her knowledge that she had missed two of her periods, but lately there had been slight vaginal bleeding. She had experienced only occasional nausea; was she pregnant or was it part of her general winter malaise? She was confused and frightened. Daily she felt herself growing weaker; she had chest pains and her coughing bouts were more frequent and intense. Blood was often present in her phlegm - she had told no-one. She leant closer to the fire in an attempt to warm her chilled body. It had rained now for the past two weeks with barely a break. Everywhere was damp and cold.

From that point onwards each day the family feared the arrival of the postman and the dreaded letter from the War Office. Mary would come home from the mill hardly daring to enquire. Every day without news kept hope alive and brought the possibility that the boys would come home unscathed. The following Saturday, 3rd February, she was late leaving the mill.

The paper-boy called out his headlines: "Spion Kop! Terrible Casualties!"

She ran home. Her father passed her the paper; she read with trepidation:

THE TERRIBLE LOSSES OF THE 2ND BATTALION LANCASHIRE FUSILIERS

33 LOCAL MEN KILLED, WOUNDED OR MISSING

> *Their friends will be pleased to know that according to all accounts that have reached us, the Boers treat their prisoners kindly.*

She scanned the list of killed and wounded: Holden, Brierley, Cody, Dawson ....

"Their names aren't there lass, 'I've already looked. Could be all's well," her father attempted to comfort her.

It had been a hard day at the mill, and with her strength draining each day seemed to be longer and more physically demanding. She walked home linking arms with Sally, partly as a gesture of friendship, partly for the physical support. The lack of news about her brothers and Jack was a continuing strain and worry. They hurried through the rain with shawls drawn over their heads for protection, chatting idly as they turned off Albert Street into the courtyard; something was amiss. There was an unusual atmosphere; you could almost feel a heaviness. At first it wasn't clear, but then they stopped and stared. The curtains in the windows of their two houses were drawn closed - someone had died. They ran, clattering over the cobbles and burst through their respective front doors.

"Who is it? Who is it?" gasped Mary.

Her mother was sat silently, sobbing; her whole body heaving. Her head was heavy in her hands. She wiped her eyes with her food-stained apron. Unusually, her father was home from the mill before her; he was standing impassively with his back to the fire.

"We've a letter. It's John … he's dead." He hesitated and then added as gently as his normally brusque manner permitted, "Next door they've 'eard that Jack's dead." He turned and banged his pipe on the mantle-piece spilling the spent tobacco. He was not one for emotions. Above the crying of the two women he proclaimed stoically, "Thank God that it's not Bill as well. At least wen this is all over, one of 'em might cum 'ome."

Mary was distraught; John and Jack, both dead. Suddenly she felt cramps and pain around her pelvis. She was nauseas and dizzy. She must be alone. She struggled to climb the steep stairs, pulling herself up with the banister. She threw herself onto her bed and screamed.

Her father was hardly surprised that his daughter had taken the news so badly. It wasn't just a brother, but her young man too – he had thought it certain that they would eventually marry. "Celia," he spoke kindly to his wife, "get yerself together lass, and go and see to yer daughter."

Celia felt wretched. She was in torment, overwrought with grief. She could barely think straight, but her daughter needed her. She mounted the stairs, her whole body still shaking from her inconsolable crying. She opened the bedroom door, for a moment she was held rigid as if in a vice, and then she shrieked hysterically; Mary was curled up on the bed protectively; blood covered her thighs; a tiny foetus lay lifeless between her legs.

CHAPTER 17

Betrayed

(August 1900)

Warren pushed through the revolving doors and entered the opulent surroundings of the Officers' and Military Club on Piccadilly. He sought out his old friend, General Sir Alexander Montgomery-Moore, presently General Officer Commanding Aldershot Garrison.

"General Montgomery-More is waiting for you in the Marlborough ante-room, sir," advised the clerk at the reception desk. "I'll send up a waiter."

"Ah! There you are." Warren strode into a small room crowded with heavy, leather chairs; the walls were lined with bulging bookcases. His friend rose to greet him; they shook hands warmly. Warren turned to the waiter who had dutifully followed him into the room, "Tonic water for me …Alex?"

"The same, but with some gin; thank you. You haven't become teetotal during your time in Africa?"

"Not completely, but you know me; it's too early to take alcohol," explained Warren.

They sat down together.

"I am sorry to hear about that nonsense in Canterbury," remarked Montgomery-Moore.

"Yes; I am scheduled to speak on native races at Saint Augustine's College, but the Mayor has refused the request of the College authorities to give me a civic reception. After all, he couldn't possibly offer official recognition to one who had incurred the Queen's displeasure – the man who lost Spion Kop." He smiled ruefully, "I have been passed over for the award of any decorations; so-called friends avoid me; I feel I'm being ostracised by society."

Montgomery-More smiled reassuringly, "We are old friends, and always will be."

The waiter reappeared and offered the drinks from a silver tray. When he had withdrawn Warren continued, "I find it difficult to understand how Buller could make such accusations about me."

"You know that in April, while you were still in Africa, when the despatches were published there was an outcry in the press and a heated debate in the Commons. There is much suspicion that all the despatches relating to the goings-on at Spion Kop have not been revealed."

"I find it strange," lamented Warren. "I thought that Buller and I were friends. He never gave any contrary indications. Indeed, such was our relationship that others would put their petitions to Buller through me saying that I was the only person capable of cutting through his brusqueness. He used to come over to lunch with me, or I lunched with him, and on these occasions we might argue, but amicably – we are both opinionated and had different ideas on how to conduct the campaign. When I left Natal we parted on excellent terms. He assured me that he had spoken well of me. We shook hands and he wished me future success." Warren paused and sipped his drink. He continued slowly, contemplatively, "You know, I received hints that he was against me, but I didn't believe them. But to be so vindictive. I think his misstatements were due to poor field intelligence and his surmising of many details."

"You're too generous in your defence of Buller," offered Montgomery-Moore. "Could it be that Buller felt that his position could not sustain two serious failures and so you became the scapegoat-in-chief? I remember the headlines when the news first broke here about Spion Kop: "Warren's garrison abandons Spion Kop". Wasn't Buller supposed to be the Commander-in-Chief? And yet he seems to bear no responsibility." He paused to sip his drink, "Did you ever get a reply to your correspondence from Roberts or the War Office?"

"I was in Cape Town when I first read the accusations in the newspapers; I was on my way home. You'll recall that after the fall of Ladysmith I was sent to put down a rebellion in Griqualand and Bechuanaland. I wasted no time in sending a despatch to Roberts in which I explained Buller's points under a very different light. I particularly refuted his unfounded assertion that the defence of the summit and preparations for the following night had not been properly taken in hand." He rose; ruefully he exclaimed, "And to state that Thorneycroft made a wise decision to withdraw – and that without any consultation, and totally contrary to all my orders!"

He walked over to the window and gazed out at the splendid, red-brick church of St James'. One of Christopher Wren's more beautiful buildings, he thought. The sun was shining; it was a glorious day. For a moment he allowed his thoughts to drift as he surveyed the London sky line. He forced himself to focus. He turned to face his friend.

"Buller attacked again at Vaalkrans. He lost his nerve and retreated. He boasted of having found the key to victory; it was a key which I gave him. I developed the tactics of the sustained bombardment as a prelude to the infantry attack. I refined the creeping barrage and the infantry skirmish. And where did we finally attack successfully? Why at Hlangwe. From my very first meeting with Buller I identified this as the enemy's Achilles' heel. What is most galling is that after his outrageous and insulting remark about my ability to command, he left the conduct of the final breakthrough battle entirely with me."

"And did Roberts reply to your correspondence?" pursued Montgomery-More gently.

"My petition was met with a deafening silence."

"And the War Office?"

"I wrote a total of four letters. Their instructions to me are clear: I am not to discuss the matter further, or to attempt any defence of my cause."

Silence descended between them. The ticking of the mahogany-cased clock, which sat on the marble mantle-piece, was accentuated in the quiet.

"What should I do? I value your advice," asked Warren of his trusted friend.

Montgomery-Moore replied thoughtfully, deliberating over each word, "Nothing ...nothing. You know, as I know, that according to military etiquette no subordinate officer, right or wrong, can controvert hostile remarks of his commander-in-chief. The Country is still at war; the Army cannot have its senior generals squabbling in public."

"Am I to grin and bear it? I want to do something."

"What you must do is wait twenty years… then you can do what you like."

"I'll probably not live another twenty years; what can I do now?" Warren's exasperation was mounting.

"I can think of only one thing," advised Montgomery-Moore. "Begin all over again in some other line. Show the world that you are not the idiot Buller makes you out to be. Show that you can lead men, and that you have superior ability."

CHAPTER 18

Homecoming

(September 1900)

For ten days Jack had sweated with a fever, often delirious, only occasionally conscious. His body had been fighting infection. Whenever he came around he was tormented by excruciating pain in his thigh. The doctors had worked hard to save his leg, but the cutting, probing and cleaning had left a raw gaping wound. He was thankful for their skill and commitment. He recalled that in his more lucid moments he had been aware of a soldier in the next bed who was forever ranting and screaming: "There! They're on the 'ill! Shoot! Shoot! For God's sake shoot!" One morning he was gone.

"Oh him," replied the orderly when Jack enquired. "He had battle fever – couldn't stop fighting in his mind. We've put him with the other insanities."

Later the orderly had returned; Keith was his name; from Oldham - a good sort. "Well Jack, I've some news for yer. Accordin' to the records yer dead."

"Well if am not, I bloody well soon will be, food we get 'ere!"

"Dead or not, this is the nearest you'll ever get to 'eaven," chided Keith. "But seriously: 4070 private Jack Clegg … that's you? But they've got yer identification slip from yer tunic; collected it on Spion Kop; and they insist they had a body."

Jack was quiet. He had managed to wipe out the image, to delete it from his consciousness, but now once again he could see the tortured lump which was Bill. He choked up as he spoke, "Me tunic were covering the body of private William Naylor."

……………………………………………………………………

As he was stretchered aboard the hospital ship the *Maine,* he was bemused to see it boasting three flags: American, British and that of the Red Cross. He later learnt that it was an old cattle vessel which had been converted and equipped by a committee of American women formed in London by the mother of that famous young war correspondent, Churchill. It was plush and well fitted-out. The nurses were compassionate, attentive and pretty. He slept a lot between the unaccustomed, clean cotton sheets, ate his fill and gradually felt the tensions in his body dissolve in the calming environment – the harrowing scenes returned less frequently. But by comparison, the short train journey from Southampton docks to Netley station, and onward by rigid, horse-drawn ambulance to the hospital, was uncomfortable and painful; it brought back the memory of that awful journey across country from Spion Kop to the Field Hospital – agonies he would prefer to forget.

Four orderlies carried his stretcher through the entrance of the imposing central tower-block. As they halted inside, awaiting instructions, he glanced about to see numerous, wooden, glass-faced display-cabinets containing a bewildering assortment of body parts. He was disturbed by this macabre introduction to Netley Hospital which lay on the shores of Southampton Waters. From the outside it was an impressive architectural masterpiece, but inside it was cavernous and cold.

The sound of four pairs of metal studs on the stone floor echoed around the corridor as Jack was conveyed to his allotted ward.

"This building's a quarter of a mile long," remarked one of the orderlies. Jack presumed the information was for his edification. "More than a hundred wards; nearly one thousand beds; and we're almost full. You lot keeps us busy." Jack detected a note of complaint in the last remark as if he had conspired to be wounded.

"We're 'ere."

The party turned into a dingy room with about twenty iron beds lining the walls. He was helped onto a vacant bed, after which the orderlies left abruptly. More than two hundred casualties had arrived on the *Main*; the ward filled rapidly.

It was almost two months since he had been wounded. His body had fought off the infection; he wouldn't lose his leg, but the slightest movement triggered agonizing pain as the bone ends rubbed together. The doctors replaced his splint with plaster of Paris dressings wrapped from crutch to toe. They declared themselves pleased with his progress and confided in him that few casualties suffering from a broken femur survived; they prophesised a long period of convalescence.

His boredom was eased by occasional letters from Mary and his sister, Sally. Apparently, the news of his survival had provoked highly emotional, contradictory reactions of ecstatic joy and screeching sorrow. Whilst his parents and siblings celebrated, next door the Naylors sank further into a quagmire of pain - two sons killed on the same day. Mary wrote how she was torn between relief at him being alive and grief for the loss of Bill.

The hospital library provided a trolley service to the wards, and for the first time in his life Jack had plenty of time to discover the joy of reading; Charles Dickens was a must; he gobbled down *Oliver Twist*, *Great Expectations* and others; he was gripped by the dark tensions of Emily Bronte's *Wuthering Heights*. But he also had time to think; he concocted a plan. He had little to spend his money on in the hospital and was able to save. He could pay for Mary, with Sally as travelling companion, to come by train and visit him in the hospital. Taking time off from the mill would normally be impossible, but then there was the week of the annual town wakes. Through a hospital orderly he would be able to arrange accommodation for three nights with a family in one of the cottages in the village.

On the Monday morning which marked the beginning of the Rochdale wakes, Mary and Sally boarded the train for London. Neither had been beyond Blackpool before; this was to be a great adventure. As she settled back in her seat, Mary sensed a tautness in her stomach; was it the eager anticipation of being reunited with Jack, or anxiety for the future? Perhaps both?

They had managed to secure seats by the windows, and during the seven hour journey they alternatively watched the unfamiliar scenery roll by, or dozed.

"Are yer eatin' yer butties?" enquired Sally as she unwrapped a small gingham parcel.

"Not 'ungry yet."

"That's yer problem; yer never are. Yer need to eat; put on some weight; build up yer strength."

Mary smiled fatalistically. She was grateful for Sally's concern; for her gentle bullying. For months her parents had been so consumed with their own grief, that they barely noticed her, as if she was immune from hurt and pain following the loss of her child and of her brothers. She had rarely eaten a full meal since that awful day back in February.

They arrived at Euston and needed to cross London to Waterloo in order to catch the train to Southampton. A railway official directed them to the Underground; they found the descent frightening, the tunnels smokey and claustrophobic; they were relieved to finally burst out into the fresh air. However, their spirits sank when they learnt that the last train to Southampton had gone, and that they were faced with the prospect of spending the night in the ladies' waiting room. The wooden seats were hard and uncompromising. As the night progressed, shadowy figures passed by the windows of the room; occasionally a hand would rub the soot-layered glass and a face attempt to peer inside. They felt nervous and intimidated in the alien surroundings. They determined that one should remain alert whilst the other tried to sleep. In the twilight of dawn they jumped on the first train to Southampton, and for several hours slept fitfully as they chugged through the sun-lit countryside. They were pleased to discover that recently the railway had been extended into the very grounds of the hospital.

As the train groaned to a halt Mary and Sally half crouched as they strained to search for Jack through the windows. Mary thought she saw him; a figure sat on a bench holding a crutch in each hand; but in the swirling engine smoke she couldn't be certain.

The girls spilled from the coach dragging their carpet bags with them. The heavy bag became weightless as Mary dashed excitedly towards the exit with Sally in tow. She emerged from the station arch to be dazzled by the glaring sun. She shielded her eyes and scanned the expansive greenness. Standing twenty yards away was a figure dressed in a drab, serge, grey-blue uniform; he lent heavily on crutches, his left leg was swathed in dirty-white plaster. It was Jack. She couldn't contain herself and dashed forward. Dropping her bag she threw her arms around him; her tears flowed with the release of suppressed tensions and emotions.

"Steady lass! Yer'll 'ave me over," he said gently, almost laughing.

She released her grip and drew back a little.

"Sorry I can't hug you lass; can't stand without these crutches."

Sally stepped between them and gave him a hug and a kiss on the cheek. "I'm so happy to see yer. We all thought yer were dead."

"Hi, sis; 't were a near thing," he replied pensively. Then shaking off a momentary gloom, "I'm so pleased to see yer both. Cum on!"

Beaming, Jack led the way, swinging expertly on his crutches. The girls struggled to keep up with him, bags in hand. They all chatted enthusiastically about home: the mill, the weather, the crowd at the Spinners', the recent turns at the Circus. Sally confirmed that their mum and dad were in reasonable health – of course so relieved and happy that he was alive and now back in England.

"And 'ow are yer parents?" he asked Mary guardedly.

What could she say? They've lost their two sons, but otherwise all's well. Or the truth: they're in the depths of despair; they blame you for being alive when Bill and John are dead. "They're all right … as well as can be expected."

They walked around the vast park-like ground s of the hospital before Jack took them to a canteen set aside for visitors, "Wat will yer 'ave?" he asked.

Mary ordered a cheese and pickle sandwich with a mug of tea.

"Yer nibbling like a mouse. I've seen more meat on a butcher's pencil," he commented with an air of seriousness. "Yer needs to eat, lass."

Mary was stung by his criticism. Of course she was thin - she was ill. She felt a pang of insecurity, didn't he want her any more?

In the afternoon they wandered along an iron jetty which stretched from the hospital grounds out into the sea. "Not a scratch on the Blackpool piers," remarked Jack. "No amusements and variety halls; but it's all we got."

Mary was unaccustomed to the heat; how she appreciated the cooling breeze wafting in from the sea. She was hot and exhausted after the long journey. She examined Jack; it was becoming evident that he was tiring – occasionally he screwed up his face as he tried to hide obvious pain. So she wasn't sorry when he explained that he had to return to the hospital by tea time – rules and regulations were strict – but that he would see them mid-morning after the doctors had completed their ward rounds; "There's a ruined abbey in the village, see you there about eleven."

He watched as the girls disappeared in the distance heading for the cottage where they were to stay. He lingered, gathering his thoughts: Mary was looking so thin and wan; her troublesome cough was never far from the surface. At times during their walking he and Sally had had to slow down to allow Mary to keep up – she was breathless. And there were tensions; she wasn't relaxed. Was it just that she was still pining at the loss of her brothers?

Mary left the cottage and wandered through the woods to the shell of the church and monastic buildings. She sat on a broad round stone, the remains of a pillar. She absorbed the comforting warmth of the sun; alone; quiet; only the frantic chatter of birds in the trees and the soothing hum of bees in the nettles intruded upon her peace. She relished the solitude. At home it was so difficult to be alone. As she waited for Jack she determined that important things had to be said. Yesterday she had been tired, but she had detected some awkwardness between them; there was an unspoken tension. She had to know her future. Did he still find her attractive? Did he still love her? Were they to be married?

"Penny for yer thoughts."

She swung around to see Jack shuffling towards her, silent on the grass.

"Yer by yerself? Wer's Sally?"

"She'll cum later. She thought we deserved time together."

Mary moved to greet him. She desperately needed to hug and kiss him; she couldn't halt the tears which dribbled down her sallow cheeks. Jack sat on the stones, threw down his crutches and with hands freed, held her to him tightly. She didn't want to let go, but eventually she broke the embrace and eased away.

"There's sommat yer should know," she started hesitantly.

"Yer parents?" interrupted Jack. "I can understand 'ow they feel. And after thinkin' Bill was alive."

"Mam and dad are shattered. They've taken the loss of Bill and John badly; wat else can yer expect? They blame yer. Without yer, they wouldn't 'ave joined the Army. They think yer should be dead instead of Bill. But there's sommat else."

"Sommat else?"

"Aye. Mam and dad don't want me to 'ave anythin' to do with yer. I've cum 'ere against their wishes … 'ad a flaming row."

"I'm sorry about yer brothers, I really am. But they was grown up; they 'ad minds of their own. We all took the same chances. I can't be 'eld responsible for fate." Jack was almost pleading. He needed to be exonerated for any part in their deaths. He needed acceptance.

"There's sommat else!" she reiterated, now almost shouting. She released his hands and looked down at the ground. She calmed herself, "After our time in the barn, I got pregnant. I 'ad a miscarriage."

Jack looked at her in stunned silence. "Why didn't yer tell me? Why did yer carry this sorrow all by yerself? Yer should 'ave shared it with me."

"But it were the news of yer death which brought on the miscarriage; it wer the shock. Then we 'eard yer were badly wounded. It wasn't right to burden yer then. As time passed it got more difficult to say."

He grasped her hands. "Look at me, lass. The luv of yer kept me goin'. Wenever I 'ad a minute to meself I only though of yer. I've 'ad plenty of time to think, and I'd remember our times together and plan for our future." He looked at her intently; this pallid, frail, sorrowing young woman whom he loved so much. His eyes watered, a consuming inner warmth welled up, "I'm sorry … I'm so sorry that you lost the baby. I'm so sorry that I wasn't there for yer. I love yer Mary Naylor; I always will.

There'll be no more soldierin' for me with this wonky leg. So as soon as I gets back to Rochdale we'll marry. We'll 'ave a family – boys, girls. I loves yer so much."

Mary's face brightened. For the first time since Jack had left her for South Africa she felt a hope; she wouldn't be alone; there was to be a future. She cried with joy.

……………………………………………………………………

He stood outside the railway station leaning on his walking stick waiting for the tramcar to arrive. It was raining and the drops dripped from his sodden, flat cap down his neck. The clouds hung low, heavy with the weight of moister; they trapped the pungent smells and pollution from the numerous, belching, mill chimneys. His left leg and hip ached.

The tram arrived to the metallic sound of wheels scraping on rails and the grating of brakes. The height of the car platform appeared formidable and presented a challenge to Jack's reduced mobility. The conductor saw his plight and took charge of his kitbag. Jack moved unsteadily down the aisle and collapsed thankfully onto the wooden seat which ran the length of the car. Once he was settled the conductor moved to him.

"Junction Albert Street and College Street if yer please mate," said Jack.

"Yer back from South Africa?" enquired the conductor.

"Aye."

"Thought so; yer kitbag an' all. Been discharged?"

"Aye…. It's all over for me."

The conductor held a board to which were clipped tickets of various colours. He tugged one free and punched the appropriate destination giving it to Jack in exchange for a half-penny. Jack looked across the aisle and out of the opposite window. He found it reassuring as the tram trundled through the streets, once again to see the familiar landmarks: the fire-station, the Mason's Arms, the Palace Music Hall, and on the corner of Drake Street, the Wellington Hotel. The car dropped down to the level of the River Roche which flowed through the centre of the town, and there it turned left. Looming to his front was the magnificent, neo-gothic town-hall; still standing sentinel were its four golden lions. He was almost home.

The tramcar halted outside the town-hall to allow the ebb and flow of passengers, then, with a clatter of bells, it moved off down the Esplanade, passed the public library and turned right over the bridge into Manchester Road.

"We're 'ere lad; was Albert Street yer wanted? Yer alright?" It took a moment for Jack to realize that the conductor was talking to him; his ears still buzzed with the sound of battle – sometimes it almost sent him mad.

"Aye; aye; ta". He rose stiffly, moved to the platform and descended carefully grasping the hand rail. The conductor passed down the bag.

"Take care lad," he said with a genuine concern in his voice.

With the clang of the internal bell, the tram car disappeared wobbling gently on its tracks as it pulled away. Jack was alone outside the mill and only minutes from home. The rain had stopped. He threw the kitbag over his right shoulder, and leaning on his stick, limped painfully to the turning which brought him to Joseph's Court. He stopped, put down the kitbag and absorbed the familiar sights which often he had thought he would never see again. The cobbles gleamed in the wet of the recent rain. The door-steps and window-sills were clean and bright having been recently scrubbed with off-yellow donkey-stone; always such a contrast to the grimy brickwork. He had been away for a lifetime; several lifetimes; but in those nine months nothing seemed to have changed. It was the courtyard where he had grown from scruffy urchin to returning hero.

Then he saw it - the Naylors' curtains were drawn closed.

EPILOGUE

Retribution

(October 1901)

Buller had enjoyed the meal, and the venue was magnificent. The Queen's Hall, Westminster was a marvel of medieval architecture. His gaze drifted to the beautiful, hammer-beam roof constructed with Irish black oak – some say from County Galway; a place he knew well from his tenure as Permanent under-Secretary. He was aware of the building's great historical significance; a place of important trials: Charles I, Sir Thomas More, Guy Fawkes. But latterly used for coronation banquets and royal lyings-in-state. In fact, he recalled that only two years earlier he had visited the Hall to pay his last respects to the only statesman ever to be so honoured, the then recently deceased Prime Minister, Gladstone; a person he revered. So much had happened in the intervening period, not least his recent encounter with the Boers.

He was feeling persecuted; bruised even. Ever since his return from South Africa and his reinstatement as General Officer Commanding First Army Corps at Aldershot, he had faced virulent criticism from certain quarters: ministers, right-wing back-benchers, and even the King. Admittedly, there may have been difficulties in the early days of the War, but then it took time to weld a Field Force together and to evolve new tactics. Following the relief of Ladysmith his handling of the Field Force had been virtually flawless; he had out-manoeuvred and defeated the Boer at every turn. In the wake of these attacks on his competence, he took solace in the knowledge that there were still many in the Country who believed in him. Almost a year had passed, but he was still basking in the warmth of his triumphant return to Aldershot – an event which surpassed anything previously experienced by that military town. His personal, beflagged train had drawn into the station decorated with colourful bunting. He had been greeted by the sound of a children's choir singing "Home Sweet Home". Dignitaries had clamoured to watch his arrival from temporary grandstands, while brass-helmeted fire-men had drawn his carriage through streets densely packed with adoring, cheering throngs. Banners declared: "He obeyed the Empire's Call"; while a military band struck up, "See the Conquering Hero Comes".

He was startled from his troubled reflections and thrust into the present by the noise of the President of the Mess banging his gavel on the table. A hush descended upon the distinguished luncheon guests, "My Lords, ladies and gentlemen, please be upstanding for the loyal toast."

With the noisy scraping of chairs everyone rose to their feet and formally held their full port glasses in front of them. No-one drank.

The President waited until all was still: "The King".

The guests echoed: "The King." Port was sipped sparingly. Everyone sat down and once again the buzz of wine-soaked conversation filled the hall.

Buller was wearing the green mess-kit of the King's Royal Rifle Corps - suitably tailored to accommodate his burgeoning frame. He had been invited to the luncheon after which he was to award medals to local volunteers who had been on active service in South Africa. He looked down the length of the tables at the splendid, ornate silver-ware, and upwards at the line of majestic chandeliers. Guests were wearing mess uniforms or black frock coats; City dignitaries sported generous, officious gold chains. Ladies were present, including his wife. These society ladies flaunted the fashionable, hour-glass silhouette - most flattering to mature women of ample curves and full bosoms. Cascades of lace fell from bodices of pastel colours.

Again the gavel summoned everyone to their feet for the second obligatory toast: "My Lords, ladies and gentlemen … the Regiment."

"The Regiment".

Then he saw him. He tensed. A couple of weeks previously *The Times* had carried an aggressive article demanding reform of the Army and his removal from it. It protected the author under the veiled pseudonym "Reformer", but everyone knew who it was -that carping war correspondent, Leo Amery, who had been with the Natal Field Force and had hounded him during the battles for Ladysmith. He knew him well: troublesome, arrogant, pugnacious. And he was here.

"More port Sir Redvers?" It was his host, Colonel Sir Howard Vincent MP, Commanding Officer of the Queen's Westminster Volunteers.

"Thank you Sir Howard." He took the decanter and filled his glass before passing it to his left as custom demanded.

"Are you ready? Should I call order?" enquired the Colonel.

"Yes … yes; I'm ready, thank you." Furtively he glanced one last time at his notes.

Colonel Vincent banged his glass on the table; silence followed. "My Lords, ladies and gentlemen, today we are gathered to pay tribute to the gallant volunteers from the City of Westminster. May I remind you that in May of last year our men embarked for South Africa there to join the great army under Sir Redvers Buller. By all accounts they gave good, brave service. Sir Redvers is our guest of honour today, and we are gratified to also have present Lady Audrey Buller, who has set an example of fortitude to the wives of every soldier throughout the country."

Tables shuddered and glasses rattled as the men banged the polished surfaces in approval; the ladies politely clapped their gloved-hands. Voices cried: "Here! here!"

"It is my honour and great pleasure to ask Sir Redvers to say a few words before we retire to present medals to our loyal soldiers."

Buller rose; he spoke slowly, a little awkwardly. He was uncomfortable making speeches; always conscious of his slight speech impediment. "My Lord Duke, Sir Howard Vincent, Ladies and Gentlemen; I must thank Sir Howard Vincent for having given me the pleasure of being able to be here to-day; and I must tell you how grateful I am to him, and to you all, for the very kind way in which he has proposed and you have received the toast to which I have now to reply.

"I am especially grateful to him and to you for the manner in which his references to my wife have been received. "Men must work and women must weep," is an old truth, though perhaps, a comparatively modern saying. It is perfectly true, and there is no doubt that all the men who have been serving the Crown in

South Africa have reasons, individual or general, to be grateful to a great many gracious ladies at home."

He looked towards his wife and they exchanged a mutual smile:

"In regard to your references to this detachment of your Regiment, they served in South Africa with, what I know they will not complain of me for saying, was bad luck. They were caught for probably the most disagreeable and least pleasant of all a soldier's duties - work on the line of communication …"

He could see; glaring at him contemptuously was that damned, scurrilous reporter. He continued with his tribute, but he felt strangely detached, floating on another plane, looking down on the scene as a spectator; gazing on his accuser, Amery. He must make the most of this unforeseen opportunity. Today he would flush him out; like a ferret down a rabbit hole he would drag him into the open. He concluded his prepared speech: " … so far as I know, and I think I fairly know, they performed their duties most admirably."

Unexpectedly, Buller did not sit down. He continued to stand, pensively gathering his thoughts. He picked up his port glass and sipped calculatedly; his audience waited politely. He placed down his glass, surveyed the warm, friendly faces staring back at him in eager anticipation. With resolve and resolution he began to speak again, this time stridently: "I have been attacked and I do not care what they say about me. One of my comrades wrote to me the other day and said: "We know you do not mind it, but we do, your army does and is furious." I know that there is a Correspondent of *The Times* here, and I want to send a message to *The Times*. *The Times* has attacked me. It has published a letter by "Reformer". He may be a penny-a-liner; he may be the greatest man in the world." His voice now shrill, ""Reformer", an anonymous scribe in *The Times,* has attacked me and says I am not fit to be in command of the First Army Corps, and I assert that there is no one in England junior to me who is as fit as I am!"

The heat of temper surged within him. He drew breath. His eyes caught those of his wife; bright blue, but now moistened and sad. Were her eyes pleading for him to stop, or was she grieved by his torment? She smiled. He assumed encouragement. The guests were riveted, engrossed, hanging on his every word, surprised by the unexpected vehemence of his pronouncements.

"I say so! I challenge *The Times* to say who is the man they have in their eye more fit than I am? They attack me, and they say that I wrote a telegram in which I ordered Sir George White to give up Ladysmith, to destroy his books, and so forth. I attacked Colenso on December 15. I was unsuccessful. It was a very trying day; I was 36 hours at work; I was 14 hours in the saddle. It was the hottest day we had the whole of the time I was out there, and I had rank bad luck. I attacked Colenso and I failed, and, having failed, I had to consider the people in front of me, in Ladysmith. Ladysmith was held by Sir George White. I knew that horse sickness was almost certain to become very prevalent in the Tugela Valley. I knew that enteric fever was endemic, and was likely to become an epidemic in the Tugela Valley at that time. I believed also that the Boers were engaged in putting dead horses into the water which the garrison was obliged to drink. I knew that the garrison would have trouble, and great trouble, with their sick."

He paused to wipe the perspiration from his brow; the hall was becoming hot, stuffy. He glowered angrily at his impassive accuser: "The message I had to send to Sir George White was that I had attacked, that I had failed, that I could not possibly make another attempt for a month, and then I was certain I could not do it except by slow fighting, and not by rushing. That was the message I had to send.

"I was in command of Natal! And it was my duty to give my subordinate some assistance, some lead, something that in the event of his determining to surrender, he would be able to produce and say, "Well, Sir Redvers Buller agreed." I, therefore, placed into the middle of that telegram a sentence in which I suggested if it would be necessary to surrender the garrison, what he should do when he surrendered, and how he should do it. I put in that sentence in order that if he found he was obliged to surrender it would be some sort of cover for him. In fact, what I felt at the time was that if surrender came I should be just as responsible for it as he was, and I did not mean to stand up and say it was all his fault."

The hall reverberated to the cheers and shouts of support. Now he had justified himself; he glared at his tormentor; he was shouting above the trialing applause: “I challenge *The Times* fairly to bring their scribe, "Reformer", into the ring! Let us know who he is; by what right he writes; what his name is; what his authority is; let him publish his telegram. It was a perfectly secret telegram. I challenge them to produce the telegram and say how they got it, and when they do that, I will publish a certified copy of the telegram I sent and the public shall judge me. I am perfectly ready to be judged!”

He was flushed, agitated. His high collar rubbed against his thick, sweating neck. Perspiration bubbled on his forehead. But he felt vindicated; he had thrown down the gauntlet. He stopped talking and picked up his glass; it was empty. Flustered, he replaced it clumsily on the table. He was breathing heavily. Gradually he gathered his composure and looked out at the sea of empathetic faces.

He reasserted his self-control and concluded calmly: “I thank you for the kind manner in which you have welcomed me and the kind sympathy and support you have given me today. I have found among my own men, and in this detachment of the Queen's Westminster’s, the same generous support and the same brave and confident spirit that I have found manifested towards me throughout the nation since my return home.”

As he sat down the cheering swelled to fill the cavernous hall. The empathy of the diners towards Buller was almost palpable.

Leo Amery closed his notebook with its accurate shorthand transcription of Buller’s tirade. He smiled inwardly, unmoved by the noisy adulation being showered upon that popular anachronism; an adulation which he understood to be a direct condemnation of himself.

....

Field Marshall Lord Roberts stood looking out of his office window into the seasonable gloom of a wet October day. On his return from South Africa he had been hailed as a conquering hero; the dying Queen had insisted on giving him a personal audience and awarded him the Order of the Garter, while Parliament made him a grant of £100,000 in recognition of his services. He had succeeded his old rival, the increasingly senile Wolseley, as the Commander-in- Chief of the Forces; the most senior post in the Army. He had reached the pinnacle of his career. But there was an emptiness in his life; he stilled grieved for his only son, Freddie.

He was realistic. Freddie had never been a bright child, but he had been big-hearted, open, gregarious, and had excelled at sport. He had been loved by his family and friends. As a father he had encouraged him into the Army where he had displayed great courage and won several mentions in despatches. Unsurprisingly, he had badly failed the written examination for entry into the Staff College, and so had sought experience and promotion through active service in South Africa.

He visualized Freddie's grave on the treeless veld. Before leaving South Africa he had gone with his wife on a pilgrimage to Chieveley where, during the Colenso battle, had been sited Number 4 Field Hospital. A cluster of dilapidated brick and tin houses identified the railway station next to which was sited a small graveyard. Freddie's grave was set apart from a group of five others - the final resting place of soldiers who had similarly died while in the care of the Hospital at that location. Captain Walter Congreve had been with his son when he died. Together they had been on Buller's staff. While Commander-in-Chief South Africa he had sought out Congreve to learn the details of his son's death.

"General Buller first realised that something was wrong when Colonel Long's guns stopped firing," Congreve explained to the Field Marshal. "We could see from our vantage point on Gun Hill, close to the naval guns, that the field artillery had deployed forward of their infantry protection. Now they were abandoned; men, horses and empty shells were strewn around the guns. It soon became apparent that the survivors were sheltering in a nearby hollow. The naval guns were further back, about half a mile, by a donga. They seemed to be out of range of aimed rifle fire, but there were plenty of random bullets flying about."

Roberts offered the young officer a drink to help put him at ease.

"Thank you, sir." Congreve took the beer in its silver tankard from the orderly, waited for him to leave the tent, and continued, "As we rode forward we became an obvious target for the Boers. One staff officer had his horse shot from under him, and the General was winded by a shell fragment. But he was calm and self-controlled at all times – an encouragement and inspiration to us all. It was as if he was enjoying the exhilaration of battle. It was at this time that Captain Hughes was virtually bisected by shrapnel."

"Yes, very unfortunate," remarked Roberts, eager to move on.

"When we reached the donga General Buller rallied some gunners hiding there. I remember his words: "Now, my lads, this is your last chance to save the guns; will any of you volunteer to fetch them?"

"A Corporal and six men stepped forward, but it wasn't enough to make up two teams. The General turned to us: "Some of you go and help." I volunteered, together with Captain Schofield and your son, Freddie. We hooked two teams into limbers and galloped for the guns."

"And Freddie? How was Freddie?"

"You'd have thought he was riding point-to-point. He was in front of me, looking back and laughing, slapping his leg with his stick." Congreve paused as the Field Marshall absorbed all he had to say. He saw a man tortured by grief; unfamiliarly old, drawn and grey. "Sir … Freddie was fearless."

"Thank you, Walter." Roberts appreciated the comforting remarks. "Please continue."

Congreve paused a few moments as he determined to accurately recall events; "There were bullets whizzing everywhere. The Boers were determined to stop us. I dismounted and hooked up a gun with Schofield; Freddie held my horse. I'm afraid that it was then that he was hit. I was consumed by the task of hooking up the second gun. Then I was hit in the leg and fell from my horse. I crawled into a ditch for safety. There were others there."

"I believe you brought Freddie in from the open."

"Yes, sir. I managed to pull him into cover. He was hit in the stomach and two other places. I covered him with my tunic, but we lay in the scorching sun for over five hours - until a truce was agreed with the Boers."

"Were any other attempts made to retrieve the guns?"

"Yes, three teams from 7th Battery limbered up and galloped forward, but the Boers were waiting. They ran into a wall of fire. More than half the horses and six men were shot before they could get anywhere near the guns. General Buller then halted any further attempts."

"Did you see Freddie in the hospital?"

"No, sir. But he was attended to by the eminent Surgeon Frederick Treves. I understand that with his abdominal wound there was no hope of recovery."

To hear this first hand account of his son's death had been an essential part of his mourning process. He continued to stare out, quietly, unseeing, unable to dispel the varied images of his son as they flicked across his memory. Suddenly his reminiscing was rudely shattered. The door burst open unceremoniously as Sir John Brodrick swept into the modest-sized, oak-panelled office. On the last Cabinet reshuffle he had replaced Lansdowne as Secretary of State for War. Roberts reluctantly, unhurriedly, turned to face his visitor not surprised at the intrusion. He had been expecting it.

"You've seen it?" blurted out Brodrick waving a copy of *The Times* and advancing meaningfully. "Ever since he was sent out to South Africa, he's been a blasted mill-stone around the Army's neck!"

"Do sit down, Sir John," offered Roberts reassuringly, pointing to several leather chairs around a low table.

"Have you read it?" persisted Brodrick ignoring Roberts' gesture.

On the table was a collection of that morning's papers: *Spectator, Mail, The Times.* "I was assailed by rumour and innuendo as I entered the building, but the papers have only just been brought to me. I've not had time to read them."

"Then let me read to you," insisted the disgruntled Minister. Before Roberts could react he opened *The Times* at a marked page and began:

> *"I must explain, first of all, that the purpose of my letter was not to attack Sir Redvers Buller-if it had been possible I would gladly have abstained from any personal references - but to criticize the Government for the unmistakable signs it has shown of its indifference to the burning question of Army reform. Not the least striking of those signs has been the appointment to the most important military command in England of a General whom they themselves believe and know to be unfit to conduct an army in the field."*

"Who's the author of this article?" enquired Roberts.
"Reformer – but we all know who that is!" Broderick continued to read aloud:

> *"Sir Redvers Buller asks me to produce "my telegram," which he suggests has been purloined in some illicit manner. If he will look at my letter he will find that I never stated that I had the "telegram" in my possession or that I had even seen it. I simply referred to the well-known fact that Sir Redvers Buller had, in a message sent immediately after Colenso, suggested the surrender of Ladysmith to that gallant soldier, Sir George White. I could, if it were necessary, produce evidence for that statement, but what better evidence can there be than the astonishing admissions made yesterday by Sir Redvers Buller himself?"*

"Minister, let me read this myself." Roberts was irritated that he should be read to like a child or imbecile. He picked up his own paper and turned to the article:

> *Sir Redvers Buller declares that his failure at Colenso was due to "rank bad luck." It may have been; but was it "rank bad luck" to make a frontal attack upon a strong*

> *position protected by an unfordable river? Was it "rank bad luck" not to seize Hlangwe Hill, the one point of vantage on the south bank of the river? Was it "rank bad luck" to abandon two batteries, half a mile from the river, and not taken away by the Boers for some hours after they were abandoned?*
>
> *Whatever the reasons for the failure at Colenso, the result of it was that Sir Redvers Buller gave up all hope of relieving Ladysmith for the next month, and without consulting the Government, without giving himself a day or two for reflection, "suggested" to Sir George White that "it would be necessary to surrender.*

Brodrick, waiting on Roberts could not tolerate the silence which had descended. “Have you read his excuse for sending that telegram? Listen:

> *“Sir Redvers Buller declares that his suggestion to Sir George White was an act of generosity, was meant to "cover" him in the event of surrender.”*

Roberts walked across the room and sat in one of the leather chairs. Broderick followed.

“Was he drunk?” enquired Broderick.

“I understand that he enjoys his drink, but I believe he holds it well.”

“Then why this idiotic outburst?” Broderick was almost shouting. He answered his own question, “It seems Buller has been goaded by an anonymous journalist into making indiscreet and unacceptable remarks. He is publicly discussing military and confidential matters – a clear breech of discipline. It has come to the point where his very continuance in command brings the Army and the Government into disrepute.” Broderick was surprised at Robert’s lack of response. “You don’t like the man … you’ve confided in me many times,” he prompted.

“I have never been impressed by Buller. He showed his true colours in South Africa. Brave …yes. But one expects a private soldier to be brave. As a subordinate general I found him to be ponderous, given to procrastination, lacking in imagination and initiative, to be argumentative and uncooperative. Several times I considered removing him, but I hesitated in case it might be seen as an act of vindictiveness following the loss of Freddie when he was on Buller's staff."

Roberts smiled sinisterly, his eyes brightened; his countenance relaxed, "However, Buller's speech yesterday is really an extraordinary help to us, and I am strongly of the opinion that we should take advantage of his indiscretion and remove him from command. But we must plan carefully. He still has many supporters among the public and the Establishment. And we can hardly be seen to bend to the agitation of a young propagandist who has never fired a shot in anger; has never been subjected to making life and death decisions in the heat of battle."

"How should we proceed?" asked Broderick cautiously.

"You need to ensure that the Cabinet fully understands that on this matter the very integrity of the Army is at stake and that I, as Commander-in-Chief, must be free to enforce the appropriate disciplinary measures. They must appreciate that this is within my jurisdiction and is not a political issue. Should they feel unable to support me, then I must assume that they have no confidence in me, and so my only course of action would be to resign."

They both smiled knowingly. Roberts continued, "Buller will fight. We must presume that he will wish to appeal at the very highest level. Since the death of the Queen I believe he has little support at Court. I will approach the King and I anticipate his ready approval for our actions.... Edward has never displayed any warmth towards Buller."

Broderick became quiet and thoughtful. "I am very glad that we are at one over the Buller question. I think, as you say, this *faux pas* on Buller's part may relieve us of a great difficulty."

....

It was Thursday 17 October, just one week after his speech at Westminster Hall. He had really put the cat among the pigeons. What a furore! Again he had been fiercely attacked in the press with *The Times* leading the pack. The Adjutant-General had responded by writing to him conveying his displeasure – Roberts' proxy. The War Office had demanded a written explanation. He had promptly replied defending his conduct; yes, he had been polite but firm in his reply. He had also written personally to Broderick to explain his actions and to request an interview to clear the air. He was pleased that his request had been accepted so promptly.

Buller stepped from the handsome-cab; it was still raining. He half jumped to avoid a large puddle but stepped short; dirty water splashed from the gutter over his shiny black shoes and silk suit. Damn! He was annoyed. He hurried inside the confused jumble of decaying buildings which constituted the War Office. He had spent many years in this cramped, dingy environment. Thank goodness work had at last begun on a substantial replacement building in Whitehall.

He was greeted by an usher; an old retainer who knew him well, "Welcome, sir; we've missed you."

"Good to see you Alfred," responded Buller. "I though you'd have retired by now."

"Just another two years to go, sir, before I get my pension." Respectful preliminaries over, he continued, "I'm to take you to the Secretary's office. If you would follow me, sir?"

Buller was very familiar with the layout, but dutifully followed his ageing guide with his lolloping gait, through the labyrinth of corridors; the noise of leather soles on flag floors marked their progress. They stopped outside a door on which a brass plaque announced its occupant: "Secretary of State for War". The usher knocked on the door, opened it and stood to one side allowing Buller to enter. Broderick was seated behind a worn oak desk; the diminutive Roberts stood slightly to one side.

"Good morning General Buller. Please sit down." Broderick indicated a chair on the near side of his desk. There was no warmth in his voice.

Roberts half nodded in scanty acknowledgement, "Good morning, Sir Redvers."

"Good morning gentlemen." Buller was immediately struck by the imposed formality and negatives vibes; the atmosphere was cold; in fact it was menacing. He met the stony glare of his antagonists. He had no regard for Broderick, who to his mind was another of those callous, absentee Irish landlords who inflicted such misery upon their tenants. Buller's regular forays into the countryside during his Irish service had opened his eyes to the injustices suffered by the indigenous peasant farmers. He compared their lot and treatment with that of the tenants on his own extensive estates in Devon and Cornwall, whom he new personally and managed with benevolence and compassion. He had publically castigated Broderick and others like him when serving as Under Secretary at Dublin Castle. He knew then that he had made life-long enemies amongst the Tory landlords. And Roberts; he had always been jealous of his predecessor, Wolseley, and vindictive towards those officers whom his rival had mentored and groomed; not least himself. It was common knowledge that Roberts had been distraught and disgruntled at Buller's appointment as Commander-in-Chief South Africa, and that he had vigorously schemed to replace him. Unfortunately, the reverse at Colenso had presented him with an opportunity to achieve his aim.

Broderick dispensed with polite preliminaries and went straight to the point, "You used the occasion of your speech in Westminster Hall to utter a vindication of your conduct at Colenso. It was a speech without parallel in the history of the British Army, and a clear breach of military discipline. Your outspoken and unguarded language has encouraged others to air perceived grievances; mischief is spreading like wild fire. I have concluded that a stern example needs to be made."

Buller interjected, "Minister, I have been goaded past endurance by a constant stream of misrepresentation and falsehood. As far back as January of this year I requested of the War Office that the full text of the telegrams be published to clear the air, but this was refused. This inaction simply added fuel to the fire. I am attacked, and what does the War Office do? Defend me? No; they damn me with faint praise and publish an official communiqué! "Oh; We are getting rid of him, and have appointed him to command a garrison of half-trained recruits to finish his final two years and then put him out to grass to die decently." Was this fair? I call it hitting below the belt!"

Broderick swept aside the criticism of his Department, "I have consulted with the Prime Minister and have the agreement of your superior, Lord Roberts, to request your resignation. You have served this country with great distinction and valour, but it is time to go, and to go quietly and with dignity, not just for your honour, but to safeguard the reputation of the Army".

Buller was taken aback at the finality of this suggestion. He half-spluttered his defence, "I accept that my speech was, in places, a little ill-judged and intemperate, but in my defence I have dedicated my life to the service of my country. I have received many accolades and decorations, and the gratitude and praise of public and monarch alike for my not inconsiderable achievements. Is all this to be forgotten? Does it count for naught? Am I to be eternally damned for one small indiscretion?"

Buller shifted in his chair, fidgeting with agitation and rising anger. He was confronted by his enemies who were trying to exploit a minor mistake for which he had already apologized; using it as a rod with which to unjustifiably beat him. He would have none of it. "The press criticizes my appointment to Aldershot. I didn't ask to be given command of the First Army Corps. It came to me unsought, and I may say undesired. It was offered to me by the War Office in the full knowledge of the circumstances surrounding Colenso and my telegrams. But now I am to be hung out to dry! Beware of giving the press the opportunity of saying that the War Office look to the public for a lead and instruction. Is policy to be dictated by a young, fanatical imperialist looking for a scapegoat? Am I to be that scapegoat?"

"To say that your speech was ill-judged is to condemn it very lightly, interjected Roberts. "It was almost incoherent and nearly unintelligible!"

"You will resign!" ordered Broderick.

"No … I'll go for court martial!"

"I'm afraid I could not support such a request," stated Roberts speaking slowly and pointedly.

Buller pushed back his chair. He stood towering over his opponents; a sense of injustice swelling up inside him, "I will appeal to the King!"

Broderick stood. He leaned forward slightly, resting his clenched fists on the desk. He relished striking the *coup de grace;* "I have already spoken to the King and he accepts my recommended course of action. You will resign or be dismissed."

The Times Newspaper 23 October 1901

SIR REDVERS BULLER RELIEVED OF COMMAND

In consequence of the speech delivered by General Sir Redvers Buller V.C., G.C.B., on October 10th, the Commander-in-Chief, after full consideration of all the circumstances and of the explanations furnished by Sir Redvers Buller, has recommended that he be relieved of his command. Action has been taken accordingly, and Sir Redvers Buller has been placed on half pay.

::

Denouement

(3 June 1908)

"Charles! Charles!"

He looked up. Striding across the grass was his old friend from South Africa, Baden-Powell; he was staying with him for a few days as a guest at his home, The Oaks, in Westbere. The house sat on a hill about three miles to the east of Canterbury, and was blessed with a fine view of the spires of the Cathedral. The grounds were ideal for children, with rambling shrubberies, belts of pine trees, small meadows and clumps of ancient oaks and fruit trees. At the back of the house was a sand-pit used as a miniature rifle range. It had become a Mecca for scouts from Ramsgate and Canterbury; they would cycle over to camp most weekends and through the summer months.

"Have you seen this? The driver has just returned from Canterbury and he collected the paper from the station."

He handed a copy of *The Times* to Warren who read of the death of General Sir Redvers Buller the day before. Well, mused Warren, his extravagant appetite and love of alcohol has caught up with him at last. He stood quietly.

"He never did you any favours," intruded Baden-Powell.

"You know," pondered Warren, "in South Africa there were two Bullers: the benign friendly Buller I had known well from our many years of acquaintance, and the vindictive, morose Buller others spoke of, but I never knew. The first Buller was my old friend; the second, a phantom of the first, full of uncertainty and suspicion." As he spoke a buried sadness welled to the surface, "I long believed that Buller would come to understand his unfairness to me, and that he would write and acknowledge his injustice. But he never did."

Together they strolled over the field towards the cluster of white bell-tents, Warren lost in his thoughts.

At last Baden-Powell interrupted, "Have you considered my offer? Do you have an answer for me? You've done a marvellous job with the Scout Troops at Ramsgate and Canterbury, but I desperately need someone to be my Travelling Inspector to encourage and organise other troops throughout the Country."

"I think not. I am enjoying the experience of being with my own group of boys too much. Do you know? They call themselves "Warren's Own"."

He joined a group of about forty boys sitting cross-legged on the grass, eagerly awaiting his arrival. He stuck the point of his shooting stick in the ground and splayed the seat, sitting on it he began:

> *"To be a good scout you require an enormous number of qualifications, and among the first a humble mind, a clear judgement, a determination to think for yourself, a constant perseverance, a desire to help others, and a clear understanding that you cannot succeed on your own. You need help inwardly and outwardly, you must*

have friends in every proceeding, and you must know where to turn when you wish to use the experience of others.

But let me warn you not to expect friends from those you help; it is the nature of things that they may dislike you. The friends you are likely to make are the band of brothers existing in the world who are on the same errand as yourself, who recognise you instinctively by your acts and welcome you to their party..."

AFTERNOTES

Subsequent Course of the War

On 5 February 1900 Buller again attacked across the Tugela at Vaalkrans only to lose confidence in the prospects of success and to withdraw for a third time. Following this failure Warren once more recommended an attack on Hlangwane. This time Buller, devoid of alternatives, accepted – "The Key to Ladysmith". This attack proved successful. The fighting raged from 14 to 28 February and is designated the Battle of Pieters.

Ladysmith was finally relieved by Buller's Field Force on 28 February 1900. Concurrently, Field Marshal Lord Roberts advanced from the Cape and on 13 March 1900 captured the capital of the Orange Free State, Bloemfontein. On 5 June he captured the capital of the Transvaal, Pretoria. Both Republics were annexed by Britain.

Many Boers refused to accept defeat with the annexation of their Republics, and entered into a phase of guerrilla warfare which was to last for a further eighteen months, concluding with the Treaty of Vereeniging on 31 May 1902.

Casualties

The official British casualty figures for the fighting in the Rangeworthy Hills include all actions taken together, and do not show those for the fighting on Spion Kop separately. Thus casualties between 17 and 24 January 1900 are given as below:

	Killed	**Wounded**	**Missing**	**Total**
Officers	27	53	7	87
Other Ranks	245	1,050	351	1,646
Total	272	1,103	358	**1,733**

During the battle the Boers took 187 prisoners. That leaves 171 British "missing" unaccounted for. Could these be dead with no known graves? In which case the actual number killed would be closer to 443.

The number of British dead recorded as buried on the plateau is 243. Subtract that from the official total of dead (272) and it leaves only 29 fatalities during the remaining four days of actual fighting - 20 to 23 January. Consider that one unit alone, the Lancashire Fusiliers, lost 15 men in their first attack on 20 January as recorded by name in their regimental journal; add to this the casualties of the King's Royal Rifles during their aborted attack on the Twin Peaks; extrapolate this across the whole Field Force for 4 days, and the official figures are not credible.

On mounting Spion Kop on the morning of 25 January 1900, Louis Botha ordered one of his senior officers to conduct a body count. He reported more than 600 British dead and half that number wounded and awaiting recovery.

In similar vein, the Boers admit to 68 killed and 134 wounded during the battle for Spion Kop. This sits uncomfortably with personal accounts, and the practice of the Boers in repatriating their dead for home burial in the Transvaal and Orange Free State.

By the end of the War more than 400,000 British imperial and colonial troops were deployed. Of those 5,774 were killed by enemy action, and 16,168 died of wounds or were killed by disease.

Suffering on the Boer side was proportionately much higher. The total number of combatants for the two Republics is thought to have been 87,365 of whom 2,120 were foreign volunteers, and 13,300 were Afrikaners from the British colonies of the Cape and Natal. An estimated 7,000 were killed. 26,370 Boer women and children are said to have died in the British concentration camps and are commemorated on the National Women's Monument in Bloemenfontein.

No one bothered to keep records of the number of black Africans who died. Contemporary sources suggest that about 7,000 perished in concentration camps; modern estimates place the figure closer to 20,000. To these must be added the unrecorded deaths by summary execution by the Boers of black Africans suspected of working for the British in such capacities as scouts and spies.

Union of South Africa

On 1 June 1910 the South Africa Act came into being which created the Union of South Africa from the British Colonies of Cape of Good Hope, Natal, Orange River Colony and Transvaal Colony. Louis Botha became the first Prime Minister.

ABOUT THE AUTHOR

William (Bill) McDonald

Bill McDonald was born in the mill-town of Rochdale, Lancashire. In 1965 he joined the Army and was a professional soldier for 24 years. He was subsequently involved in the Territorial Army in different capacities for a further 10 years. He began his military career as a Fusilier in the Lancashire Fusiliers and retired with the rank of Major. As a Colour- Sergeant he was decorated for meritorious service during the Northern Irish troubles and selected for commissioning. He attended the Royal Military Academy Sandhurst and later the Army Staff College. On leaving the Army he worked in Africa for a humanitarian aid organization. He is married with three children and two grandchildren. He is now retired and lives with his wife in Northumberland.

The Lost Victory is his first novel – a sequel is planned

Made in the USA
Charleston, SC
05 April 2013